THE SECRET OF BORGES

A Psychoanalytic Inquiry into His Work

Julio Woscoboinik

Translated by

Dora Carlisky Pozzi

University Press of America,® Inc.
Lanham • New York • Oxford

Copyright © 1998
University Press of America,® Inc.
4720 Boston Way
Lanham, Maryland 20706

12 Hid's Copse Rd.
Cumnor Hill, Oxford OX2 9JJ

All rights reserved
Printed in the United States of America
British Library Cataloging in Publication Information Available

Library of Congress Cataloging-in-Publication Data

Woscoboinik, Julio.
(Secreto de Borges. English)
The secret of Borges : a psychoanalytic inquiry into his work / Julio
Woscoboinik ; translated by Dora Carlisky Pozzi.
p. cm.
Includes bibliographical references.
1. Borges, Jorge Luis, 1899— Criticism and interpretation. I. Title.
PQ7797.B635Z9813 1998 868—dc21 98-29604 CIP

ISBN 0-7618-1238-5 (cloth: alk. ppr.)
ISBN 0-7618-1239-3 (pbk: alk. ppr.)

∞™ The paper used in this publication meets the minimum
requirements of American National Standard for Information
Sciences—Permanence of Paper for Printed Library Materials,
ANSI Z39.48—1984

This is a translation of *El secreto de Borges. Indagación psicoanalítica de su obra*, by Julio Woscoboinik, 3rd ed., September 1991, Grupo Editor Latinoamericano, Buenos Aires, Argentina (1st. ed., 1988; 2nd. ed., July 1991). French translation: Paris, Césura Lyon, 1989. Awards: Sociedad Argentina de Escritores, 1988; Ministerio de Cultura y Educación (Argentina), 1992.

Acknowledgments
I dedicate this book to my son, Sebastián.

I wish to express my special gratitude to my wife, Polita, for providing the tireless collaboration that no one else could have offered. Throughout the long years it took to write this book, I shared my quandaries with her, the two of us exchanged ideas, and she assisted me in clarifying many concepts.

I thank Dora Carlisky Pozzi, of the University of Houston, for producing this accurate English translation with minute attention to detail and a congenial dedication to the task, as well as for representing me ably in the U.S. We are both indebted to Dr. James Houlihan for his revision of details of English style.

Excerpts from Borges's prose and poetry are reproduced by permission granted by the following copyright holders:
From "The Circular Ruins," tr. A. Kerrrigan and "Tlön, Uqbar, Orbis Tertius," tr. A. Reed, in *Ficciones*, ed. A. Kerrigan (Grove Press, 1962) by courtesy of Grove/Atlantic, Inc.
From "The Draped Mirrors," "Poems about Gifts," "Mirrors," "The Moon," tr. M. Boyer and H. Morland, in *Dreamtigers* (University of Texas Press, 1985); and from "On the Cult of Books," "The Flower of Coleridge," "The Analytical Language of John Wilkins," and "The Mirror of Enigmas," tr. R. L. C. Simms, in *Other Inquisitions 1937-1952* (University of Texas Press, repr. 1985) by courtesy of the University of Texas Press.
From R. Burgin, *Conversations with Jorge Luis Borges* (1968), by courtesy of the author.
From "A New Refutation of Time," "The House of Asterion," "The Immortal," and "The Sect of the Phoenix," tr. J. E. Irby; from "Emma Zunz," tr. D. A. Yates; and from "The Zahir," tr. D. Fitts, in *Labyrinths: Selected Stories and Other Writings*, ed. D. A. Yates and J. E. Irby (New Directions Publishing, 1964) by permission of New Directions Publishing, New York, and of Laurence Pollinger Limited, London.
From "Doctor Brodie's Report" and "Rosendo's Tale," in *Doctor Brodie's Report*, tr. N.T. di Giovanni in coll. with Borges (Dutton, 1972); from *Evaristo Carriego*, tr. S. Ashe (Dutton, 1984); from *The Book of Imaginary Beings*, tr. N.T. di Giovanni in coll. with Borges (Dutton, 1970); from *Borges, Selected Poems 1923-1969*, ed. and tr. N.T. di Giovanni in coll. with Borges (Delacorte / Seymour Lawrence, 1972); from "The Aleph," "Streetcorner Man," "The Dead Man," and "An Autobiographical Essay, in *The Aleph and Other Stories*, ed. and tr. N.T. di Giovanni in coll. with Borges (Dutton, 1970); from "Ulrike," "The Night of the Gifts," "Undr," and "Afterword," in *The Book of Sand*, tr. N.T. di Giovanni (Dutton, 1977); and "Preface" and "The Masked Dyer," in *A Universal History of Infamy* (Dutton, 1972) by permission of Penguin U.S.A.

Contents

Acknowledgments		iii
Prologue		vii
Introduction	Borges in Two Metaphors	1
Chapter 1	A Psychobiography of Jorge Luis Borges	17
Chapter 2	The Literary Style. The Man	41
Chapter 3	The Unthinkable in Borges	61
Chapter 4	From Asterion to Oedipus	77
Chapter 5	Borges, the Man at the Pink Streetcorner	87
Chapter 6	Emma Zunz: the Enigma of a Name	105
Chapter 7	The Unspeakable: Primal Scene and Secret	127
Chapter 8	Endymion in Buenos Aires	143
Chapter 9	The Man Resembled the Voice	171

Chapter 10	Dreams and Nightmares in Borges	179
Chapter 11	Borges, Author of Hamlet	207
Chapter 12	Circular Time: Another Borgean Tautology	223

Prologue

Over twenty years ago my colleague, M. Th. Guilbaud, Professor of Social Mathematics in a Psychology department which I chaired, mentioned to me an Argentinian writer I did not know at the time. He said that this writer's short stories, translated into French several years earlier, were studied with real passion by a small group of researchers interested in the logical structure of literary works. My friend suggested that I read them and undertake a psychoanalytic study of these stories. Thus, in 1968, I went on a summer vacation carrying several books by Borges, among them *Ficciones*, *The Aleph*, and *L'Auteur et autres textes* ("Pierre Menard},the Author [of Don Quixote] and Other Texts). It was for me a dazzling experience, since then constantly renewed. A fresh reading stimulated me to interpret these writings as a psychoanalyst. As a result my article, "Le corps et le code dans les contes de Borges," was published in *Nouvelle Revue de Psychanalyse* in 1971.

Borges continued writing, publishing, and giving interviews wherein he explained details concerning his work. His oeuvre only concluded (save for the posthumous addition of unpublished texts) with his death in 1986. Literary critics have scrutinized his style, the sources of his inspiration, his themes, and the resources involved in the composition of his stories. Borges's humor, or rather his irony, dazzles us like the many facets of a skillfully cut diamond. It is possible now possible to undertake a new psychoanalytic inquiry. Julio Woscoboinik has all the assets for succeeding in such an enterprise. He lives in Buenos Aires, where he practices psychoanalysis. He loves the writings of Borges but has never sought to meet the man personally. He is in possession of important documents that are not available in France. The most interesting writings by the Argentine critics to whom I refer above have led him to new perspectives on some of the short stories. Woscoboinik writes clearly and persuasively yet never seeks to direct the reader's attention toward himself. A good commentator always fades behind the author. He often cites, sometimes at length, fascinating passages from Borges's work. He keeps before his eyes the texts of which critics speak and can thus judge whether or not their comments are well grounded.

The subtitle of Woscoboinik's book, Psychoanalytic Inquiry, signals the respect a psychoanalyst, no matter how talented he may be, must have for the genius of creative writers. We have Freud's own example of such a respectful attitude. The psychoanalyst inquires, Why do these works please me, why do they move, seduce, and disturb me; what is it in my reading that reflects myself? A psychoanalyst who analyzes literature should not be thought to be omniscient, able to dispense gratuitous interpretations concerning one who never lay down on his couch, one whom he knows only through the mediation of texts. Julio Woscoboinik adopts in this respect a method I consider exemplary. He does not interpret, but rather parallels a page by Borges and a page by Freud or by a later psychoanalyst. He places both side by side just as if they were bilingual inscriptions on an ancient tablet. It is the reader's task to verify the translation—never totally accurate and sometimes nonsensical—which requires corrections and offers variants.

This book on Borges captures both his original creative talent and the psychological processes involved in all literary creation. Woscoboinik shows Borges utilizing childhood memories, erudition, nocturnal dreams; he shows us how he transmutes his quasi-hallucinatory fantasies and phobias into litterary matter that receives a definitive aesthetic form from another labor, the labor of style.

I read *The Secret of Borges* reordering its rich table of contents into four parts. The first is an overview of Borges's life where the events that triggered a creative regression or provided the plot of a short story are emphasized. His youthful works receive more detailed consideration than the short stories he wrote as a mature man. Julio Woscoboinik particularly underscores the common experiences of Jorge Luis and his younger sister Norah: the fear of mirrors, the horror of incest, imaginary games.

The innovative second part of the book presents and expands several studies, mostly by Argentine critics, on the style of Borges. Which rhetorical figures are utilized, with the intention to produce which linguistic results? Which spatial configurations (rhombus, hexagon, labyrinth, diverse figures of symmetry, structure *en abîme*), which temporal ones (e.g. circular time) govern the logic of his stories? A fundamental aspect of the Borgean art is shown here, the art of tightly interweaving in the story two different logics, the logic of discourse and that of the spatial forms which I have dubbed "formal signifiers." Here Woscoboinik reviews speculations on proper names and numbers worthy of the Cabbala (well-known by Borges).

In what I term the third part we find the stories presented in chronological order yet with thematic regroupings. This analysis includes sources, structure, levels of signification, and the discussion of previous criticism. The fourth and last part, more diverse, addresses first Borges's relations with women (by whom he felt threatened), then his voice (he was prone to a stuttering of sorts that impeded him when speaking in public), and his dreams. Borges described his dreams each morning to his mother, who in turn told him hers. He jotted down his oneiric experiences and on that basis of sometimes painful personal experiences he wrote a study on the dynamics of the nightmare.

The Secret of Borges then reviews the salient events of the writer's old age: the death of his ninety-nine-year-old mother, his own marriage at eighty seven with Maria Kodama, a forty-year-old woman of Japanese descent, or the recuperation of his poetic creative power. Finally, Woscoboinik attempts to decipher the "Secret" of Borges: uncertainty about his own identity, doubling of the self, the fragile distinction between reality and imagination, the impression that he was but a shadow of his ancestors, who had themselves turned into shadows, or even that he had been dreamed by another and was in his turn limited to dreaming up fictional characters.

The reader should not be misled concerning the secret of Borges. It is not a question of a fact, real or imaginary, hidden by Borges and now at last revealed. It relates rather to what remained a secret for Borges about himself, something that the biographer and the psychoanalyst may dare hypothesize, with the limitations of which Rossolato reminds us when he formulates the "relation of the unknown." The "navel" mentioned by Freud, which engenders a work or a dream, eludes all interpretations. What remains unexplained is the hollow space, the lack, the vacuum around which the work is constructed, that which persists after such construction as the reverse of the work, as the absence of another work which might have been the same work if it had been constructed from the inside out.

In my article "Le corps et le code dans les contes de Borges," I attempted to balance the roles in this author of the physical and the intellectual, narrative and logic, narcissistic problems and Oedipal fantasies. Now, having read *The Secret of Borges*, I cannot disprove the evidence: the narcissistic is at the same time predominant, natural, and authentic. I can see that Borges resorts to Oedipal topics more infrequently, in a more forced, more factual manner. I am not referring just to the narcissistic folding back upon oneself and the overinvestment of the self that are necessary conditions of any creative work. Narcissism is the very content of Borges's work, which offers us an inventory of its figures, beliefs, and typical ways of reasoning. I must however make some qualifications, for the narrative texts by Borges are representations of masculine narcissism. It is not therefore surprising that they are read by men more than by women. With which feminine images (prostitute, submissive servant, naïve young girl) could these male readers identify? Yet this is not the place to develop a comparative analysis of masculine and feminine narcissism. As I reread Borges in the light of Julio Woscoboinik, I perceived in the characters' speech, in the psychological laws governing their interactions, and in the operational signs underlying progressions and regressions of the action, symbolism, enunciations, emotions and singular ideals pertaining to the large modalities of psychological narcissistic dynamics in the scenarios.

Borges's fascination with mirror images, a point of departure for narcissism, is symbolized by the figures of the double, the reflection, the echo, reversed symmetry, and the horror of mirrors which distort or de-multiply the image of the self, which make an individual their captive, just as do a tiger in a cage or the minotaur in his labyrinth, which confuse the self-image with the images of others, and which, to sum up, are as prone to folding back upon themselves as they are to turning around. Another figuration of narcissism is the circle ("circular ruins," circular time) turning around upon itself and claiming to be the center of the world. The statements made by the main character or by the narrator are equally characteristic of a narcissistic stance. For one to live the other must die; one man is every man; there is a place which condenses all places. "Everything is everywhere and everything, no matter what, is all things." Differences are often denied.

On the other hand, the feelings and emotions of the characters are more narcissistic than Oedipal. These are: defiance, shame, humiliation, spite, laziness, submission, irony, revenge, coldness. Characters act like puppets, concerned only about their self-image. They ignore the emotions that might be considered natural—love and the fear of death, which they gamble on in the lottery.

Finally, the ideal of narcissistic omnipotence runs like a thread through the stories: creating a new language (so as to be the only one speaking it), manufacturing other societies, other worlds, gathering in a single library all the books—those that have been and those that will be written—avoiding coitus and generation in order to engender onself... To have known so well such a subjective dimension of the human gives Borges's oeuvre, by virtue of a paradox that would have delighted him, its universal scope. Let us thank Julio Woscoboinik for allowing Borges's readers to draw this conclusion.

Didier Anzieu
Preface to the French edition, 1989.
Translated (1998) by permission.

Introduction

Borges in Two Metaphors

The Blind Minotaur

Among the engravings of the Vollard suite at the Picasso Museum in Paris there is an 1934 aquatint by Picasso entitled "The Blind Minotaur Guided by a Young Girl at Night" (*El Minotauro ciego guiado por una joven niña en la noche*).[1] I was surprised when I could see in this wonderful work the image of Borges. With hesitating steps that he measures and supports by means of a stick or staff, the Minotaur moves forward, with that vague alertness of the blind, as if he were gauging the void by listening into it. A young girl whose face looks mature holds his hand, and turning to look at him, moves ahead. In her arms is nested a white dove that spreads its wings.

The tenuous light of the moon in a starry night illuminates this dramatic scene. Yet the figures appear to have a magic light of their own. On the right, two fishermen pull a net just beginning to show on the surface. On the left a young sailor of beautiful adolescent countenance observes the scene. He seems to be awed, as are the fishermen, by the powerful and controlled bestiality of the Minotaur. A spurious son of Queen Pasiphae and the marvelous white bull of Minos, the Minotaur, a symbol of orgiastic drives, walks here bent over himself, in the solitary night. He is like a strange oneiric condensation: in the cruel majesty of the labyrinth, he might represent both Asterion and Oedipus—the wretched figure of Oedipus holding Antigone's hand. While the sailors, midwives of the sea, pull out the net and the white dove rests in the girl's fragile arms, the Minotaur moves forward, blind and defeated, as if he were praying to the heavens.

Borges's image imposes itself. It takes residence precisely at the fractious ridge that separates the blooming from the faded; the lavish from the needy; it stands on the thin line between glory and disdain, between power and castration, between Narcissus and Oedipus.

Don Quixote, Don Borges

> ... You must know, then, that the above-named gentleman whenever he was at leisure (which was mostly all the year round) gave himself up to reading books of chivalry with such ardor and avidity that he almost entirely neglected the pursuit of his field-sports, and even the management of his property; and to such a pitch did his eagerness and infatuation go that he sold many an acre of tillage-land to buy books of chivalry to read, and brought home as many of them as he could get.
>
> ... Over conceits of this sort the poor gentleman lost his wits, and used to lie awake striving to understand them and worm the meaning out of them... and what with little sleep and much reading his brains got so dry that he lost his wits.
>
> ... In short, his wits being quite gone, he hit upon the strangest notion that ever madman in this world hit upon, and that was that he fancied it was right and requisite, as well for the support of his own honor as for the service of his country, that he should make a knight-errant of himself, roaming the world over in full armor and on horseback in quest of adventures, and to put in practice himself all that he had read of...[2]

I find the beginning of *Don Quixote* pertinent as I begin this study of Borges, for if Don Quixote went out to the world in order to live the books, Borges made of the books his world. The citation is also suitable because, if Don Quixote goes, as he puts it, "in quest of adventures, and to put in practice himself all that he had read of," Borges remains in the solitary adventure of rewriting, recomposing, deforming and transforming the adventures he has read. Don Quixote read the world so as to demonstrate the books; Borges reads the books to justify his life.

Literary Creation and Psychoanalysis

> The roots of language are irrational and of a magical nature.
>
> Jorge Luis Borges[3]

Whenever a psychoanalyst attempts a work such as mine, some preliminary remarks are in order, spelling out the aim and method of his project, and forestalling some of the objections he expects it may cause. Freud, to whose work we can always resort for a pertinent quotation, expressed this concern in 1910, as he was studying Leonardo da Vinci, "When psychiatric research, normally content to draw on frailer men for its material, approaches one who is among the greatest of the human race, it is not doing so for the reasons so frequenty ascribed to it by laymen. 'To blacken the radiant and drag the sublime into the dust' is no part of its purpose,[4] and there is no satisfaction for it in narrowing the gulf which separates the perfection of the great from the inadequacy of the objects that are its usual concern. But it cannot help finding worthy of understanding everything that can be recognized in those illustrious models, and it believes there is no one so great as to be disgraced by being subject to the laws which govern both normal and pathological activity with equal cogency."[5]

The world of creation is intricate. Even more intricate are the psychoanalytic paths to approach creation. One is always teased by the fear that analyzing might be an intrusive penetration, rummaging, as it were, through the dark cellar of the origin of literary or artistic creation, through its fascinating mystery. Perhaps it is like inquiring, with a child's eyes, into the primal scene where children are engendered.

In therapeutic analysis a patient approaches the psychoanalyst and asks questions, but in the analysis of a work of art we snatch an author's life and work, posing questions and making statements from outside, unilaterally, without giving the author an opportunity to respond. The absence of a dialogue creates another difference: there is no exchange that brings to light unknown regions, that is responsible for structuring the symptoms that the patient wishes to resolve.

The analysis of a literary or artistic creation involves contemplating an aesthetically pleasing object. Perhaps this contemplation intensifies the guilt experienced while attempting to penetrate such an object. But, as Freud says, we are trying to find out what the great paradigms are able to reveal to us. This is an aspect, by no means the least important, of the psychoanalysis of culture. For a student of the human psyche, the work of art is an object rich in suggestions and discoveries. We approach literary works such as those by Borges, saturated with signifiers, and this wealth is even greater. Just as not all analysands are alike, so some works lend themselves more readily to our inquiry, offering us fascinating knowledge.

Yet the psychoanalysis of cultural products is similar to inquiries that have been carried out universally and immemorially, such as innumerable interpretations of the Bible or commentaries on legends, fables, tragedies, and myths. All are attempts to discover what lies beyond (or just this side of) words and images.

None of these discourses should be silenced. From the here and now, we should all be able to speak, each one of us within our posibilities. The vantage point we adopt is not even that of psychoanalysis as a science; it is rather the current, limited knowledge of the psychoanalyst who authors the interpretive work. All writers enjoy the pleasure of discovery and creation, as much as they can reveal mysteries and dispel enigmas.

Such a task is unusually complex when the writer is Borges, a crafty player, astute and tricky. A Proteus of elusive disguise, intangible as sand, erudite encyclopedia, a millionaire with a fortune of beauty and words, Borges is a Minotaur of poetry, an unhappy Asterion who is imprisoned, alone, poor, and blind.

There are aspects of literary creation that might deserve to be called "transnarcissistic" because they communicate two narcissisms: the writer's and the reader's. I will do my best to avoid any hermeneutic idealization, in other words, the temptation to reshape Borges's works along the lines of my own theories.

Borges the psychoanalyst?

> We forget that a literary work is fictional and that the vivid characters that move us and sometimes outrage us, the reprobates, the penitents, the blest, the ministers of anger or grace, 'Dante' protagonist of the poem and God himself, are projections of Dante's mind, figures of his dream. (...) The poet is each and every man of his fiction, each breath, each detail. (...) Dante, therefore, would have symbolized in those passages a mental conflict. Dante was Ulysses and deep down he may have feared the punishment of Ulysses.
> From Borges's prologue to *The Divine Comedy* [6]

Is this not the best authorization, the best model of psychoanalytic reflection upon Borges? In the same prologue, Borges continues: "I am convinced that Dante constructed the triple architecture of his poem in order to insert this encounter.[7] Constantly rejected by Beatrice, he dreamed a very stern Beatrice, an inaccessible Beatrice, he dreamed her on a chariot drawn by a lion that was a bird and which became all bird or all lion according to the reflection in Beatrice's eyes... " This may prefigure a nightmare. He adds, "I read and reread the chances of their illusory encounter and I think of the two lovers dreamed by Alighieri in the Hurricane of the Second Circle, obscure emblems (whether he understood it, whether he wanted it or not) of the happiness he did not achieve... I think of Francesca and Paolo, united for ever in his Inferno. Dante must have forged that line with horrifying love, with anxiety, with admiration, with envy."

With remarkable analytical insight, Borges comes close to an interpretation of Dante that we might produce using our own code. He even suggests symbolic interpretations that he calls allegories, and which he explains in footnotes, associating the eagle with pursuit and the she-fox with heresy, the prostitute with the church, and the dragon with the devil.

Imaginary Dialogue

In 1908 Freud wrote, "We laymen have always been intensely curious to know—like the Cardinal who put a similar question to Ariosto—from what sources that strange being, the creative writer, draws his material, and how he manages to make such an impression on us with it and to arouse in us emotions of which, perhaps, we had not even thought ourselves capable."[8]

In an imaginary conversation with Freud, Borges might have answered,

> **BORGES**: By perceiving, I believe, what is received through the muse, through the spirit, or through the subconscious, as psychology would say. The writer receives something and then he must find the words and the cadences that will express it. I am always certain that I am receiving something that is alien to me. Now I don't know whether it seems alien because it comes from deep within myself or from far outside...
> **FREUD**: Shouldn't we seek the traces of poetic creation in the "Spiel," in children's play, and in the fantasies of daydreams and nocturnal dreams?
> **BORGES**: Yes, I find no difference between dreaming and living, although reading was my only childhood play. Yeats believed in

what he called "The Great Memory" and did not think it necessary that the poet have many personal experiences since he can rely on that vast receptacle that is the memory of the human species.

FREUD: I believe there is some truth in what you say. I spoke of "Urphantasien," protofantasies inherited along the vicissitudes of human history. I agree with you in that the relation of a fantasy to time is quite substantive. Past, present, and future, are like the beads of a necklace threaded by desire. It seems to me that you affirm, even when denying it, the great weight of personal experiences in the creative process.

An impossible dialogue? I think not. We must listen to it. If we do, we will discover that Borges intuitively perceived many aspects of the unconscious and with his insights often paralleled Freud's explanations and concerns.[9]

Revelation and Word

Diverse are the paths chosen by psychoanalysts to approach literary and artistic creation. Some emphasize content, others form and style; others base their study exclusively upon the text, others investigate the author's life as well. Yet it is always a search for the unknown, for the unconscious, for what is named in the third person. Its goal is to discover what is only shown disfigured, what eludes censorship in dreams, in metaphors and metonymies, or is ransformed into its opposite. It is a quest for nervous tics, slips, and errors.

Some authors prefer to characterize creation as a product of the preconscious, because it verbalizes phantoms which can be named and recognized. Thus, Lawrence Kubie states that the symbolic process, at the *unconscious end* of the spectrum, is fruitless, stereotyped, not creative, and unable to communicate even its limited meanings. In the unconscious the symbolic process only represents memory traces from a past where it is anchored in a rigid and immutable manner.

The registers of preconscious functions are, on the other hand, automatic and subtle. They involve multiple perceptions. Recollection is immediate, their chains of association are analogical and juxtaposed; they have direct connections with affective processes. The rich play of preconscious operation occurs freely in states of abstraction, in dreams, when we write, paint or allow our mind to wander in free association.

Kubie adds, "The uniqueness of creativity, i.e., its capacity to find and put together something new, depends on the extent to which preconscious functions can operate freely between these two ubiquitous concurrent and oppressive prison wardens."[10] The preconscious activity may be favored or hindered by the influence of environment and education, something that does not occur at the level of unconscious fantasies.[11]

How important is the preconscious? On the basis of collaborative research with David Liberman, David Maldavsky points to the preconscious as a system of transformations, crossed by various logics and barriers and controlled by a double demand: that of expressing unconscious thinking and that of obeying the mandates of the second censorship (which resides between the preconscious and the conscious). This is the ground upon which psychoanalytic work operates. He concludes that the preconscious is structured, as it were, in a combination of styles.

Didier Anzieu distinguishes five stages or phases of creative activity, to each one of which is hooked a specific resistance.[12] In the first stage there is a regressive motion, linked to an internal crisis and to archaic psychic representatives. The second is the process of perceiving those representations, making it possible to fix them in the preconscious as an organizing nucleus. The third stage presupposes a special gift, a creative genius capable of structuring images, effects, and rhythms and inscribing them in different materials and codes. Fourth is a composition task starting from several previously elaborated transcriptions. And finally, in the fifth moment, comes the proof of reality, exposing the work to the judgment of the public.

We know that regression stumbles against neurotic and character defenses, justified by the fear of facing archaic and/or psychotic anxieties of dismemberment, pursuit, depression, etc. What is important and difficult is to endure or control the sometimes catastrophic and destabilizing overflow of the regressive process. I believe Borges achieves this control, though I am not necessarily stating he always does so. Ehrenzweig argues that creative work is able to oscillate between differentiated and undifferentiated modes and, assigning them very precise tasks, fuse them together. The non-creative psychotic subject succumbs to the tension between the conscious (differentiated) and unconscious (undifferentiated) modes of mental functions."[13] Hans Sachs states, "Art offers important satisfactions to the synthetic function of the ego by restoring to it dissociated parts of the personality. In this sense art does perceptually what psychoanalysis does cognitively."[14] Interestingly, Borges claims that he cured his insomnia by writing the story "Funes the Memorious."[15] In his own words, "I must have adequately symbolized my pain."

For Otto Rank, form in a work of art is a means for the artist of containing, controlling and ordering "chaotic creative forces within himself... which otherwise threaten to overwhelm him."[16] Can we, reflecting in this manner, conceive form and style as a container and apply to this concept the psychoanalytic theory that José Bleger developed concerning framing as the repository of the most archaic and terrifying anxieties?[17] Rank adds, "Form... embodies man's continual quest for spiritual elevation over his biologic and communal dependencies."[18] In other words, he is referring to the process of sublimation, an important and controversial concept. No doubt in Borges, sublimation has had a restorative role, an intense function of reparation.

"The formal organization in a work of art," in Ehrenzweig's view, "serves to bind and neutralize libidinal energy and thereby win it over into the service of the ego."[19] E.H. Gombrich also refers to the libidinal transformation of impulses into fantasies and then into art.[20] All this can occur because the Ego has the ability to delay the discharge of energy and to impose order and organization. What Borges does is transform the Ego's delay of impulses into a kind of infinite delay. A representative of the American Ego School, Ernst Kris, treats "the formal qualities of a work of art... primarily in regard to their *defensive function*... [Form] provides the structure which facilitates the neutralization of psychic energy."[21] For Philip Weissman, however, the Ego does not use regression in creativity; rather, the Ego avails itself of a dissociative or desynthesizing function which it puts into the service of the synthetic or integrative activity. He views it as the Ego's capacity to withdraw and dissociate itself from both Id and Superego demands. This, he states, is a more precise approximation of how a non-regressive Ego functions in the creative process. Weissman then examines pathological states in which the dissociative function does not operate in the service of the synthetic function and here depersonalization, feelings of unreality, fugue states, and so forth, may occur.[22] Perhaps occasionally Borges too may have experienced such pathological conditions.

While Kris contends that inspiration reflects the emergence of the Id material and the primary process into consciousness, Weisman believes that in inspiration the Ego controls the primary process; this does not occur in psychosis, where the Ego is overwhelmed by its irruption. Clearly for Weissman psychosis and creative process are not compatible. For H. Hartman, the more creative an artist is, the greater the dissociation between personal and creative life. In this regard Phyllis Greenacre distinguishes in the artist a conventional and a creative self.

Another psychoanalytic approach, that of the English School, may offer us a different view and enrich our understanding of artistic creation and of Borges. I am referring to the valuable book by Didier Anzieu, *Body and Code in Borges's Stories* (*Le corps et le code dans les contes de Borges*), where the author points out that psychic phenomena discovered and conceptualized by Melanie Klein and her disciples contribute priceless theoretical referents for an understanding of artistic creation; some of these are massive projective identification, fragmentation anxiety, the constitution of internal objects, processes of splitting and integration, symbolic equation, and symbolism.[23] For Melanie Klein, primary unconscious forces find gratification in artistic creation. Infantile wishes and destructive fantasies give rise to guilt due to the fear of harming the object or losing it. Yet they also give rise to the need to restore it. The work of art speaks to us about this reparation.[24] Thus creativeness, symbolization processes and sublimation are intimately connected.

In regard to the origin of the symbolic process, Klein adopts the point of view of Ferenczi and Jones: (primary) identification and the pairing of two different objects through an affective bond enable the Ego to elaborate fantasies and to develop symbols which bridge the internal and the external world. From a Kleinian perspective, Hanna Segal conceptualizes the first developmental attempts as an Ego activity striving to integrate primary anxieties (the fear of "bad" objects) with the desire of total union with the idealized object. In the paranoid-schizoid, by projective identification and other basic mechanisms, parts of the self and of the internal objects are located outside. Now there occur what Segal calls, using a Klein term in a different sense, "symbolic equations." While these are a first step in the development of the symbolic ability, they nonetheless continue to display—being as they are moored in the object—a pairing between the symbol and that which is symbolized. They provide the basis of the psychotic's concrete thinking. Segal gives the well-known example of the patient, a violinist, who refused to play before an audience, claiming, "You don't want me to masturbate in public." Playing the violin was not just a symbolic equivalent of sexual activity: it was rather its concrete realization.[25]

As the Ego matures and relations with the total object are developed, the depressive position occurs. Henceforth internal and external reality start to become differentiated; there is a stimulus for the creation of true symbols, as substitutes of the absent object, allowing sublimation and reparation.[26]

The concept of sublimation is highly controversial in psychoanalytic theory. Its dynamic effects, and the obvious links with Oedipal repression during the latency period, were described by Freud. However, as Jean Guillaumin points out, "A detailed study of the interplay of the functional mechanisms involved is not available yet."[27] Sublimation is seen in a somewhat magic light, as an exceptional mechanism of sorts, characterized by a change in the target of the drive, often accompanied by a change of object. Freud particularly singled out as sublimatory activities, artistic creation and intellectual inquiry; in these the drive derived toward a new end, one that is not sexual, points toward socially valued objects. Melanie Klein, as we have seen, emphasizes the tendency in sublimation to restore the object attacked and harmed by destructive drives.

Géza Róheim proposes the notion of an *intermediary object*, since the cultural or sublimatory object stands half-way between the narcissistic and the object-seeking attitudes, writing that "in sublimation this oscillation must disappear and something more stable must take its place."[28] Róheim prefigures concepts that D. W. Winnicot will develop with great clarity.[29] The transitional object, the first "not-me possession," has the developmental function of protecting the baby from separation anxieties. It leads to an attachment to a teddybear, the corner of the blanket, or any other soft object available. Those anxieties materialize when in the course of emotional development the infant must abandon the idyllic relationship with the mother. This gives rise to a conflict between "the inability to recognize and accept reality and the growing ability to do that." A space is created as outlet and relief of this conflict, an intermediate zone between the subjective and that which is perceived objectively, which does not involve a challenge of the emerging "reality principle" and where the child is allowed the use of illusion, of the "as it were." Transitional objects and events will develop in this realm. Here the child is the "supreme creator."

In adult life this very illusion and its nature are inherent in art and in other cultural manifestations. It can, however, turn into the mark of madness when its true essence is not grasped and when belief is demanded from others. For Winnicott, therefore, the notion of artistic creation is connected with the concept of that third realm, a potential space where the free play of illusion is allowed and authorized. This shared illusion bridges the space between the creative artist and the public.

Not only the infant babbling but also words themselves are transitional objects for Roland Gori. In his view "The act of speech does not belong to the symbolic order. It is rather like an almost stationary *point of equilibrium* where the continuous oscillation of narcissist and eroticoobjectal investings maintain him between the libido and the death pulsion, between the body and the code, the imaginary and the symbolic orders."[30] Structuring of the word starts from the bodily image. We are approaching here the important reflections offered by French psychoanalysts, which permit a peculiar approach to understanding literary creation. The statement, "The unconscious is structured as a language" synthesizes the seminal ideas that Lacan opens up from Freud, structuralism, Saussurian linguistics and Hegelian philosophy.

The concept of "dream work" is based, as we know, upon the diverse mechanisms of the primary unconscious process, particularly condensation and displacement. Lacan avails himself of these elements to found and consolidate the analogy he poses between unconscious processes and some aspects of language. He equates condensation with metaphoric process and displacement with metonymic process. "Language is a subtle body, but a body nonetheless," writes Lacan (1953).[31] The "empty word" in the discourse of the imaginary contrasts with the "full word" or language of desire. The latter carries, insofar as it is inscribed in the Oedipal, the means of releasing desire captured in the narcissistic image or mirror stage. Literary creation is a text that may be deciphered like a dream. Oral language differs from writing because it has intonations perceived only by a listener. Different listeners play with phonic approximations as they attempt to find sense, but this sense will be attained only through the concatenation of signifiers. Saussure's bi-univocal relationship, therefore, does not apply. The writer may (or may not) achieve the production of poetic meaning, starting from the adventure of the signifier, rather than starting, as conventionally assumed, from a meaning and looking for its expression.

The notion that language is a condition of the unconscious is discussed by Laplanche and Leclaire, who reverse Lacan's thesis and see "the unconscious as the condition of language." André Green criticizes Lacan for ignoring affection in his statements. He reclaims the important role affection deserves. Didier Anzieu also points out the clinical and technical disadvantages of seeing in the patient "just a text," one, in the last analysis, without a subject matter.

Clearly, it would not be easy, in studying Borges, to consider the literary work as only a text to be deciphered with no help but the web of its signifiers. Sometimes it is fascinating to investigate, especially in

Borges, the concatenation of signifiers, yet it is not sufficient. The themes that stubbornly recur in his entire work in multiple and various forms, I shall attempt to discover, while the Borgean style and subject matter, the thematic recurrences, and the interviews with him and the facts known about him, are the materials with which I have to work.

I have briefly reviewed some psychoanalytic approaches to creative activity. Freud wrote on leonardo Da Vinci, on Dostoiewski and patricide; on Michelangelo's Moses, on the sinister in Hoffmann's story "The Sand Man," on the painter Cristopher Haitzmann and "A Demonic Neurosis of the Sixteenth Century"; on "A childhood memory of Goethe," in *Poetry and Truth;* on "Creative Writers and Daydreaming"; on delusion and dreams in Jensen's "Gradiva." Ever since, psychoanalysts have been eager to learn from certain creative personalities, and this curiosity has been productive. It is interesting to remember, by the way, that the only prize Freud, an exceptional researcher, ever won, was a literary prize named after the great German writer Goethe.

What is the significance an investigation of Borges's work has for our discipline? Didier Anzieu replies, "It permits us to glimpse into the unconscious psychic processes in the work of a disabled man, a grand master of shyness, a boy raised under a glass cover by abusive women, one who remained dependent upon and under the protection of his mother during his entire life, without seeking in other women anything more than brief encounters. These unconscious processes have allowed him to create a work of genius on a cultural level; on a personal level he has liberated himself by means of a restitutive sublimation."

Personally, my interest is prompted by the desire to discover the wealth of genius blooming in the feeble sand of a vital desert, the abundant production of an enlightened brain in blatant contrast with a blind body; the sane adventure of a lucid capacity for regression; the framing in the ironlike destiny of a name, Jorge Francisco Isidoro Luis Borges, a name that imprisoned him for life in an idealized genealogical tree, which controlled and subjected him. I wanted to discover the infinite manners of saying his pain, as he walked, strong and patient, in the limited space of a library-jail, even as the Asiatic tiger in the zoo that so fascinated him and in whose mirror he might seem to have been captured. I wanted to understand the possibilities his avid and monstrous memory offered him, while at the same time alienating him and creating identity conflicts such as feeling as if he were just an echo or a dream of others.

Because we are reluctant to agree with Angelus Silesius that "the rose is because it is, it blooms because it blooms," psychoanalysis attempts to inquire and at the same time enrich itself in the search for the seed, the land, the garden where the rose bloomed.

Such is my endeavor.

Notes

1. *Picasso's Vollard Suite* (London: Thames & Hudson, 1956).
2. Miguel de Cervantes Saavedra, *Don Quijote, el ingenioso hidalgo de la Mancha* (Don Quixote, the Ingenious Gentleman of La Mancha), trans. John Ormsby (New York: Heritage Press, 1950).
3. Jorge Luis Borges, Preface to "El Otro, el Mismo" in *Selected Poems 1923-1967*, ed. Norman Thomas di Giovanni (New York: Delacorte / Seymour, 1972), 279.
4. Freud is citing here from a poem by Schiller.
5. Sigmund Freud, "Leonardo Da Vinci and a Memory of his Childhood," *The Standard Edition of the Complete Psychological Works of Sigmund Freud*, trans. James Strachey, 24 vols. (London:The Hogarth Press and the Institute of Psycho-Analysis, 1978) 11, 63. Hereafter SE.
6. Dante Alighieri, *La Divina Comedia* (Buenos Aires: Colección Jackson, 1856), 31, ix.
7. He refers to the encounter with Beatrice.
8. Freud, "Creative Writers and Day-Dreaming," SE 9, 143.
9. The preceding imaginary dialogue has as its source an interview with Borges by Amelia Barilú, published in *La Prensa,* 8 April 1984, and it paraphrases Freud's essay (cited above).
10. Lawrence S. Kubie, *Neurotic Distortion of the Creative Process*, Porter Lectures 22 (Lawrence: University of Kansas Press, 1958), 45.
11. Regardless of the debatable nature of this theory, some of its aspects invite reflection. It moved me to wonder what would Borges have been, had he been born in a different milieu? The first idea that crossed my mind was: chief of a train station, perhaps because the task of such a man is a nearly automatized control of travel along multiple distinct paths. His role is that of a railroad organizer. In reality Borges was a librarian, who—curious and avid reader that he was—controlled an intellectual station, an archive that organizes knowledge, abstracted from the world and crossed by many paths of thought.
12. Didier Anzieu, "Vers une métapsychologie de la création," in *Psychanalyse du génie créateur* ed. D. Anzieu et al. (Paris / Bruxelles / Montreal: Bunod, 1974), 13-17.
13. Anton Ehrenzweig, *The Hidden Order of Art: a Study in the Psychology of Artistic Imagination* (Berkeley: University of California Press, 1976).
14. Hans Sachs, cited by Marshall Bush, "The Problem of Form in the Psychoanalytic Theory of Art,"*The Psychoanalytic Review* 54 (1967), 19.
15. "Funes, the Memorious," in Borges, *Ficciones*, trans. Anthony Kerrigan (New York: Grove Press, 1962).
16. Otto Rank, as cited by Marshall Bush in "The Problem of Form," 16.
17. José Bleger, "Psicoanálisis del encuadre psicoanalítico," *Revista de psicoanálisis* 7 (Buenos Aires 1964), 2.

18. Ibid.
19. Ibid., 22.
20. E. H. Gombrich, *Meditations on a Hobby Horse and Other Essays on the Theory of Art* (London: Phaidon Press, 1963).
21. Cited by Bush in "The Problem of Form," 24.
22. Philip Weissman, "Theoretical Consideration of Ego Regression and Ego Functions in Creativity," *The Psychoanalytic Quarterly* 36 (1967), 37-49.
23. Anzieu, Didier, *Le corps et le code dans les contes de J. L. Borges* (Paris: Gallimard, 1981).
24. Melanie Klein (ed.), *New Directions in Psychoanalysis* (London: Tavistok, 1955).
25. Hanna Segal, "Notes on Symbol Formation," in *The Work of Hanna Segal. A Kleinian Approach to Clinical Practice* (New York / London: Jason Aronson, 1981), 49-65.
26. Taking departure from the Kleinian theory some speak of psychotic aspects or nuclei of the neurotic personality. These studies provide a basis for Wilfred Bion's important contribution on thought-processes in psychosis. See his *Second Thoughts* (New York: Jason Aronson, 1977).
27. Jean Guillaumin, "La création artistique et l' élaboration consciente de l'inconscient, avec des considérations particulières sur la création poétique," in Anzieu et al., *Psychanalyse du génie créateur*), 216.
28. Géza Róheim, *The Origin and Function of Culture*, Nervous and Mental Disease Monographs 69 (New York, 1943), 75.
29. D. W. Winnicott, "Transitional Objects and Transitional Phenomena," in *Playing and Reality* (New York: Basic Books, 1971), 1-25.
30. Roland Gori, *"Entre cri et langage: l'acte de Parole," Psychanalyse et Langage* (Paris: Dunod, 1977).
31. Jacques Lacan, *Speech and Language in Psychoanalysis*, trans. Anthony Wilden of *"Fonction et champ de la parole et du langage en psychanalyse," La psychanalyse*, v. I, Paris 1956 (Baltimore: Johns Hopkins, 1981).

Chapter 1

A Psychobiography of Jorge Luis Borges

> The reason a literary work moves us is that it was constructed around a complex.
>
> Gaston Bachelard
>
> Il faut connaitre toute la littérature et la philosophie pour déchiffrer l'oeuvre de Borgès.
>
> Jean Wahl[1]

The decision to attempt a psychoanalytic approach to Borges's work increased my wonder and my fear. I was full of trepidation when I considered the difficulties of a task of such scope, the responsibility it involves, and how hard it would be to study an author who until recently lived in our midst. My awe, my admiration for Borges's monumental work also grew. María Esther Vázquez, Borges's close friend and collaborator, begins her book with the statement that he is far more often written about or commented upon than read. Yet dwelling on his writings involved surprise and wonder for me. I could not help admire the profuse oeuvre he produced during over sixty years of constant literary production, for he started writing when he was twenty years old and continued all his life.

Borges was truly addicted to words, and thanks to his extraordinary memory and his undisputed erudition, he left a beautiful and vast body of essays, criticism, poetry, and short stories. I am tempted to compare him to Picasso for the scope and diversity of his work, for a stylistic process that encompasses the most remarkable variations, and for the power of synthesis he achieved in many years. In stories and poetry, he takes the reader from fascination to horror, from compassion to hatred, from tenderness to pain. One can perceive the harshly conflictive condition of someone trying arduously "to be," to wrestle himself free from a mirrored labyrinth where he is a prisoner in chains. "Even as an unfortunate character who cannot detach himself from the figures on a book," he has struggled throughout his life, as his writings reveal, with and sometimes without energy, to climb out and flee from that garden *behind the fence of iron palings*, or to traverse a crossing impossible for him to go through. The Preface to *Evaristo Carriego* reads,

> For years I believed I had grown up in a suburb of Buenos Aires, a suburb of dangerous streets and showy sunsets. The truth is that I grew up in a garden, behind a fence of iron palings, and in a library of endless English books. The Palermo of the knife and guitar throve (I am told) just around the corner, but those who populated my days and gave a pleasant shiver to my nights were Stevenson's blind buccaneer, dying under the horses' hooves, and the traitor who left his friend behind on the moon, and the time traveler who brought back from the future a withered flower, and the genie imprisoned for centuries in a Solomonic jar, and the Veiled Prophet of Khurasan, who hid his leprosy behind silk and precious stones.
>
> What was going on, meanwhile, on the other side of the iron palings? What everyday lives were fufilling their violent destinies only a few steps away from me in some unsavory saloon or ominous vacant lot? What was Palermo like then, and how beautiful would it really have been? This book, which is less documentary than imaginative, tried to address itself to these questions.[2]

A trained ear, or even one untrained, may hear or read in this text the half-resigned, half-pained voice of imprisonment, isolation, terror. There is dread and horror in readings filled with crime, treason, veils and withered roses. There is fear of clouded, violent and unpredictable destinies.

"Less documentary than imaginary." This is how Borges always wrote, from his infinite memory, from his amazing archive of early readings and encyclopedias, from his insomnia populated by nightmares.

He was shy, extremely reserved. He adored his sister and they both invented an infinite number of extraordinary games. They never quarreled and they were always together before Georgie found in Switzerland some schoolmates.
Q: Borges, what were you like as a boy? As a "pibe" (a kid), as we say in Argentina, were you playful, naughty?
A: No, not at all. I was a reader; somehow I was a writer, even though I did not write. I think I haven't changed; I think I'm the same. And I even keep reading the same authors. I always see myself as a reader. I knew that my destiny would be literary.
"I knew early on that he would be a writer," states his mother. "When he was six he wrote a short story in old Spanish, entitled 'The Fatal River.' It was four or five pages long. When he was very young his language was remarkably unusual. Perhaps he was not hearing well? He totally disfigured many words."[3]

Mrs. Leonor Borges adds: "He was passionate about animals, especially wild beasts. When we visited the zoo, it was difficult to make him leave. And I, who was small, I was afraid of him, so big and strong. I was afraid he'd get into a rage and beat me .... However, he was very kind. When he did not want to give in, I took his books away. That was decisive."[4]

I believe that such memories constituted for Borges a fantasy system of sorts, with unique characteristics. The persistence and recurrence of these themes in his literary production seem to me to identify the thanatic elements of an obsessive version.

Even before he knew the alphabet, his paternal grandmother, Frances Haslam de Borges, read to him English magazines for children, bound in a heavy volume he called "leccionario," a composite of dictionary and lecture. He was insatiable. His favorite readings had to do with animals, the more ferocious the better. The other grandmother, Mrs. Leonor Suárez de Acevedo, was saddened by his enthusiasm for tigers. He clamored for them in his child prattle. "No, baby," the maternal grandmother advised him, "a little lamb is nicer." Yet Georgie would stick to his "ferocious tigers," as he called them, drawing them everywhere. One of his books has been preserved, an English book of children's stories and poems, where all the blanks are covered by the tigers he drew. He always started from the legs, elastic and divergent. Their most notable traits were "teeth and stripes."[5]

> In my childhood I was a fervent worshiper of the tiger: not the jaguar, the spotted "tiger" of the Amazonian tangles and the isles of vegetation that float down the Paraná, but that striped, Asiatic, royal tiger, that can be faced only by a man of war, on a castle atop an elephant. I used to linger endlessly before one of the cages at the zoo; I admired encyclopedias and books of natural history for the splendor of their tigers. (I still remember those illustrations, I, who cannot rightly recall the brow or the smile of a woman.) My childhood came to an end, and the tigers and my passion for them grew old, but they are still present in my dreams.[6]

This is just one example of the fervor, the phantom of desire, that would in diverse ways and forms prowl around the intricate Borgean forest. With his sister he later developed a passion for antediluvian animals, whose difficult names he knew accurately. Just as all his other hobbies, this one was violent and it corresponded to a definite stage. The elementary zoology earned as a child was followed by paleontology and Egyptology, which lasted long. Then came Buddhism, then ancient languages, Anglo-Saxon and Icelandic. "... as if there were a tenacious quest for origins."

Borges learned English first, then Spanish. Neither his sister nor he attended school at the same age as most children. Their father, "who was afraid of infectious diseases," chose to have his children taught at home by an English governess, Miss Tink. Georgie did not start school until he was nine years old.

"I attended fourth grade at a school on Thames Street, where I was taught the elements of *lunfardo*,[7] the rudimentary *lunfardo* of those times. Maybe there were ten or fifteen obscene synonyms. I thought, 'how strange that I don't know the most common words.' I was intimidated by the indigent children who disdainfully taught me the basic *lunfardo* of the day. Surely, I was surprised that at home I had not been instructed in the most common words of the language. In contrast with this, my sister was the leader of her schoolmates. She told the silliest among them some nonsensical stories that they couldn't manage to understand. As a matter of fact, our world was not a closed one."

"*Like all children,*" he told Alicia Jurado, "I was a real snob. In those early days I thought that literature ought to be arduous and that what is easily accessible and pleasant can not be good literature." Many a time Borges, almost defensive, as if he were accused of being different from other children, said, "I was like everybody else." "Like everybody else," he would repeat in different circumstances. *Like everybody else*, he would say again, when he suffered some woman's emotional rejection

and felt humiliated because he did not feel loved. "When we played, Norah would always be the leader, and I used to timidly lag behind. She went up to the terraces, climbed the trees, the hills. I followed her, with more fear than excitement. This contrast also occurred at school."
Norah could see Georgie always reading, lying on his stomach on the ground. He didn't like any manual work or any game of skill, except the diavolo,[8] but he liked to reenact with her scenes taken from books: "he was a prince and she the queen, his mother"; standing on a staircase, they leaned over to hear the acclamations of an imaginary multitude; or they traveled to the moon in a "missile" built by folding a red silk Chinese screen... into which they tumbled after sliding down the banister of the staircase. Sometimes, they traveled dangerously on the flat roofs, searching for a room where they'd never been, a mysterious place that ought perforce to exist.[9]

During the holidays they used to visit their mother's cousins, the Haedos, who had a country house in Montevideo, at a location called Paso del Molino. There all three, Georgie, Norah, and their cousin Esther, played. There was a lookout tower, with a spiral staircase and colored windows, doubtless the origin, as A. Jurado points out, of Triste-le-Roy's red and green diamonds in Borges's story *"La muerte y la brújula* (Death and the Compass)." My own observation is that this gazebo also appears in the story "Emma Zunz," as a memory masking infantile sexual play. A *"mirador"* is a place where one looks, peers, satisfies one's curiosity concerning sex.[10] Walking up a spiral staircase is something children find delightful. In that solitary place the three kids founded the Society of the Three Crosses, where the two girls ought to defend the boy from an imaginary enemy who wanted to kill him. I dwell upon these memories because they would be significant for a psychoanalytic session.

Headquarters was a painted wooden kiosk surrounded by a balcony and reached by means of a small bridge. They wrote messages to each other in a code invented by the presumed victim, and they wandered in the country house wearing cloth masks. The theme of pursuit, expressed in their games, later persisted in Borges's stories, fashioned in innumerable fantastic variations.

Borges was born on August 24th, 1899, in the same house where his mother had been born, on Tucumán Street between Esmeralda and Suipacha. He came to this world after eight months of pregnancy, and one can easily imagine the anxiety of a mother over her first child, a mother who always relied on the help of her own mother. When he was nine months old and was beginning to crawl and break away, his mother became pregnant again. Her attention was henceforth divided between Georgie and the new baby she was carrying in her womb.

A sibling's birth is always a traumatic experience, even more so if they are separated by just eighteen months.[11] Might this be the reason that Borges—he of the prodigious memory—when interviewed by Burgin in Cambridge, in 1974, told him that his sister was three or four years younger than he was?

His early years were spent in that old rambling house with huge rooms, furnished with antique and robust oak pieces that in the silence of the night would stretch and yawn with terrifying whispers. The walls imposed the worship of swords. The serious countenances of military men who had fought in the war for independence seemed to be ordering cavalry charges. Georgie and Norah grew in this atmosphere of an antiquities museum, amid the smell of old halls and the sound of fanfare, of pomp and ceremony.

Norah still remembers the terror-filled nights when they were left alone upstairs, in their bedrooms, facing an enormous antique wardrobe with three big moon-shaped mirrors that reflected their images as they lay in bed. When I was very young," Borges confesses, "I never dared tell my parents to leave me in a totally dark room so as to be free from that fear.[12]

> As a child, I felt before large mirrors that same horror of a spectral duplication or multiplication of reality. Their infallible and continous functioning, their pursuit of my actions, their cosmic pantomime, were uncanny then, whenever it began to grow dark. One of my persistent prayers to God and my guardian angel was that I not dream about mirrors. I know I watched them with misgivings. Sometimes I feared they might begin to deviate from reality; other times I was afraid of seeing there my own face, disfigured by strange calamities.[13]

In a poem entitled "Mirrors" he wrote,

> Today at the tip of so many and perplexing
> Wandering years under the varying moon,
> I ask myself what whim of fate
> Made me so fearful of a glancing mirror.
>
> I see them as infinite, elemental
> Executors of an ancient pact,

> To multiply the world like the act
> Of begetting. Sleepless. Bringing doom.[14]

Antonio Carrizo relates that in 1914, shortly before the beginning of World War I, the Borges family traveled to Europe.[15] Borges was fifteen, and when asked why that trip was made, he replied:

> **BORGES**: You see, my father wanted to live in a city where no one would know him. Besides that, he saw a picture... the one, I think, with the Rhone, where one can see the old city, the Alps... and he said, "I'll take a walk here." And we chose to go to Switzerland.
> **CARRIZO**: That period in Geneva branded you for ever, didn't it, Borges?
> **BORGES**: "Well... that was my adolescence, those were years of beautiful experiences. Friendship, too. And my studies. Because I attended secondary school in Geneva and that gave me the French language as a gift."[16]

It seems that some poems written in French at that time were lost. His mother remembered one grimly poetic line with this metaphor for a coffin, *"petite boîte noire pour le violon cassé."*

There he taught himself German. He read *Der Golem,* by Gustav Meyrink. Also Verlaine, Montaigne, and especially Schopenhauer, whom he admired, and with whom he felt he identified.

After a sojourn to Spain (there, in Palma de Mallorca, his father wrote a novel entitled *El caudillo* (The Leader), the family returned in 1921.

> **MARÍA ESTHER VÁZQUEZ**: If you were summarizing your life, which moments in it would you say were the most important?
> **BORGES**: My first return to Buenos Aires. And also very intimate moments that were happy, and the times when I write.

Returning, he rediscovered Buenos Aires, and about this "reunion" with Buenos Aires he wrote in 1943:

> ... I felt Buenos Aires,
> This city I thought was my past
> Is really my future, my present;
> The years I have lived in Europe are illusory,
> I have always been (and will be) in Buenos Aires.[17]

Borges published *Fervor de Buenos Aires,* his first book of poetry, where, as he states himself, an understanding reader may find the heartaches, the sadness, the ghosts and the concerns which will be apparent in his entire work.[18]

It was a period of high youthful enthusiasm. With Eduardo González Lanuza, Norah Lange, and Francisco Piñero, he founded the mural journal *Prisma*. The ultraist manifesto written by Borges and published in the journal *Nosotros* is also dated 1921.

The following year, Borges, Macedonio Fernández, González Lanuza, and others published the first issue of the journal *Proa*. Three issues of this journal saw the light between August 1922 and July 1923. I have culled a direct testimony about this period in Borges's life, published by the Spanish writer Ramón Gómez de la Serna. He visited the Borges family and published this piece in *Revista de Occidente* simultaneously with a review of *Fervor de Buenos Aires*. I transcribe it at some length because I believe it contains valuable information.[19]

> The image of the remote Borges that I have had for quite some time will serve to explain to me this nearer Borges, who has just sat down on Pombo's couch, the hard couch of these heirs of the past. My image of the remote Borges revealed a pale, sensitive youth, hiding among thick drapes lined in off-white, a boyish youth you never find when you call him.
> "Jorge!... Jorge!... Come on, where are you hiding?"
> The boy was behind the drapes, peering at things he would always remember.
> I always remember Jorge Luis by the side of his sister Norah, the intriguing girl whose skin was as pale as his, who was lost, as he was, among the drapes, peering at everything in the distinguished Borges house, full of pictures, of great open halls, mirrors with rain, candle-holders where flames that no one had lit shone on mysterious and effusive occasions.
> While Jorge Luis kept silent, Norah Borges showed us this house "*that the tightly bonded patriarchal Borges family never left.*" [20] Norah depicted in her wooden etchings, and described to us confidentially, her evenings with some girlfriends who, when alone, revealed their shapely legs, crossing them 'like a T." They spent the time (silly girls!) playing chess by locating themselves on the checkered floor of the hall. She talked about the small magic lamps with fringed shades, the large flower pots, each worth a garden and a grotto, the man-eating sofas, the cages of artificial birds, the *tresillo* tables whose vests contained table pockets.[21]
> Afterwards, Norah took us out to those terraces where the steps echo as if in rooms, as though the immense night gained deep intimacy

Psychobiography

over them, as though it were a starred room draped with wildly caressing velvet.

What Norah revealed was witnessed, I knew, by a brother who reserved himself for poetry, was amassing poetry. I expected great things from him as soon as he wrested himself away from the drapes of the great nostalgic house and untied the distinguished strings with the sort of tassels that decorate drapes with a San Fernando tie.

Unsociable, remote, rebellious, he only occasionally let a poem fly like an exotic, exquisite bird into the daytime sky.

Ramón Gómez de la Serna describes as follows a traditional Argentinian home in those times. He provides a backdrop for the contrasting presence of two siblings: one "hiding among thick drapes" and one "revealing shapely legs" in the night's "wildly caressing velvet." It seems that Norah was a self-asssured, seductive adolescent, while Jorge Luis was "unsociable" and "remote," an introvert, a poet.

His literary endeavors and the new friendships he had been able to develop filled him with enthusiasm. Yet something clouded those years. And his father's blindness compelled them to travel to Europe again.

These reports make me think that the family nucleus moved *en bloc*, in a manner rather symbiotic and phobic. Leaving Buenos Aires this time was quite painful to young Georgie. He had fallen in love with a girl whose hair was tied in long braids and dedicated to her, before departing, these lines:

> Three hundred nights like three hundred walls
> must rise between my love and me
> and the sea will be a black art between us.
>
> Time with a hard hand will tear out
> the streets tangled in my breast.
> Nothing will be left but memories.[22]

"This poem," says Alicia Jurado, "was prophetic."[23] When he returned, the girl had cut her braids, and with them went too the inconstant poet's passion. Borges always was, of course, a man inclined to one-on-one exchanges. And he always preferred women for this manner of dialogue—rather a cautious, full of questions monologue into which he gradually brought his interlocutor so as to develop his own ideas. He had many female friends, so diverse that it is impossible to find a single common trait among them, not even stupidity, as some mischievously say, because several were intelligent. Borges, however, did not choose them on account of their intelligence, or their beauty, or any identifiable attribute. I think he applied to women the same criterion he used for pictures: he did not consider the totality, nor did he judge the value, but rather became interested in some minimal detail that had escaped notice until then, and this detail allowed him to decide whether he liked the picture. Perhaps when it came to a woman it may have been her name, her braids, a shared pleasure in something, or some association of ideas that moved him to seek her friendship. Habit, an effective factor in his life, may have done the rest.

Borges stayed forever a boyish man, an adult boy. The relationships he had with the different women who figured in his life have qualities typical of filial relationships, in which he showed the nuances characteristic of a tender, arbitrary, willful, seductive, and demanding son (or father).

Jurado continues the description of Borges,

> Though superlatively strange, terribly introverted, quite maniacal, contradictory, and disconcerting, this human being arouses great affection. He always seems insecure, pessimistic, and somehow profoundly helpless. That must be the trap he sets for our tenderness. Often, deceived by his sweetness and by some touching childish trait, I looked at him with the sort of tender maternal superiority we women feel toward men who seem defenseless. Yet soon I realized, with some alarm, that I was the one who needed him. I found support in his firm intelligence, as any young girl would who is only beginning to live.

And Alicia Jurado confesses, not without a touch of understandable feminine disappointment,

> And during all the hours spent in more than twenty years of friendship, with very rare exceptions, we talked endlessly about literature. I don't know if I should deplore it. It may be a mistake to expect that a man will be everything. In these times of specialization we should accept the fact that he was only a writer, rather than demand of him that his life encompass 'life and death' like anyone else's.

"Life and death have lacked in my life—from that indigence— my toilsome love for these minutiae," says the poet. The thought process has been libidinized for Borges. Words have been charged with passion and that has left him indigent as a human being. And then, again, perhaps he arrived at resentment and asceticism starting from a certain indigence, which, real as it was for Georgie's soul, may or may not have been factual.

As we have seen, he wrote in "Dreamtigers," "I still remember those illustrations, I, who cannot rightly recall the brow or the smile of a woman." Thus a woman appears as a confused memory, or at times only a film-clip, a partial recollection of a brow, a countenance, a smile. At times, as something given or withdrawn, something to take or leave. Just as the love that for Borges is played only in dark hallways and tortuous houses of prostitution, "woman" is assimilated either to "prostitute" or to "unfaithful and incestuous." I develop this theme of woman and love in Borges's life in later chapters, especially in "Endimión in Buenos Aires."

Why so much resentment, such disdain, so much contempt? They are surprising in someone who has developed such a close bond, first with his mother and sister, and later with the women who collaborated with him, assisted him as secretaries, and guided his blind steps. Since approximately 1956, Borges has been compelled by blindness to dictate his work, and this naturally created a situation in which others, especially his mother, participated. As a matter of fact, doña Leonor confessed her dislike of some themes, such as the *compadritos* (city swaggerers), Evaristo Carriego, certain fantastic stories, etc.. Some poems Borges did not dictate to her so as to spare her suffering (such as "*Los dones*," because it alluded to his blindness). She wrote the last few lines of the story "The Intruder." Actually he himself made frequent references to his mother's opinions, in attitudes ranging from the greatest dependence to an almost adolescent rebellion.

Emecé published in 1974 the first edition of his *Obras completas* (Complete Works). Borges dedicated it "To Leonor Acevedo de Borges." He wanted to record in writing a confession, that he never felt deserving of presents. But of that shy childhood he says,

> You have given me so many things, and the years and the memories are so many. Father; Norah; all four grandparents; your memories, and in them the memories of your forefathers—the patios, the slaves, the water seller, the charge of those Peruvian hussars, and the shame of Rosas—your honorable imprisonment, when so many of us men kept silence; the mornings in Montevideo, Geneva, and Austin; the bright and dark times shared; your youthful old age; your love of Dickens and of Eça de Queirós—Mother, you yourself. These words are just between us two, et *tout le reste est littérature*, as Verlaine, in his fine literary way, wrote.[24]

In the year following that publication (July 8th, 1975), Borges's mother died at the age of ninety nine years. María Esther Vázquez says,

"To this day, her room remains untouched. He enters in the morning the empty sunlit room and silently salutes the invisible presence." This is a negation of death, of what is lost, of the passage of time. "The inwardness of Good-bye is tragic / like that of every event in which Time is manifest." (From a poem by Borges dedicated to Rafael Cansinos Assens.[25])

> **CARRIZO**: Who gave the tone, the style, to the household, to your upbringing, to the shaping of these children, Norah and yourself? Was it Doña Leonor or was it your father?
> **BORGES**: It is so difficult to tell! Because I do not see them as different. Possibly my mother was more concerned. My father was an indifferent man. And he had become skeptical about many things. I don't really know. It is a question I have never asked myself. My father was a lawyer and a psychology professor. He used much irony; he was a friend of Macedonio Fernández; he revered Macedonio, they cared greatly for one another; later I inherited Macedonio's friendship.
> He told me to read, to write when I felt the need to do it and advised me not to publish. Or to publish as late as possible. He knew that my destiny was literary. And he helped me, by letting me into his library; but he never gave me direct advice. I showed him the manuscript of my first book, asking him to edit it, and he said, 'No, you have to edit it later.' Later I gave him a copy and he never expressed an opinion on the book; yet after he died we found that he had saved that copy, which was... well, full of editing marks.
> My father was a very brave man and I am not. Yet we both accepted our blindness. My paternal greatgrandfather and my grandmother were also blind.

How does one listen to these recollections? I for one feel almost physically uneasy. What a great distance, how much coldness flows through these veins pried apart in words, empty of passion. So much tenderness is absent, there is so much formality. One can see no emotion, not even for the first fruit of his talent. What a cuirass, what a blind heart, how much feeling has been frozen; how obstinate and harsh is the demand.

In "*Un ensayo autobiográfico* (An Autobiographical Essay)," Borges reminisces about his father:

> He also wrote (and destroyed) a book of essays, and published a translation of Fitzgerald's Omar Khayyám in the same meter as the original. He destroyed a book of Oriental stories—in the manner of the

Arabian Nights—and a drama, *Hacia la nada* (Toward Nothingness), about a man's disappointment in his son.[26]

Borges's father, we should not forget, was also blind. He strikes me as a narcissistic personality, with remarkable obsessive and phobic traits. He was nihilistic and skeptical, a perfectionist with ambition, and he placed in Georgie (and encouraged in ambivalent and contradictory ways) all of his own hopes and aspirations.

From the time he was a very young boy, Borges toyed with the aporias of Zeno and the tortoise, with Berkely and Hume, with *The Arabian Nights*, with Shelley, Keats, Swinburne, and the psychology of William James. Clearly what he did not do was play with other children in his neighborhood. A bodily, warm and affectionate contact with others was missing.

Borges's relationship with his father may be rather seen as almost resembling the relationship of a professor and his pupil. And it is not devoid of "a disturbing aspect," as Emir Rodríguez Monegal writes.[27]

Jorge Luis Borges's translation of Oscar Wilde's *The Happy Prince* was published in one of the Buenos Aires dailies, and because he signed it merely "Jorge Borges," people assumed the translation was his father's, while the father's translation of Omar Khayyam was thought to be the son's work. Might this be the origin of the false bibliographic references he had so much fun with in many stories?

The books written by Georgie that his father could read before he died were *Fervor de Buenos Aires*, five volumes of essays, three of which he did not publish again, the biography of Evaristo Carriego, and *Historia universal de la infamia* (A Universal History of Infamy).

It is significant and striking that Jorge Luis Borges never had a job until his father's death, in 1938. At thirty nine, he became a librarian at the Municipal Library of Caballito, a neighborhood in the city of Buenos Aires. His retiring nature and his shyness limited and hampered him to the point that twice his friend, the writer Pedro Henríquez Ureña, had to read the speeches that Borges had written and was supposed to deliver. He called himself a "veteran of panic."[28] A few months after his father died he had an accident that waylaid him for two weeks. His mother describes it as follows,

> Georgie had two serious accidents, the first when he was very young. He fell from the first car of a streetcar and the wheels of the second car missed his head by a few inches. Some of his hair was pulled, his glasses were not broken but his nose was badly hurt. He had another

horrible accident, and after that he started writing fantastic stories, something that had never happened to him before; *I believe something changed in his brain.* In any case, for a while it was touch-and-go whether he would live or die. It was Christmas Eve, and Georgie went to pick up a guest we had invited to dinner. It seemed that, the elevator being out of service, he had climbed the stairs very quickly and did not see an open window; he walked right into it, and pieces of broken glass pierced his scalp. The scars are still visible. Because the wound had not been properly disinfected before it was sutured, the next day he was running a high fever, which persisted until it was finally necessary to operate, in the middle of the night. For two weeks he was between life and death. At the end of the first week, the fever began to abate and he told me, "Read me a book, read me a page." He was hallucinating, he saw animals coming into the room, and the like. I read him a page and then he said, "That's all right."—"What do you mean?"—"Yes, now I know that I'm not going to be insane, I have understood everything." He began to write fantastic stories afterward, a thing that had never happened to him before... As soon as he was back home again, he began to write a fantastic story, his first one... And afterward, he wrote only fantastic stories, which scare me a little because I don't understand them very well. I asked him once, "Why don't you write again the same things you used to write?" And he answered, "Do not insist, do not insist." And he was right.[29]

The mother made a mistake in this testimony published, as I mentioned before, in the Paris journal *L'Herne*. When she heard Georgie was in a hospital emergency room, "My husband and I," she says, "hurried there." Years later she rectified the error, explaining that it was her son-in-law, Guillermo de Torre, who went with her. Is this slip a simple lapse of memory? Or does it reveal a denial of her husband's death, just as Borges will later deny his mother's passing away?

This accident on Christmas Eve, 1938, marks a milestone in the life and the work of Jorge Luis Borges. Psychoanalysts who specialize in accidents usually emphasize the fact that the probability of accidents increases in situations of change. How else could we understand this injury, this accident that led to the complication of septicemia, a few months after the death of the father? Is it just the expression of his anxiety before meeting with a woman? Might this injury be like a self-circumcision that allows him to access an adult, autonomous life? And, pursuing this line of thought, can this cut on the forehead be interpreted as a symbolic displacement of another cut, one that did not occur at the appropriate time, on account of the absence of the father as paternal function? What is certain is that "something," as *doña* Leonor says, "changed inside his brain."

Rodríguez Monegal (who is not a psychoanalyst) interprets it as follows, "After the accident (the trial, the ordeal) Borges reappears transformed into a different writer, engendered only by himself. Before the accident he was a poet, a book critic; after the accident he will be the author of complex and fascinating verbal labyrinths, the producer of a new form, the story which is at the same time an essay. The new Borges (the new writer) goes much farther than any of his father's projects. That the accident also occurred in romantic circumstances (let us not forget, he was on his way to pick up a young woman to bring her to the house) only adds the necessary erotic element to the symbolic patricide that the act itself (the death and resurrection of the Hero) implies."[30]

In his important study on the work of Borges, Didier Anzieu distinguishes, coincidentally, two stages in the writer's entire production, one before and one after, the death of the father and the 1938 accident, which he takes as indicators.[31] He says, "Borges must renounce the Oedipal competition and must develop his work at another level." My own study of Borges leads me to believe that his set of problems travels the ambivalent winding paths of narcissistic dependence rather than the open field of the Oedipal conflicts. The itinerary is one of subjection rather than struggle, one of dual bonding rather than triangular passions.

Indeed there is a cut, a relative liberation from narcissistic attachments from a symbiotic bond with an authoritarian father who held his son prisoner in a mirror relationship that paralized him. The injury, the septicemia and the risk of death allowed Jorge Luis to be re-born toward his own style, toward his own ideas. He unconsciously paid the relief of guilt for his father's death and thus was able to wrestle himself from the figure, imagined or real, of an idealized father who was his pursuer.

His liberation was furthermore relative, it took place exclusively in literary terms. Borges realized this and deplored it. For that reason he often felt as a wretched individual who could only repeat, who could only be someone else's echo or dream. Let us remember "*Las ruinas circulares* (The Circular Ruins),"[32] "*El Golem,*"[33] and these lines:

> Echoes, undertow, sand, lichen, dreams
> Nothing else am I but those images.[34]

He attempts time and again to rescue himself as a subject but he finds it impossible: "I am destined to repeat myself, I am definitely monotonous."

I transcribed earlier (p. 18) Borges's description of the garden and the library where he grew up, citing it from a prologue Borges wrote in 1974. He had expressed the same sentiment in 1945, when he earned the Sociedad Argentina de Escritores' highest award for his book *Ficciones*. Fernando Pessoa writes, "Art lives on the same street as life, but has a different address; this is the art that gives relief from life but no relief from living..."[35] Borges wanders inside himself and seeks that relief by transforming all his intricate and arduous interior world into a rich and beautifully crafted palace, where he makes up with words his poetry and his tortuous stories. With them and through them he lives, enjoys, realizes himself as a human being. What is more, I believe that by means of them he was able to survive.

"*Funes, el memorioso* (Funes, the Memorious)" cured his persistent insomnia. "*Pierre Menard, autor del Quijote* (Pierre Menard, Author of the *Quixote*)" allowed him to realize that he had recovered after his accident. He acted courageously in the stories about knife-wielding felons, he took revenge in "*Hombre de la esquina rosada* (Man at the Streetcorner)." He calls "revelations" the themes that occur to him, in a manner very much like free association. That is what makes his work so rich and so suggestive for a psychoanalytic reading. Due to his erudition and his personal traits these associations often turn out to be excessive, bizarre, extensive, convoluted and confusing.

After *Ficciones* and *El Aleph* one can observe an attempt to write in a more sober, a simpler language. Perhaps this effect is more apparent than real, because he never loses sight of the complex web of multiple allusions, half mocking and half erudite, esoteric, cabalistic.

All the learning and all the books are condensed in one point; in one word, there is the universe. Just as in *El Aleph,* his entire life, past, present, and future form a sinister teratoma where endless memories, images, and fantasies occur, as it were, in packets of mnemonic traces scattered and fragmented without binding cement.

In "*El jardín de senderos que se bifurcan* (The Garden of Forking Paths)," he writes, "In all fiction, when a man is faced with alternatives he chooses one at the expense of the others. In that of the almost unfathomable Ts'ui Pên, he chooses—simultaneously—all of them."[36]

"The complexity and the originality of the stories," writes Noé Jitrik, "equally trace the heightened torment of a spirit that struggles, torn by his total appetite, and his inability to satisfy it." The expression "torn" chosen by a literary critic reminds me of what Wilfred Bion says in "Language and the Schizophrenic," "In order to control such greed the patient splits and establishes the mechanism of *Spaltung,* or Ego cleavage."[37]

The French critic, Pierre Macherey, attempts to approach Borges's fiction in *Pour une théorie de la production littéraire* as follows, '"How is it possible to write the simplest story, since it implies an infinite possibility of variation, since its chosen form will always lack other forms that might have clothed it? The art of Borges is to respond to this question by means of a story: by choosing among these forms precisely that which, on account of its imbalance, its obviously artificial nature, and its contradictions, best preserves the question."[38]

Which question does the chosen form preserve? That of the narcissistic, omniscient, divine, and megalomaniac desire of possessing all at one point and simultaneously; possessing it all and giving nothing up, possessing it all in one moment rather than in sequential time, and fashioning it in a single, sublime, and impossible word. The chosen forms allow him to express himself by means of ambiguous, contradictory, artificial, and imaginative characters. Deep down, however, they don't allow him to rescue himself from the circle and the labyrinth, the garden and the library, the book and the crime. Indeed the crime, for Borges is considered a master of the detective story. Moreover, we know that he was a learned, an erudite bibliophile. Book and crime are recurrent themes: the books are those of his father's library "with numberless English books," and the crime is what lies outside that "fence of iron palings. Palermo, the knife and the guitar wandered (they assure me) the street corners."

Insofar as the imagined reality has those qualities, action is limited to the book. The book is therefore a shelter from overflowing fantasies, where he projects, as if upon a screen, his own persecutory anxieties. Borges gives clear signs of his schizoid personality by dissociating and locating outside all that is impulsive, passional, perverse. And he does this dispassionately. Graham Greene wrote once that, had he not been a writer, he'd have been a criminal.

Borges sublimates himself by writing. He admires the epic, and is moved by it. In the political arena we know that more than once he declared himself conservative and reactionary. "I distrust democracy, that curious abuse of statistics."[39] He writes stories where crime has its own value, as a plain affirmation of power, rivalry, challenge. Thus he even comes to identify, as he recognizes himself, arrogance with courage, defiance with valor. Borges's frequent and successful incursions into the genre of stories dealing with knife-wielding hoodlums, *compadritos* (city swaggerers), and criminals, usually perverse and with homosexual traits, is indeed surprising. Alicia Jurado points out in this respect, "The knife is one of the main characters of stories and evocations of ruffians, the sect of the knife and the courage that Borges can not admire rationally yet appeals to some irrational zone of his complex psychology."

In the book on Evaristo Carriego there is a page where he describes a knife from Toledo that once belonged to his father,"In a drawer of my writing table, among draft pages and old letters, the dagger dreams over and over its simple tiger's dream. On wielding it the hand comes alive because the metal comes alive, sensing itself, each time handled, in touch with the killer for whom it was forged. At times I am sorry for it. Such power and single-mindedness, so impassive or innocent its pride, and the years slip by, unheeding.[40]

What is striking is that he speaks about himself in similar terms in his poetry,

> In vain have oceans been squandered on you, in vain
> The sun, wonderfully seen through Whitman's eyes.
> You have used up the years and they have used up you,
> And still, and still, you have not written the poem.[41]

A knife that does not fulfill the mission for which it was created hurts him. A life that weaves and unweaves nothingness fills him with guilt. He is tormented by the figure of a superlative hero, out of reach, for which he was engendered yet one that, despite all his monumental work, he cannot meet. So much greed!

His entire libidinal ability has been displaced, absolute and violent as it is, toward purely intellectual work. Perhaps it is thus he feels and does not feel love; feels and does not feel hatred and cruelty. Are these experiences alien to him because they have been discharged of emotions? Or is it the case that, because they have discharged their affection, they are *experienced* as if they were alien? He needed to conterpoise the irresistible force of his pulsions with an infinitely greater force of control and rationality.

This apparently frozen poet, this purely intellectual, ascetic man, conceals passions that are dramatic, absolute, total, tremendous. There are two Borges, and they don't know one another.

> Years ago, when my mother was still alive, I was taking a bath, enjoying the cool water in that state resembling a dream, and suddenly I heard myself saying something, and that something (which I will not repeat) was the first line of a poem, and then came another. I could see that

those two lines had a theme and that theme had to be necessarily a painful one, because that was the tone the poem required. Then I could more or less discern a poem that I dictated to my mother so as not to lose it, and my mother said with genuine alarm, 'But Georgie, I did not know that you were so sad: why haven't you told me anything?' And I replied: 'I have told you nothing because I did not know it.' Or perhaps, if we resort to current psychology (but I prefer not to resort to it), I was subconsciously sad, did not realize it. What is remarkable is that I did not know that I was going to say what I said, just as I did not know that I was sad and yet that desperate poem came out.

Once again Borges's fine psychological perception is amazing. In another anecdote he reminisces,

One of my friends, a professor from Paraguay, took me to his home in Texas. He said he had tangos and asked if I wanted to hear them. I said, "Yes, of course." He played all the tangos I loathe, actually. For instance, "*Flaca, fané y descangallada*," "*La cumparsita*"... I thought to myself, "What a disgrace; these aren't tangos, how horrible this is!" And while I was thus judging them intellectually, I felt my own tears. I was crying with emotion. That is to say, I condemned that music intellectually and yet at the same time it had touched me and I was crying.[42]

This is the Borges to whom poems and stories are revealed; they come to his mind as random thoughts. They are his own feelings. This is Borges, the narrator, immersed in dreams and nightmares. This insightful explorer of rugged and strange internal landscapes is a true fountain of perplexity and amazement for psychoanalysis and psychoanalysts. As a child, he tells us, he cherished the fantasy of possessing a prodigious magnifying glass that would let him discover the Minotaur in the center of a picture of the Cretan Labyrinth.

I don't know whether my attempt to peer into Borges may share in that magic and that impossible yearning.

Notes

1. Jean Wahl, *L'Herne* 4 (1964), 258
2. Jorge Luis Borges, *Evaristo Carriego* (Evaristo Carriego: a Book about Old-time Buenos Aires), trans. Susan Ashe (New York: Dutton, 1984), 33-34.
3. Leonor Acevedo de Borges, "Propos de Mme. Leonor Acevedo de Borges," *L'Herne* 4 (1964), 9-10. English translation as cited in E. Rodríguez Monegal, *Jorge Luis Borges: A Literary Biography* (New York: Dutton, 1978), 27.
4. Ibid., 37.
5. An image of one of those tigers drawn by Borges as a boy is found in E. Rodríguez Monegal, *Borges par lui même* (Paris: Editions du Seuil, 1970). The shape suggests a rather successful drawing by a five- or six-year-old. Two traits are striking: the intensity with which the mouth is enhanced, and the position of the rear legs, rather flaccid, without firm support. The first of these characteristics relates to great oral greed, while the second may be interpreted as a weak stance in reality, with the realm of fantasy being privileged. Other qualities deserve comment as well. The stripes on the body and the legs overlap the boundaries of the skin (lack of discrimination of Self and non-Self?). The figure does not create a sense of texture, and this suggests difficulties in physical contact. More generally, this tiger does not impress as a "ferocious" one, and he lacks feline elegance. He is a bit flat, weak, lifeless. One might even say he looks like a *poor* old, blind tiger.
6. Borges, "The Maker," *Dreamtigers*, transl. Mildred Boyer and Harold Morland (New York: Dutton, 1964), 24.
7. Name given to the slang of Buenos Aires and surrounding areas. [Translator's note.]
8. A game played with a wooden hoop.
9. Alicia Jurado, *Genio y figura de Jorge Luis Borges* (Buenos Aires: Eudeba, 1980), 29.
10. "*Mirador*," Spanish for lookout tower, or gazebo, derives from the root of "*mirar*," watch or look. [Translators' note.]
11. Sigmund Freud, "Three Essays on the Theory of Sexuality," SE 7, 194-95 writes, "The threat to the bases of a child's existence offered by the discovery or the suspicion of the arrival of a new baby and the fear that he may, as a result of it, cease to be cared for and loved, make him thoughtful and clear-sighted... the first problem with which it deals is not the question of the distinction between the sexes but the riddle of where babies come from.. This, in a distorted form which can easily be rectified, is the same riddle that was propounded by the Theban Sphinx."
12. María Esther Vázquez, *Borges, imágenes, memorias, diálogos* (Buenos Aires: Monte Ávila, 1977), 52.
13. Borges, "The Draped Mirrors," *Dreamtigers*, 27.
14. Borges, ibid., 60.

15. Emir Rodríguez Monegal, *Jorge Luis Borges*, 110-111 comments on the arrival of his grandmother in Geneva as World War I was being fought:

> Fanny Haslam's courage is a subject Borges loves to discuss. She had proved it in her early years in Argentina when she shared frontier life with her husband, Colonel Borges. Now, in facing the German submarines, Grandmother showed her truly British spirit. With her arrival in Geneva, the original Borges clan was restored. Life in Geneva began to take on features of life in Palermo (Buenos Aires).
>
> Before his grandmother's arrival, Georgie had sent her postcards which revealed his homesickness... He trie[s] to make more acceptable the fact that he was still so attached to his grandmother's apron strings.
>
> Grandmother was not the only relative to visit the Borgeses in Switzerland. Arund 1916 some of Mother's Uruguayan cousins came to Europe. They belonged to the Haedo branch of the family. To celebrate the visit, Father took some photographs which show at least three generations of Haedo women surrounding *doña* Leonor, the maternal grandmother. Among these women (eight in all), Georgie cuts a strange figure. Even with his closest relatives he seems the odd man out, the stranger. The difference is visible in the expression of the face, the sadness of the eyes behind the thick glasses, and the terribly unhappy mouth. It is also evident in the way he sits or stands, always so clumsily, as if his body, growing too quickly and with a will of its own, bothered him too much.

In those difficult days Georgie could not forget he had a body."
16. Antonio Carrizo, *Borges el memorioso* (Buenos Aires: Tierra Firme, 1982), 257.
17. Borges, *Dreamtigers*, xi.
18. Borges, *Fervor de Buenos Aires, Obras completas* (Buenos Aires: Emecé, 1969).
19. Ramón Gómez de la Serna, cited by Jurado, 182.
20. The emphasis is mine.
21. *Tresillo*: omber, an old-fashioned card game. [Translator's note.]
22. Borges, *Selected Poems 1923-1967*, ed. Norman Thomas di Giovanni, (New York: Delacorte / Seymour Lawrence, 1972), 28-29. Transl. W. S. Merwin.
23. Jurado, 28-29.
24. Borges, Preface to "*El Otro, el Mismo*," in *Selected Poems*, 278.
25. Borges, ibid., 248. Trans. Robert Fitzgerald.
26. "A man's disappointment in his son" is in English in the original. Borges, "An Autobiographical Essay," *The Aleph and Other Stories. 1933-1969*, ed. and transl. Norman Thomas di Giovanni in collaboration with the author (New York: Dutton, 1970), 211.
27. Emir Rodríguez Monegal, *Borges hacia una interpretación* (Madrid: Guadarrama, 1976), 87.

28. A personal recollection of Alicia Jurado.
29. Acevedo de Borges, "*Propos*," 10.
30. Rodríguez Monegal, *Borges hacia una interpretación*.
31. Anzieu, Didier, "*Le corps et le code dans les contes de J. L. Borges*," *Nouvelle Revue de Psychanalyse* (Paris: Gallimard, 1971), 177-210.
32. Borges, "The Circular Ruins," *Ficciones, 1933-1969*, ed. and trans. Donald A. Yates and James E. Irby (New York: New Directions, 1962), 50:

> Not to be a man, to be the projection of another man's dream, what a feeling of humiliation, what vertigo! All fathers are interested in the children they have procreated (they have permitted to exist) in mere confusion or pleasure; it was natural that the magician should fear for the future of that son, created in thought, limb by limb and feature by feature, in a thousand and one secret nights.

33. Borges, "*El Golem*", *Selected Poems*, 113, 115. Trans. John Hollander.

> Less a man's than a dog's eyes, less a dog's, well,
> Even than a thing's, the creature's eyes
> Would always turn to follow the rabbi's
> Steps through the dubious shadows of his cell.
> . . . .
> The rabbi gazed on it with tender eyes
> and terror. How (he asked) *could it be done*
> That I engender this distressing son?
> *Inaction is wisdom. I left off being wise.*

34. Borges, "*El hacedor*," in "*La cifra*," *Obra poética* (Buenos Aires: Emecé, 1960). 585.
35. Fernando Pessoa, *Livro do desassossego* (Lisbon: Atica, 1982).
36. Borges, "The Garden of Forking Paths," *Ficciones*, 98.
37. Wilfred Bion, "Language and the Schizophrenic,"*New Directions in Psycho-Analysis*, ed. M. Klein et al. (London: Tavistock, 1974, 220-239.
38. Pierre Macherey, *Pour une théorie de la production littéraire* (Paris: Maspero, 1966), 281:

> *Comment écrire la plus simple histoire, alors qu'elle implique une possibilité infinie de variation, alors que sa forme choisie manquera toujours des autres formes que auraient pu l'habiller? L'art de Borgès c'est qu'il répond à cette question par un récit: en choisissant justement parmi ces formes celle qui, par son déséquilibre, son caractère évidemment artificieux, ses contradictions, préserve le mieux la question.*

39. Prologue to *La moneda de hierro* (Buenos Aires: Emecé, 1976).
40. Borges, *Carriego*, 126-27.

41. Borges, "Mateo XXV:30, *"El otro, el mismo,"* *Selected Poems*, 93.
42. Carrizo, *Borges el memorioso*, 77.

Chapter 2

The Literary Style. The Man

In a famous definition, Buffon identifies style with self: *"Le style est l'Homme."*[1] In this chapter I attempt to investigate the style in order to discover the man. It goes without saying that mine is not a literary reading but a psychoanalytic one. That, however, does not exempt me from considering the literary aspects of his work. On the contrary, it dictates that I take a detour along all aspects of the narrative art, along rhetorical figures and along the diverse *in-scriptions* or stylizations offered by language, or rather, achieved by the writer by means of language.

The two most important collections of stories produced by Borges were published between 1939 and 1949. They were *Ficciones* (1944) and *El Aleph* (1949). That decade brought about the recognition of Jorge Luis Borges in the forum of international literary criticism.

In his early work, poetry alternated with essay. In 1923 he published *Fervor de Buenos Aires*, in 1925 *Luna de enfrente* (Moon across the Way), and in 1929 *Cuaderno San Martín* (Notebook of San Martín), all books of poetry.[2] Essays of this period are: *Inquisiciones* (Inquisitions, 1925), *El tamaño de mi esperanza* (The Dimension of my Hope, 1926), and *El idioma de los argentinos* (The Language of the Argentines, 1928). Later he said about these books that they were "forgotten and forgettable," and refused permission to reprint them. One can perceive in them, however, a vehement concern with style, with rhetorical patterns, and a quest for new expressions.

In 1930 Borges published *Evaristo Carriego*; in 1932, *Discusión*, an anthology of diverse essays and lectures: "*El arte narrativo y la magia* (Narrative Art and Magic)," "*Postulación de la realidad,*" "*Films,*" "*Una vindicación de la cábala,*" etc. *Historia universal de la infamia* was published in 1935. The prologue presents it as "... exercises in narrative prose... stem[ming] from my rereadings of Stevenson and Chesterton, and also from Sternberg's early films, and perhaps from a certain biography of Evaristo Carriego. They overtly exploit certain tricks: random enumerations, sudden shifts of continuity, and the paring down of a man's whole life to two or three scenes. (A similar concern with visual aims gives shape to the story "Man at the Streetcorner.") They are not, they do not try to be, psychological."[3]

These "tricks" foreshadow the style of his future prose, so different and personal, already reflected in these stories. Borges assimilated and transcended the findings of modernism, ultraism and other literary forms he first adopted and later critiqued. He says, concerning his beginnings, "I used to write in a Baroque, highly artificial manner. I went through what many young writers were going through, I think. Because I was shy I thought that if I spoke simply, people would think I could not write. I felt the urge to show that I knew many rare words and that I was able to combine them in surprising fashion. I believed literature was just technical skill and nothing else, but I am no longer of that opinion."[4]

Commenting upon neologisms coined by Unamuno, Borges has in mind the semantic rather than the rhetorical aspect of language. Words ought to offer ideas, instigating an activity that creates ideas. He made up new words to express something never said before, something that could not therefore be conveyed by existing words. The virtues of Borges's fantastic prose are its austerity and rigor and its effectiveness and precision. He abjures the Hispanic ornamental style, he rejects what is beautiful yet superfluous. In 1928 he defined style as "total efficiency and total invisibility."[5] Style fulfills its function in silence, just as the organs of our body, just as our heart ticks even when we do not hear it. This goal Borges achieves as the result of firm determination, living totally and singly devoted to a literary search, and especially, thanks to his personality and his talent. This extraordinary writer transforms theme into style and style into theme, just as he transforms dreams into stories and stories into dreams. The Spanish writer and critic Amado Alonso defines Borges as the sharpest case of a scrupulous literary conscience. "Words and sentences come to him replete with meaning, and even more, with meanings that do not hamper each other."[6] *Historia universal de la infamia* is seen as a leap in his production, one that foreshadows the even greater leap he would take in *Ficciones*. The youthful vocabulary, the intellectual phraseology, and any prior pomposity, are now gone. Borges's persistent interest in infamy endures. Later, however, infamy will cease to be a certain reality viewed ironically, in a sardonic caricature. Infamy will become a narrative fiction, which is intricate, labyrinthine, and philosophical, one that allows him to toy with time and with the infinite.

In 1939, Borges's style takes another important step toward self-definition. It all begins with his accident at the end of 1938, the year when his father died (see Chapter 1). Borges describes the incident thus: "In the year 1939, I fell ill with septicemia. Just as Dahlman in *El sur*... I decided to write something, something new and different, so if it did not succeed I would be able to blame the novelty of the effort. I started writing the story with the title "Pierre Menard, Author of Don Quixote."[7]

According to Didier Anzieu, the father's death and the accident are a watershed dividing Borges's work in two segments, before and after 1938.

Style and Psychopathology

Integrating psychoanalytic theory with Ruesch's study of human communication, and on the basis of his clinical experience, David Liberman published in 1962 *La comunicación en la terapéutica psicoanalítica* (Communication in Psychoanalytic Therapy).[8] Later he enriched his work with elements from semiotic theory.[9]

Each patient exhibits a specific manner of expression, a style of his own. Style involves a way of categorizing reality, a history and a language, a particular way of choosing, selecting, and articulating different rhetorical forms. The foundation that differentiates one style from another, in turn, derives from the fixation of the libido to particular erogenous zones, the mobilizing of basic anxieties and defenses, and the expression of unconscious fantasies. No human being can be equated to a pure clinical structure. That is why we see a display of various styles combined, where some prevail and others are backgrounded, some are primary and others are subsidiary. David Maldavsky has studied these matters in depth. He emphasizes the importance of the preconscious "as a system of transformations crisscrossed by different logics and different defenses." The preconscious is structured, in his view, as a combination of styles.[10] Liberman distinguishes six styles on the basis of their psychopathological structures:

1) reflexive (the observing, non-participant, schizoid personality);
2) lytic (depressive personality);
3) epic (active persons);
4) narrative (logical persons, obsessive neurosis);
5) dramatic, with suspense (fearful, fleeing person; anxiety hysteria);
6) dramatic, with esthetic effect (outgoing personality; conversion hysteria).

Both in the reflexive and in the lyric style there is a predominance of what Roman Jakobson calls the source or emitter. The difference resides in the following: the form of expression in the reflexive style is: "concerning X, I think." In the lyric style, it is rather "I feel for X." For Maldavsky, the metalinguistic factor dominates in the reflexive style: it amounts to speaking about another language in an insatiable search for an unattainable essence.[11] I find this observation felicitous, and I see it clearly confirmed in Borges's work.

While I do not consider this classification as an absolute, I take it as a point of departure. I believe that the narrative style is dominant in the Borgean text, yet as a defensive strategy in regard to the reflexive style, which is equally fundamental and dominant. This does not preclude, of course, the emergence from time to time of aspects pertaining to the other styles.

According to Maldavsky, the reflexive style typically involves a high level of generalization. Vital experiences, observed from a distance, are transformed into abstract ideas as well as possibly into unknowns. These unknowns, however, do not arouse suspense, and the themes of this style develop around revealing, or even just communicating, such unknowns. Quite frequently this style displays feelings of emptiness, of futility, which militate toward creating a mood of amazement and contemplation, a mood deprived of emotional or affective commitment. Someone with a reflexive style experiences a loss of boundaries, a fusion with a transcendent wholeness in a bond that is predominantly cognitive.

In contrast, the narrative style is characterized by a persistent striving for correctness and order. These goals are attained by means of temporal or spatial nearness, or alternatively through the play of similarities and differences. Themes tend to avoid what is chaotic, what is felt to be dirty or perverse, and the uncontrolled emergence of the like. Cancelling mechanisms typical of ambivalence become manifest, and create an atmosphere of disruption. It is common in this style to assign much higher value to the intellect than to the emotion, to value thought and language over feelings. Redundant and meticulous interest in detail creates fatigue and exhaustion.

As I consider what predominates in Borges's literary production, I see the reflexive style manifested essentially in its themes, and the narrative style in its form. The genius of Borges, however, achieves an intertwining of both styles. A system of perceptions, feelings, and thoughts makes style vivid. The Borgean worldview has its roots in his search for the unreal, as he faces a reality that he views as chaotic, a reality within which man is lost as he would be in the maze of a labyrinth. He says, "Let us grant what all idealists concede: the hallucinatory quality of the world. Let us do what no idealist has done: let us search for unrealities confirming that quality. We will find them, I believe, in Kant's antinomies and in the dialectic of Zeno."[12] If for Borges the world is the freak creature of a "decrepit deity," of a "deficient angel" or "the accidental product of a powerful intrigue by evil spirits and a final marriage," this world must suffer from latent anguish and can only pretend that it has harmony and order.

"For the European the world is a cosmos where each person corresponds intimately to the function he performs; for the Argentine it is a chaos."[13] Which is the function that Borges views as not having been accomplished by the Argentine? The enigmas of his identity, the clues to his destiny, the queries of his existence will be sought in the most diverse sources. "In the history of philosophy are doctrines, probably false, that exercise an obscure charm on human imagination: the Platonic and Pythagorean doctrine of the transmigration of the soul through many bodies, the Gnostic doctrine that the world was created by a hostile or rudimentary god."[14]

This "obscure charm" leads him to completely developing certain topics, which Ana María Barrenechea has classified as follows.[15]

The infinite and, in relation to it, the vastness of time and space; multiplications, forks in the road and the plurality of worlds; Zeno's *aporias*; mirrors opposite mirrors; infinite postponements; simultaneous and cyclical time; the eternal return of the same.

Chaos and cosmos: Gnostic theogonies and cosmogonies; the secret sense of the universe; labyrinths; mysterious clues, encoded stories.

Pantheism and identity :"everything is everywhere and anything is all things"; every man is all men; in one point, the universe; writer and reader are one and the same; all and nothing.

Time and eternity: the temporal flow and its disintegration; regressive time; Christian eternity; Platonic eternity; the refutation of time; death; memory and oblivion.

Idealism and other forms of the unreal: Berkeley's idealism; symbols of the unreal; mirrors; dreams and nightmares; levels of reality and fiction; doubt and conjecture.

We may add as "characters" playing in these greater scenarios, persistent themes such as infamy, more closely related to the narrative style. These themes emerge in connection with a "certain slanted" perception of family tradition, the cult of compadritos, of courage, duels, knives, murder. In the same catalogue belong the reiterated tigers, books, library, moon, rose, chess, insomnia, etc. All these call forth the most diverse systems of symbols.

Aspects of Borges's Creative Work

The following is part of an interview published in the journal *Cabal*:

—How different was it to start dictating your work?
—I discovered then, just as Henry james discovered, that dictating is a convenience, one feels more irresponsible. Also, because the person who is writing cannot wait forever, you keep dictating until you finish.
—And do you then edit what you dictated?
—Surely what you end up with is somewhat shapeless, you have to edit later, but you have a draft, that is to say you have the flow of the ideas. Earlier, for many years, it was different. I used to write phrase by phrase. I advanced line by line. Naturally the article had no continuity, because each line was like a disconnected isle. Emerson used the same method; that's why you can read several pages by Emerson, full of admirable sentences, but you cannot read the entire article, because each phrase does not prepare the next one, nor is it prepared by the former. The whole turns out as a sequence of sentences or aphorisms. When you dictate you cannot do that; you have to move on, like a boar, as it were, rushing forward..."[16]

And yet these statements made by Borges contradict what one of his most faithful collaborators, María Esther Vásquez, has said: "Borges has an unusual working method; he dictates five or six words beginning a prose paragraph or the first line of a poem, and he asks for them to be read immediately. As he listens, he runs the forefinger of his right hand over the back of his left hand as if he were following the lines of an invisible page. The phrase is reread one, two, three, four, many times, until he finds the continuation and he dictates another five or six words. Then he asks for all that is written to be read. Since he dictates punctuation, one has to read it out loud. That segment is reread, with his hands following it, until he finds the next phrase. Occasionally he has read a dozen times a segment of five lines. Each one of these repetitions is preceded by Borges's apology, for he is somehow quite tortured by the imposition he assumes he is making upon his scribe. In this manner after two or three hours of work half a page is achieved that does not require further editing."

This description clearly belongs in the same register as scrupulous attention to detail, obstinate sparing of words, prudent and frugal editing, persevering respect of an order, or some internal, severe and perfectionist command. On account of this obsessive obedience he is afraid of irritating his companion and he feels guilty of the ruthless self-criticism that forces upon him delays and detours. In regard to the realm of unconscious infantile drives, this attitude would correspond to the child's request for patience because of the doubts and the indecision caused by the fear of defecation. Otto Fenichel says, "The displacement of cathexes from defecation to speech and to thinking activities is sometimes betrayed by irrational modes of retaining and expelling words or thoughts; it can be seen in inhibitions of these functions as well as in their irrational hypercathexis."[17]

"Each line ... like a disconnected isle" suggests, beyond the power of synthesis, an excessive control intended to reduce the risk of that "boar" rushing forward, of ideas and feelings that might become contaminated; intended also to make sure that thoughts be at a safe distance from feelings; that what is "clean" does not touch what is "dirty." Likewise we observe how keen Borges is on multiple literary quotations and allusions, be they mythological or personal, which he reshapes with his prodigious imagination, creating a literary "collage" that is both real and fantastic. He explains it as follows in the prologue to the 1954 edition of *A Universal History of Infamy*: "[These pages] are the irresponsible game of a shy young man who dared not write stories and so amused himself by falsifying and distorting (without any aesthetic justification whatever) the tales of others."[18]

The same obsessive shyness is manifested in the story "The Flower of Coleridge": "Those who carefully copy a writer do it impersonally, do it because they confuse that writer with literature, do it because they suspect that to leave him at any one point is to deviate from reason and orthodoxy. For many years I thought that the almost infinite world of literature was in one man. That man was Carlyle, he was Johannes Becher, he was Whitman, he was Rafael Cansinos-Assens, he was De Quincey."[19]

The urgent need for a referent reveals, I believe, the essential fear to break away from those idealized figures who would be "the only reason" and the only truth, thus finding his own identity as an individual. They help him to vanquish his lack of self confidence and his phobias, in the manner, as it were, of accompanying objects. Thus his answers are quite frequently quotations he saves in the privileged archive of his memory. Thanks to them he can express thoughts eliptically while he evades feelings.

After the above mentioned accident, a few months after the death of his father, Jorge Luis Borges awakens, sets himself free, and begins writing the series of fantastic stories. Nonetheless subjection continues and it becomes evident in his nearly psychotic desire to rewrite certain classics, as shown in "Pierre Menard, author of Don Quixote."[20] And thirty years later, in his wish to become Shakespeare by purchasing his memory. Borges is not himself, he is all the classics he has read and admired: "An infinite memory seems a gift, and yet, it kills whoever possesses it or is possessed by it."

As a boy, precocious and different, he had been able to play with memory and with the enumerative classifications of different species, prehistoric and mythological animals... thus linking his avid curiosity with a controlling, obsessive systematization. We also know that he "disfigured" words, generating a new and strange vocabulary. Such were the games of a child whose intellectual overvaluation moved him to build and take apart structures of words just as other children construct and take apart castles of building bricks. Psychoanalysis has shown us the creative richness and the wealth of metaphors that naturally emerge in children. We are aware of their desires and anxieties, linked to abundant unconscious phantasmagorias.

Borges never ceased being a child who solves and takes up puzzles of erudite words. Later, when puberty awakened in him, both in a coenesthetic and a poetic way, he continued reading profusely, rereading, being his own teacher. His early readings, which Borges always remembered with delight, seem to have become structuring markers: "I must avow (not without regret and awareness of my poverty) that I reread with intensely reminiscent pleasure and that I am not excited by new readings." He adds: "I tend to contradict them, to translate them into influences and combinations."[21] Borges has a vehement desire to return again and again, stubbornly, to the same, translating, contradicting, inverting, reverting, combining, mingling.

Other methods he often resorts to are a search for mirror images, for symmetry and repetition. In the story *"El jardín de senderos que se bifurcan* (The Garden of Forking Paths)" the theme of the labyrinth is present, as well as the idea that every Being is the inverted Döpelganger of another; for one to survive, the other must die.[22] These methods pertain to magic and obsessive thinking, which plays itself out in the symmetries of the mirror, whether they are direct or inverted. Borges often manifests the fear of discovering before the mirror his real countenance, and this betrays monstrous or perhaps perverted projections. Obsessively shutting oneself up in the pleasure of rereading amounts to finding a shelter from the experiences of a risky world, one he thus succeeds in shunning.

Otto Fenichel recognizes in obsessive neurosis alternating strong anal-sadistic drives and guilty feelings of anxiety over punishment. The need for a relative balance between these two attitudes may be expressed through "compulsions of magic symmetry intended to avoid disturbances." Thus every drive tends to be cancelled by way of the symmetric counterdrive.

The basic opposition between (chaotic) life and (organized) art recurs in *"El arte narrativo y la magia* (Narrative Art and Magic)".[23] The structures that contain and control the chaotic are manifested in a "precise play of attention, echoes, and affinities." Thence arise Borges's art as theorem and his use of mathematics and geometry; the hexagonal galleries of "La biblioteca de Babel"; the structure of the rigorous diamond in *"La muerte y la brújula"*; *"La lotería de Babilonia"* with its connotations of magic and chance. That "precise play of attention, echoes, and affinities" is expressed in the reiterated theme of the mirror. "I owe the discovery of Uqbar to the conjunction of a mirror and an encyclopedia."[24]

Paul de Man observed that all of Borges's stories "have a similar mirror-like structure," adding, "This mirror-like proliferation constitutes, for Borges, an indication of poetic success."[25] The literary works that Borges admires the most include this element. He is fascinated by mirror effects in literature, such as the drama within a drama in the Elizabethan period; Don Quixote, the character, reading *Don Quixote*; Scherezade beginning one night the word-by-word recitation of *Las mil y una noches* (*A Thousand and One Nights*).

Jaime Alarazki, who studied this aspect of Borges's work in *Versiones, inversiones, reversiones*, writes: "The texts of his stories function like mirrors that invert or reverse previously perceived images. Furthermore, those images fold and turn over themselves in search of their own reflection: "The visible is but a reflection of the invisible."[26] These are "symmetrically stubborn" mirror palimpsests, which do not always succeed in protecting the balance between the pulsive and the punishing in Borges. Sometimes that balance is interfered with.

Narrative Resources and Stylistic Traits

Jaime Alazraki lists some of the most remarkable traits of Borges's stylistic resources:[27]

1) He tells a story as the rereading and summary of another story, real or apocryphal, or a combination thereof.

2) He clearly leans toward the use of anaphora (repetition), of different kinds of adjectives, and has a predilection for oxymorons and enumerations.

3) He uses certain words on account of their lost or unusual etymological meaning.

4) The narrator comments on his own text.

5) He reveals the sources of the narration at the start (most of these sources being apocryphal).

6) He makes frequent use of parenthetical comments.

7) He transforms intransitive verbs into transitive ones and viceversa.

8) He prefers figures of continuity, such as metonymy and sinecdoque.

I shall discuss in some detail a few of these resources, particularly those that may allow us to visualize with greater clarity the traits of Borges's personality that have left an imprint on his style.

The oxymoron

Borges often resorts to oxymorons in his narrative prose. Thus he expresses a paradoxical reality. He defines the oxymoron as follows in "The Zahir": "In the figure of speech called oxymoron a word is modified by an epithet which seems to contradict it: thus the Gnostics spoke of dark light, and the alchemists of a black sun. For me it was a kind of oxymoron to go straight from my last visit with Clementina Villar to buy a drink at a bar; I was intrigued by the coarseness of the act, by its ease. (The contrast was heightened by the circumstance that there was a card game in progress.)"[28]

The very title of *A Universal History of Infamy* creates a certain tension and incongruity, as Borges himself points out in the prologue. It is remarkable that almost all the titles of the first part are oxymoronic: "The Dread Redeemer...," "... the Implausible Impostor," "The Disinterested Killer," "The Insulting Master of Etiquette," "The Widow Ching, Lady Pirate." Borges's ironic, muted humor cleverly and subtly trasforms his ambivalence into stylistic traits. There are further examples: "... the great and blameworthy life of the nefarious redeemer Lazarus Morell," "Some of them were thankless enough to fall ill and die." One could cite many more.

The story "El Aleph" begins with an oxymoron: "On the burning February morning Beatriz Viterbo died, after braving an agony that never for a single moment gave way to self-pity or fear, I noticed that the sidewalk billboards around Constitution Plaza were advertizing some new brand or other of American cigarrettes."[29] And in this same story Borges refers directly to such a stylistic device: "Beatriz had been tall, frail, slightly stooped; in her walk there was (if the oxymoron may be allowed) a kind of uncertain grace, a hint of expentancy."[30] By means of these expressions, resolved with a touch of sharp caricature, Borges is able to reinforce his pejorative, hostile thoughts. The oxymoron is a condensed paradox where form is invisibly transformed into theme. Alazraki points out the presence of a real oxymoronic structure, defining, in his view, the technique of the Borgean essay.

On a psychological level the oxymoron appears as a paradigm of contradiction and ambivalence, conveying mechanisms of negation and cancelling. From this viewpoint one might consider Borges himself as an oxymoronic personality. In "Notes upon a Case of Obsessional Neurosis" Freud observes that compulsive acts develop in two stages, the second of them cancelling the first: "Their true significance lies in their being a representation of a conflict between two opposing impulses of approximately equal strength: and hitherto I have invariably found that this opposition has been one between love and hate."[31] In "Inhibitions, Symptoms and Anxiety" he describes this process with the term "*Ungeschehenmachen*" ("undoing"). He sees in this mechanism, together with the mechanism of isolation, a form of defense characteristic of obsessive neurosis. Getting rid of something by "making it not to have happened," says Freud, "is irrational and in the nature of magic."[32]

A writer's swinging between two opposites, his use of *diphasic* expressions where one thought is immediately followed by another that halts and even cancels the first, his hesitating, dubitative ruminations, all tend to resolve his own obsessive and paranoid anxieties, while they arouse the reader's amazement and perplexity.

Diversity in the Use of Adjectives

Among all expressive resources, say the students of style, adjectives are the most apt to reveal a poet's personality. In Borges they are a key element. Most remarkable in his work are the functions of the oxymoron— which is itself in a way a method of applying adjectives. I address the following: tic-adjectives, metonymic adjectives, hypallage, bivalent adjectives and adjectives derived by the addition of a prefix. These five uses of adjectives are the most active gear of his style, since they turn form into a clear vehicle of content.

Tic-Adjectives

This term itself has psychological connotations. A representation, similar to a fixed idea, takes possession of a writer's thinking processes and is repeated with the obsessive frequency of a nervous tic. In Borges they furthermore point to his personal worldview. Thus the most frequent are: "infinite," "vast," "remote," "inextricable," "intricate," "chaotic," "enigmatic," "undecypherable," "perplexed," "irrecuperable," etc. For instance: "infinite Aleph," "infinite book," "an infinite tiger," "vast evidence," "a vast school," "remote reasons." This artful device projects the simplest and smallest objects on a distorted and phantasmagoric scale. There are nouns with a similar function, such as "labyrinth," "arena," "desert," "nightmare," "chaos," "enigma," "chance," etc.

Metonymic adjectives

These adjectives implicitly carry a function of displacement. They are transferences where an object is described by the feeling it arouses: "indifferent nook," "contemplative deserts," "clumsy colors," "perplexed corridors," "vain anterooms." The adjective compresses feelings that would otherwise force greater descriptive digressions. Thus Borges emphasizes an abstract vision of reality, thus he gives to his story an allegorical color. Such a reference to feelings might suggest the characteristics of a lyric or depressive style (Liberman). And yet this is not the case, for by virtue of the described displacement those feelings are depersonalized and placed outside the subject, in the objects with which they are coupled. In *The Aleph* Borges returns to Beatriz—who is now dead—on each one of her birthdays because the whole ambiance alludes to her, makes her present without risk. Allusion is metonymic too, it is a form of avoidance that permits mediated contacts, contacts over a distance.

Hypallage

Hypallage is a commonly used figure in poetry and it refers to transferred adjectives, which modify a word they do not logically qualify. The adjective slips away from the noun that was its original destination and is transferred to another noun in the context. Thus the expected logical connection is transformed into an irrational one, which is perplexing. This is one of the effects that persons who express themselves in a reflexive style arouse in their interlocutors. "In a brazen chamber, before the *silent handkerchief* of the strangler, hope has not failed me.[33] The handkerchief is brought to the foreground, and in this reference, the *silent strangler* becomes a strong focus. In the story "La muerte y la brújula (Death and the Compass)," we read: " 'There's no need to look for a Chimera, or a cat with three legs,' Trevinarus was saying as he brandished an imperious cigar."[34] The character Trevinarus is displaced upon the cigar, which in turn acquires a certain independence and a surprisingly categoric force.

Bivalent adjectives

Borges describes this device in "Pierre Menard, Author of Don Quixote": "This effective combination of two adjectives, one moral and the other physical, reminded me of a line from Shakespeare…"[35] He is aware of his use of rhetorical tools. Through these adjectives he is trying to create new expressions that will be the result of contrast, that will conjoin the moral and the physical, the concrete and the abstract, the immediate and the emotional, fable and allegory.

The Roman god Janus appropriately symbolizes Borges's bivalent vision of everything, one that sometimes leads to non-definition and ambiguity. A character in "Death and the Compass" says, 'Nine days and nine nights I lay in agony in this desolate, symmetrical villa; fever was demolishing me, and the odious two-faced Janus who watches the twilights and the dawns lent horror to my dreams and to my waking.' "[36]

All these resources reveal his bivalent vision of things, which sometimes lead to indefinition and ambiguity. He knows it and he says in his own defense: "The text of Cervantes and that of Menard are verbally identical, but the second is almost infinitely richer. (More ambiguous, his detractors will say; but ambiguity is a richness.)"[37]

Adjectives derived by the addition of a prefix

The Spanish prefixes *"in," "de,"* and *"des"* are constantly repeated in Borges. We know that they denote negation by inverting or eliminating the original meaning. Thus, the negative rides on the positive, and they almost form an antithetical pair, with opposites cancelling each other. This is how an adjective of this type creates an effect of futility and estrangement.

I select from the story "Las ruinas circulares" the following sequences:

Adjectives with the prefix *in*: *"árboles incesantes* (incessant trees)," *"invencible propósito* (invincible purpose)," *"grito inconsolable* (inconsolable cry)," *"intolerable lucidez* (intolerable clear-headedness)," " *"incoherente materia* (incoherent subject matter)," *"hijo irreal*.(unreal son)."

Adjectives with the prefixes *de, des*: *"hojas desconocidas* (unknown pages)," *"templo despedazado* (torn apart temple)," *"desconocido socorro* (unknown help)," *"deficiente empeño* (deficient effort)."

In "Jokes and their Relation to the Unconscious," Freud points out that negative particles provide excellent allusions by slightly modifying words. He recalls from Heine, "Spinoza, my fellow *unbeliever*," and from Lichtenberg, "We, day-laborers, servants, blacks, by God's *misfortune*."[38]

Freud surveys the different resources that create the effect of a joke. Many of these resources, paired by Freud with oneiric ones, are present in the several facets of Borges's style that I am analyzing in this chapter. There is a difference, though: they are directed in Borges toward biting irony rather than toward humor and cheer.

These intriguing processes of condensation in the shaping of words, which have become apparent as the nutshell of verbal jokes, evoke the shaping of dreams, where similar psychic processes have been discovered. Techniques of intellectual jokes such as displacement, intellectual errors, nonsense, indirect representation and antinomic representation also point in this direction, and they recur, singly or in combinations, in dream-shaping processes.

Writing about condensation, Freud refers to the metaphor's ability to elicit a smile : "It is almost impossible to go through a crowd holding the torch of Truth without searing someone's beard (Lichtenberg)."

Metaphor and Metonimy

These important rhetorical forms have been studied in psychoanalysis on the basis of the dream process, since they remit to the two fundamental mechanisms of dream: condensation and displacement. A metaphor is but a signifying substitution. As a rhetorical figure, it consists in gliding from the words' literal meaning to another, figurative meaning, by means of an implicit comparison. It is therefore based upon relations of similarity allowing the enrichment of language through the creation of multiple forms, in the expression of the same thing or event. For Borges, metaphors make it possible *"to discover hidden analogies and to establish links between different ideas."* Dreams are replete with metaphors: a person is given the combined traits of several others; a known countenance is given someone else's name; a certain individual is placed in circumstances totally different from the usual ones; new, compound words are created.

Metonymy (etymologically, "change of name") involves a displacement where the essential is designated by means of the secondary, the content by its vehicle, the whole by the part, the cause by the effect. In other words, a signifier may express another one with which it is contiguous. Synecdoche is a special form of metonymy. The meaning of an object or a function has been displaced to one of its parts and, throught that chosen detail, the totality is being revealed. As a film critic, Borges transferred to literature the use of a cinematographic technique: the closeups which he turned into "synecdochal close-ups." Displacement functions like a camera that, in reducing the field, concentrates the focus on a detail and, thus, makes perception more direct and precise.

Synecdochal or metonymyc displacements occur also in dreams. There are transvaluations implying transferences of sense. "While in dreams the manifest accesory elements express the latent primordial elements thanks to metonymic construction, actually the relation of contiguity betweeen signifiers is never as directly evident as it is in the metonymic elaborations of language."[39] In dreams the contiguity can only be made manifest by means of associations. The oneiric is constantly present in Borges. On the other hand, it is true that these rhetorical figures are inherent in the creative nature of every writer and poet.

Throughout his literary development, Borges, who earlier on admired metaphor, later assigned greater worth to metonymy. In *Fervor de Buenos Aires* he wrote that a metaphor seeks "what is efficient rather than what is unheard of," and in *El tamaño de mi esperanza* (The Dimension of My Hope) he said: "... any metaphor, marvelous as it may be, is a possible experience." He emphasized their facile emergence, while at the same time he spoke of the difficulty in finding "how they may be able to hallucinate." He devoted a chapter in *Historia de la eternidad* to the study of metaphors. Curiously, here he supports his theory with ten examples of metaphors concerning death and just as many concerning woman. His conclusion is, "We feel that there is no emotion justifying them, and we judge them laborious and useless."

As he seeks to hallucinate, Borges disbelieves metaphor and prefers figures allowing more than substitutions; he wants displacements, dislocations and joltings, in an allegorical game that points to chance in time and space. Borges himself is revealed in this preference for metonymy. For metonymy accords abstract traits to his work, and it is coherent with his tendency toward the generic, the intangible, the unattainable. A pantheistic vision of the world that is dear to his ideology is essentially the same that explains that rhetorical form. "Everything is everywhere and anything is everything," he says. Archetypal examples are "The Aleph" and "The Zahir." Kenneth Burke points out that abstract and spiritual words have a metonymic origin.

Emphasis placed upon some displaced detail and its obsessive fixation is also frequent. Just so is the response to reminiscences of his childhood with Norah, when, eluding the personal aspects, he refers to the atmosphere surrounding the two of them: the tiled patio, the windmill, and so on, suddenly revealing how partial elements denote a displacement of emotion. His extreme modesty, his paranoid fears, his obsessive style conceal schizoid fragmentation, the structure of cleavages and the ensuing risks. Here is, in other words, the need to separate, avoid, shun, distance oneself from. In contrast, synecdoque operates in the opposite direction, snce it allows of a more direct contact with objects. Using it Borges leans more toward realistic illusion. Perhaps he does so as a way of dropping anchor on reality and as a method to counteract the experience of emptiness created by the intangible.

Oscillation between Metaphor and Metonimy

Guy Rosolato observes that what he calls "metaphoric-metonymic oscillation or swing" is pertinent in trying to understand Borges's preference for metonymy.[40] The narcissism that structures the psyche as an axis in every stage of life is founded, according to Rosolato, upon five basic pillars: libidinal retraction, idealization, doubling, the double bond and the metaphoric-metonymic oscillation or swing. He applies the latter label to a pendular movement grouping and gathering all possible positions around a central point. Its aim is homostatic, that is to say, it is intended to ensure balance. Such a swing or oscillation is therefore inherent in the very nature of trophic narcissism.

On the level of thought and language processes, movement takes place between a coherent, continuous development (this is how metonymy signifies) and a rupture by substitution and dislocation (this is how metaphor signifies). Hence Rosolato concludes that metonymy's reassuring continuity is more appealing than metaphor's demand of a displacement, which may sometimes be critical. This oscillation takes advantage of the potential implicit in the articulation of signifiers, and it becomes further enriched—when it does—in the conquest of the symbolic play. All kinds of vicissitudes occur at this point.

The metaphoric-metonymic oscillation supports the mirror play with the double, that is to say, the very course of the projections between good and bad and between the two mandates of a double bond. In turn, the "object fetish" is then constituted as a "privileged" example in the pathology of the metaphoric-metonymic shift, while it demonstrates how a symbolic activity is subservient to a drive. Finally, this oscillation takes its place at the center of all artistic and creative activities, of play and humor, since it is able to express the very essence of narcissism in a socially accepted mutual exchange. Thus art offers access to the primary process, and for this reason, the oscillation I have discussed is a condition of aesthetic pleasure. When the balance is broken, everything changes. We then witness the "immobile remissions of schizophrenia, the sterile plays of mania or the contorted fixation of obsessive neurosis."

Notes

1. Address given to the Académie Française, 25 Aug. 1753.
2. Between 1929 and 1954 Borges almost abandoned the poetic genre; he returned to poetry after becoming blind, in 1955.
3. Prologue to the first edition of *Historia universal de la infamia*, 1935. This book is a collection of essays published in the newspaper *Crítica* in 1933-34. The first story, with an original theme, *"Hombre de la esquina rosada,"* was initially signed with the pseudonym Francisco Bustos—actually the name of his great-grandfather. Cited from Jorge Luis Borges, *A Universal History of Infamy*, trans. Norman Thomas di Giovanni (New York: Dutton, 1971), 13.
4. James Irby, *Encuentro con Borges* (An Encounter with Borges), (México: Vida Universitaria, 1964), 14.
5. Jorge Luis Borges, *El idioma de los argentinos* (Buenos Aires: Gleizer, 1928).
6. Amado Alonso, *Materia y forma en poesía* (Madrid: Gredos, 1960), 352.
7. Borges, "Pierre Menard, Author of Don Quixote," *Ficciones*, trans. Anthony Kerrigan (New York: Grove Press, 1962).
8. David Liberman, *La comunicación en la terapéutica psicoanalítica* (Buenos Aires: Eudeba, 1962).
9. Liberman, *Lingüística, interacción comunicativa y proceso psicoanalítico* (Linguistics, Communicative Interaction, and Psychoanalytic Process), (Buenos Aires: Nueva visión, 1971).
10. Maldavsky, *"Los estilos y el problema de la estructura del preconsciente* (Styles and the Problem of the Structure of the Pre-Conscious), *Revista de la Escuela Argentina de Psicoterapia para Graduados* 12-13 (1986): 151.
11. Maldavsky, *Teoría de las representaciones* (Buenos Aires: Nueva Visión, 1977). He points out that each individual applies in his peculiar manner of expression a set of transgressions to consensual norms. These norms are phonetic, syntactic, semantic, and pragmatic or logical. Whether transgressions are sublimatory or pathological depends on which defenses are brought to bear in each case. Whereas denial or refutation dismantle those consensual norms, repression does not. The same style, therefore—Maldavsky adds—may lead to a psychotic disturbance or it may give rise to sublimation. He analyzes in this respect Borges's "The Circular Ruins" comparing it to the verbalizations of a schizophrenic patient in the course of her sessions. Such an approach, though interesting, is limited, since it relates only to defenses and it disregards the interplay of various factors conditioning a neurosis or a psychosis.
12. Borges, *Discusión* (Buenos Aires: Emecé, 1964), 136.
13. Borges, "Our Poor Individualism," *Other Inquisitions*, trans. Ruth L. C. Simms (New York: Simon and Schuster, 1968), 34
14. Borges, "Quevedo," ibid.

15. Ana María Barrenechea, *La expresión de la irrealidad en la obra de Borges* (Buenos Aires: Paidós, 1967).
16. Statements made in the course of an interview for the journal *Cabal* (no issue number nor date).
17. Otto Fenichel, *The Psychoanalytic Theory of Neurosis* (New York: Norton, 1945), 283.
18. From the prologue to the 1954 edition of *Historia universal de la infamia*, 27 May 1935, 289 (cited from Borges, *A Universal History of Infamy*, 11-12).
19. Borges, "The Flower of Coleridge," in *Other Inquisitions*, 13.
20. Borges, "Diálogo con Osvaldo Ferreri," *Tiempo Argentino*, 20 March 1985.
21. Borges, *El idioma*.
22. Borges, "The Garden of Forking Paths," *Ficciones*, 89-101.
23. Borges, "El arte narrativo y la magia," *Discusión*.
24. Borges, "Tlön, Uqbar, Orbis Tertius," *Ficciones*, 17.
25. Paul de Man, "A Modern Master," *Critical Essays on Jorge Luis Borges*, ed. Jaime Alazraki (Boston: Hall, 1987), 59.
26. Jaime Alazraki, *Versiones, inversiones, reversiones. El espejo como modelo estructural del relato en los cuentos de Borges* (Madrid: Gredos, 1977).
27. Alazraki, *La prosa narrativa de Jorge Luis Borges* (Madrid: Gredos, 1983).
28. Borges, "The Zahir," *Labyrinths: Selected Stories and Other Writings*, trans. Donald A. Yates and James E. Irby (New York: New Directions Publishing, 1964), 158.
29. Borges, "The Aleph," *The Aleph and Other Stories, 1933-1969*, ed. and transl. by Norman Thomas di Giovanni in collaboration with the author. (New York: Dutton, 1970), 15.
30. Ibid., p. 16.
31. Sigmund Freud, "Notes upon a Case of Obsessional Neurosis," S. E. 10, 192.
32. Freud, "Inhibitions, Symptoms and Anxiety" S.E. 20, 119-20.
33. Borges, *Ficciones* (Buenos Aires: Emecé, 1944), 65.
34. Borges, "Death and the Compass," *Ficciones*, 130.
35. Borges, "Pierre Menard", *Ficciones*, 30.
36. Borges, "Death and the Compass," *Ficciones*, 84.
37. Borges, "Pierre Menard," *Ficciones*, 52.
38. Freud, "Jokes and their Relation to the Unconscious," SE 8.
39. Jöel Dor, *Introduction à la lecture de Lacan* (Paris: Denoël, 1972), 72.
40. Guy Rosolato, "Le Narcissisme," *Nouvelle Revue de Psychanalyse* 13 (Spring 1976).

Chapter 3

The Unthinkable in Borges

Borgean Enumerations

Umberto Eco writes in *The Name of the Rose*, a book that often reminds me of Borges, "There is nothing more wonderful than enumerations, which are an admirable instrument for the most perfect hypotyposes." [1] This term denotes vivid, real, and powerful descriptions of someone or something by means of language. Borges admired hypotyposes in Whitman and repeatedly resorted to them, as much in poetry as in prose. Quite often these enumerative constructions achieve disconcerting, chaotic effects.

Constantly in search of simultaneous memory, Borges saturates a single word with diverse meanings. The Aleph and the Zahir are totalizing, indescribable symbols, endless circumstances, objects, and characters. When the text is multiplied with allusions to Anglo-Saxon and Scandinavian sagas and to esoteric Oriental references, Borges's erudition, the erudition of a lucid collector, floods the reader's mind and confuses him.

Even as in Dali's paintings, there are in Borges's writings multiple minuscule crutches that support him. These are the vast and endless references, which can be philosophical, metaphysical, philological, mystic, or mythological. Just so for Funes, "... the least important of his recollections was more minutely precise and more lively than our perception of a physical pleasure or a physical torment."[2]

Other stories too arouse, as does this one, the reader's admiration while irritating him with the obsessive, overflowing play of a mind that rejects the body (insofar as it involves taste, smell, touch, tachycardia, pleasure, enjoyment, kissing, sex, pain) and finds amusement in inventing a word for each number, or a proper name for each stone, each animal, each branch, "the tranquil advances of corruption, of caries, of fatigue."[3]

This rumination of ideas, words, quotations, events, finally gnaws away at his own mind and exhausts our attention. His rational, erudite and frequently cold descriptions resemble the setting of a black-and-white engraving that is flat and bidimensional, lacking color, warmth, and passion. Borges almost succeeds in making us feel physical discomfiture. One must assume that in this manner he is conveying his own suffering. He writes, "A man sets himself the task of portraying the world. Through the years he peoples a space with images of provinces, kingdoms, mountains, bays, ships, islands, fishes, rooms, instruments, stars, horses, and people. Shortly before his death, he discovers that that patient labyrinth of lines traces the image of his face." [4]

Words and Things

Can Borges think the unthinkable? What suggested this question is a passage of "The Analytical Language of John Wilkins" where he refers to a certain Chinese encyclopaedia entitled *Emporio celestial de conocimientos benévolos* (*Celestial Emporium of Benevolent Knowledge*).[5] He adds: "On those remote pages it is written that animals are divided into (a) those that belong to the Emperor, (b) embalmed ones, (c) those that are trained, (d) suckling pigs, (e) mermaids, (f) fabulous ones, (g) stray dogs, (h) those that are included in this classification, (i) those that tremble as if they were mad, (j) innumerable ones, (k) those drawn with a very fine camel's hair brush, (l) others, (m) those that have just broken a flower vase, (n) those that resemble flies from a distance." Borges is well aware that the genres and species he enumerates are contradictory and vague, yet this and other incoherent enumerations allow him to assert his nihilistic thesis,"... obviously there is no classification of the universe that is not arbitrary and conjectural." [6] And he goes even further, stating, "... we must suspect that there is no universe in the organic, unifying sense inherent in that ambitious word." (ibid)

This passage is not surprising, even though Borges appears to contradict here what he will assert in "*El Aleph*" or in "*El Zahir.*" It inspired the French philosopher, Michael Foucault to write *Les mots et les choses* (Words and Things), published in Paris in 1966. Foucault avows this in the Preface, "This book first arose out of a passage in Borges, out of the laughter that shattered, as I read it, all the familiar landmarks of my thought—*our* thought, the thought that bears the stamp of our age and our geography. It broke up all the ordered surfaces and all the plans with which we used to tame the wild profusion of existing things, and it continued long afterwards to disturb and threaten with collapse our age-old distinction between the Same and the Other." [7]

What surprises Foucault in this literary game, in this taxonomy, is the absence of a common ground, a "topos" where animals might be classified, as in the passage by Borges quoted above. By ordering them alphabetically as if these categories could be linked in some way, Borges goes beyond the limits of our imagination and our thinking.

On the other hand, from a psychoanalytic viewpoint, it is difficult to understand this "classificatory sequence" as free association. The elements are connected neither by analogy nor by phonetic similarity. They remind us of the Dadaist technique that forms phrases consisting of haphazardly combined words. Reading this text—just as when reading the literature of the absurd—may move us to laughter, just as it kept Foucault "... laughing a long time, though not without a certain uneasiness that I found hard to shake off. Perhaps because there arose in its wake the suspicion that there is a worse kind of disorder than that of the *incongruous,* the linking together of things that are inappropriate; I mean the disorder in which fragments of a large number of possible orders glitter separately in the dimension, without law or geometry, of the *heteroclite*; and that word should be taken in its most literal, etymological sense: in such a state, things are 'laid', 'placed', 'arranged' in sites so very different from one another that it is impossible to find a place of residence for them, to define a common locus beneath them all." [8]

These are the *heterotopias* that have multiplied the places infinitely. Foucault goes on to consider utopias as well as atopias, both forms of the absence of places. While u-topia connotes a real non-locus that may nonetheless be conceived as a virtual, feasible space, a-topia slips into an empty space, a great hole. Thus, while in heterotopias the absence of a common space of encounter is disquieting and disconcerting, utopias offer illusion and comfort, they give hope. Finally, the non-being and the silence of atopias plunges us into perplexity, anxiety or estrangement.

It is easy to understand how heterotopias arouse these reactions, for, Foucault says, "... they secretly undermine language... they shatter or tangle common names... destroy 'syntax' in advance, and not only the syntax with which we construct sentences but also that less apparent syntax which causes words and things... to 'hold together'."[9] Since heterotopias deprive him of the ability to think common names for things—a space of encounter—man is bereft of an organizing principle, a compass to help him find his bearings and move amidst them. He cannot access a shared code. Foucault continues, "Heterotopias (such as those to be found so often in Borges) dessicate speech, stop words in their tracks... ; they dissolve our myths and sterilize the lyricism of our sentences."

The illusion created by utopias, in turn, is displayed in thousands of alternatives, allowing the creation and recreation of fantasies, fables, myths, and discourses, summonning to the understanding of a language that is communicated and shared. But atopia's non-locality leads to a particular type of disorder, namely aphasia. There is no longer a common locus, either real or imagined, where words and things might be connected. In its stead oblivion, astonishment, disquiet occur.

The term "aphasia" literally means deprivation of speech. It is a disease including speech disorders caused by disruptions in the central nervous system which impairs the ability to understand and use words. Aphasias have been variously classified. One classification divides them into two types, sensory or receptive aphasia and motor or expressive aphasia. The young Freud's research on aphasias, in 1891, was the starting point of the theories he later developed on the representation of things. Later, he introduced in "The Interpretation of Dreams" the concept of word-representation.[10] Thing-representation emerges in relation to the primary process and to perceptual identity, while word-representation is related to the secondary process and to thought identity. In "The Unconscious," he states that "the conscious presentation comprises the presentation of the thing plus the presentation of the word belonging to it, while the unconscious presentation is the presentation of the thing alone."[11] Through thought identity it is possible to avoid the mere wish-fulfillment for the sake of the pleasure principle. It points toward achieving what logicians call identity principle.

Borges's enumerations amaze us by overflowing the boundaries of logic and the order of what is similar. He makes objective that which is unexpected, disorderly, indefinite, different. I am not referring here to the pathological reality of zones of aphasia (though they might as a matter of fact be equated with expressive zones of cleavage). I am rather pointing out Borges's lucid abilities to access archaic, syncretic and psychotic cores of the human psyche. He succeeds in making them objective with amazing regressive insight. This may be one of the most interesting aspects that psychoanalysis can point out in his work.

Heterotopia or Carry-all

In "The Aleph" the character Carlos Argentino Daneri, praising his own abysmal poem, prides himself in having "rejuvenat[ed] a process whose roots go back to Scripture—enumeration, congeries, conglomeration." [12] Congerie may be defined as an accumulation of things, a mixture of immaterial objects, words, affections, and so forth. Conglomeration is the result of joining or uniting things or parts thereof so that they will constitute a global heap.

Here another association with Foucault's heterotopias comes to mind. For Borges the common locus is actually, in my view, a "carry-all," a container where he places any word, object, or circumstance, wholly or in part. The "topos" of encounter appears thus to be that heavenly Emporium—the Borgean mind—"of benevolent knowledge." Later such "carry-all" becomes "the Aleph" or "the Zahir," a Pandora jar where both tempests and the trillings of birds may be heard. These are universal paradigms gathering the all into one. In a single place is the entire universe; in a single book are all the books, and in the author's own life there are thousands and thousands of lives. This is a greedy "carry-all" ready to ingest both heavens and dung, an embryonic teratoma harboring a variety of diverse tissues fragmented and devoured, as it were, by the force of some cannibalistic impulse. It is a utopian locus of simultaneous memory, of the here and now, of ever and now, which cannot tolerate waiting for a sequence. Objects that are so diverse can only be juxtaposed in the diversified and endless realm of language.

Rather than conveying information concerning the classification of animals, Borges tells us of the Chinese encyclopaedia and the man who wrote and compiled it. And since "there is no classification of the universe that is not arbitrary and conjectural," he introduces his own. Why not? Stirred by fixed, obsessive ideas, by oppositions, ambiguities and contradictions, he can cathartically express his anxieties, his madness over against so much Superego "sanity," he can defy with irony that which is solemn and conventional.

Borges cites Chesterton in "The Analytical Language of John Wilkins": "Man knows that there are in the soul tints more bewildering, more numberless, and more nameless than the colours of an autumn forest.... Yet he seriously believes that an ordinary civilized stockbroker can really produce out of his own inside noises which denote all the misteries of memory and all the agonies of desire." [13]

Other Enumerations

I have selected for analysis a few passages from "Doctor Brodie's Report," "The Aleph," and "The Zahir."

From the first of these stories I transcribe a passage describing the language of an imaginary tribe he arbitrarily calls "Yahoo":

> The Yahoo language is complex, having affinities with no others of which I have any knowledge. We cannot speak even of parts of speech, for there are no parts. Each monosyllabic word corresponds to a general idea whose specific meaning depends on the context or upon accompanying grimaces. The word "n r z," for example, suggests dispersion or spots, and may stand for the starry sky, a leopard, a flock of birds, smallpox, something bespattered, the act of scattering, or the flight that follows defeat in warfare. "H r l," on the other hand, means something compact or dense. It may stand for the tribe, a tree trunk, a stone, a heap of stones, the act of heaping stones, the gathering of the four witch doctors, carnal conjunction, or a forest. Pronounced in another manner or accompanied by other grimaces, each word may hold an opposite meaning. Let us not be unduly amazed; in our own tongue, the verb "to cleave" [English in the original] means both to divide asunder and to adhere. Of course, among the Yahoos, there are no sentences, nor even short phrases.[14]

The word *n r z,* insofar as it suggests dispersion or spots, through a multiplicity and variety of images gives the impression of a surrealist painting. There is no creaking sound of understanding going on because there might be some clue connecting all that is splattered or stained. On the other hand, *h r l* forces us to a difficult and fruitless search for some connections: "the gathering of the four witch doctors, carnal conjunction, or a forest." Such variety of meanings of the same word resembles a child's language when it begins to develop. Because the child lacks knowledge and also on account of his omnipotent manipulation of reality, the same word is valid for a string of objects or circumstances which are connected or associated.

Interestingly, a word may have opposite meanings. Borges grasps the qualities of primitive languages and is intensely interested too in the most ancient languages. It is another manifestation of his extraordinary erudition. Freud was equally concerned with the antithetical meaning of primal words. [15] Reading an 1884 essay on linguistics by Karl Abel he learned that in ancient Egyptian there are, for instance, words with two meanings, such as "strong" and "weak," "command" and "obey." In Latin, *altus* means both "high" and "deep"; *sacer*, "sacred" and "accursed"; *clamare* means "shouting," but *clam* means "softly, secretly." Freud points out that "Abel calls attention to further traces of ancient difficulties in thinking."

I use in this study the term "cleavage," employed in psychoanalysis to represent a split of the Ego. The English expression "splitting of the Ego" is equivalent to the French *"clivage du moi"* and to the German *"Ich Spaltung,"* a term that Freud used to designate the particular phenomenon he observed especially in fetishism and psychosis. It denotes the coexistence in the Ego of two psychic responses regarding the external reality insofar as it contradicts a demand arising from a drive: one considers reality, the other denies it and substitutes a product of desire. These two attitudes coexist without influencing one another. The reader finds Borges's choice of the verb "to cleave" and the meaning he assigns to it surprising, and he is even more amazed when Borges adds "in our language," since he is actually writing in Spanish. Could this express precisely a dissociation, a cleavage between his two maternal tongues, Spanish and English?

Freud began his inquiry into the double meaning of certain terms in relation to his studies of the dream. He thought opposition and contradiction function in an intriguing way in dreams. According to Freud, "no" does not seem to occur in dreams, which tend to combine opposites into one unit or envision them as part of an identical element. From this perspective, interpreting Borges's complex and oneiric though watchful enumerations would imply possessing a difficult or nonexistent secret clue to his waking dreams. He himself tells us so when he writes in

"*Alguien sueña* (Someone Dreams)": "He has dreamed the enumeration that treatises call chaotic, which is actually cosmic, since all things are connected by secret links." [16] In the same text, where everything pertains to an enumeration beginning with "He has dreamed...," it is possible to perceive one of those secret clues: "He has dreamed the steps of the labyrinth. He has dreamed the secret name of Rome, which was its true rampart."

The secret name of Rome, its true rampart, is Love.[17]

"The Aleph"

Aleph is the first letter of the Hebrew alphabet which has been the traditional symbol of the Cabbalists. According to Gershom Scholem it represents for the Jewish people the spiritual root of all the letters and it implies the whole alphabet. [18] It is considered in the Hasidic tradition as expression of the Will of God, since it probably was the only letter that the Jews heard directly from the mouth of the Creator. Furthermore, it is a pantheistic symbol, seeing that it translates literally a deity that expresses the totality of the universe in a microcosm. An Aleph is "one of the points in space that contains all other points," explains Daneri to the narrator in the story with this title mentioned above. He discovered this small point in the cellar when he was a child. It is "the only place on earth where all places are, seen from every angle, without any confusion or blending." [19] In the Aleph "one can babble with all of the images of Beatriz," Daneri's deceased cousin, a woman once hopelessly loved by the narrator-protagonist.

This enumeration that at times appears to be a true literary teratoma, differs from others I have analyzed earlier, in that, on account of the emotional connotations it reveals, we are able to somehow attain a precipitate of sense. Borges explains that the main problem, that is, enumerating an infinite set, has no solution.

> Really, what I want to do is impossible, for any listing of an endless series is doomed to be infinitesimal. In that single gigantic instant I saw millions of acts both delightful and awful; not one of them amazed me more than the fact that all of them occupied the same point in space, without overlapping or transparency. What my eyes beheld was simultaneous, but what I shall now write down will be successive, because language is successive.

... The Aleph's diameter was probably little more than an inch, but all space was there, actual and undiminished. Each thing (a mirror's face, let us say) was infinite things, since I distinctly saw it from every angle of the universe. I saw the teeming sea; I saw daybreak and nightfall; I saw the multitudes of America; I saw a silvery cobweb in the center of a black pyramid; I saw a splintered labyrinth (it was London); I saw, close up, unending eyes watching themselves in me as in a mirror; I saw all the mirrors on earth and none of them reflected me; I saw in a backyard of Soler Street the same tiles that thirty years before I'd seen in the entrance of a house in Fray Bentos; I saw bunches of grapes, snow, tobacco, lodes of metal, steam; I saw convex equatorial deserts and each one of their grains of sand; I saw a woman in Inverness[20] whom I shall never forget; I saw her tangled hair, her tall figure, I saw the cancer in her breast; I saw a ring of baked mud in a sidewalk, where before there had been a tree; I saw a summer house in Adrogué and a copy of the first English translation of Pliny[21] {Hilemon Holland's) and all at the same time saw each letter on each page (as a boy, I used to marvel that the letters in a closed book did not get scrambled and lost overnight); I saw a sunset in Querétaro[22] that seemed to reflect the color of a rose in Bengal; I saw my empty bedroom; I saw in a closet in Alkmnaar a terrestrial globe between two mirrors that multiplied it endlessly; I saw horses with flowing manes on a shore of the Caspian Sea at dawn; I saw the delicate bone structure of a hand; I saw the survivors of a battle sending out picture postcards; I saw in a showcase in Mirzapur a pack of Spanish playing cards; I saw the slanting shadows of ferns on a greenhouse floor; I saw tigers, pistons, bison, tides, and armies; I saw all the ants on the planet; I saw a Persian astrolabe; I saw in the drawer of a writing table (and the handwriting made me tremble) unbelievable, obscene, detailed letters, which Beatriz had written to Carlos Argentino; I saw a monument I worshiped in the Chacarita cemetery; I saw the atrocious relics that had once deliciously been Beatriz Viterbo; I saw the circulation of my own dark blood; I saw the coupling of love and the modification of death; I saw the Aleph from every point and angle, and in the Aleph I saw the earth and in the earth again the Aleph and in the Aleph the earth; I saw my own face and my own bowels; I saw your face, and I felt dizzy and wept, for my eyes had seen that secret and conjectured object whose name is common to all men but which no man has looked upon—the unimaginable universe.

I felt infinite wonder, infinite pity.[23]

The passage I have selected from this story is intensely suggestive, yet it is difficult to decipher each element of this enumeration and some of the symbols, without incurring vague generalities or, conversely, a personal hermeneutics which would therefore be dubious. I will nonetheless advance some hypotheses. Borges, as narrator and protagonist, toys once again with the deliberate intention of confusing and hiding the clues to his suffering. After emphasizing the labyrinth—this time it is the city of London, bombarded during World War II—and the mirrors—with their now familiar versions and inversions—Borges enumerates all "[his] eyes had seen": a woman's "tangled hair" and "tall figure"; "the cancer in her breast" and "a ring of baked mud in a sidewalk, where before there had been a tree." We can make various assumptions, from the reference to a diseased breast, a "bad" ("*malo*") breast, perhaps associated with an empty uterus after a ripping birth (the ring of mud where there was a tree before), to the allusion to obsessive and phobic mechanisms which, by means of breast cancer or the cold winter, discourage and cancel the excitement experienced as incestuous or impossible.[24] The erotic is played over against the tragic and uncanny: "tigers, pistons, bison, tides, and armies," "the coupling of love," obscene relationships and epistles, and death: cancer, cold, the cemetery. "The atrocious relics that had once deliciously been Beatriz Viterbo" has an overtone of cruel revenge. "Now that she was dead, I could devote myself to her memory, without hope but also without humiliation," he says in the beginning of the story. We find once again his lonely, empty bedroom, as well as images of woman and love as despicable.

While recounting his memories, Borges the narrator refers to the visit he always pays, on the anniversary of Beatriz's death, to her father and the cousin with whom she betrayed him. Reluctant as he is to uncover his private life, he reveals however, in this unique connection with Daneri, some traits belonging to the register of the voyeuristic and perverse. The bond that unites Borges to Daneri is as much his contempt as his "love" for Beatriz. "It was in this way," he says, "on these melancholy and vainly erotic anniversaries, that I came into the gradual confidences of Carlos Argentino Daneri (p. 16)."

Incest, love and death, ripping holes and cold spite[25] might relate to traumatic early stages of his narcissization as well as to later problems with sexuality. To quench his infinite frustration and his infinite hatred, to shun his sinister terrors and to bashfully hide his need for tenderness and his pressing desires, Borges takes shelter in a masturbatory feverish vertigo resulting from condensing, in a single point, multiple fragments of experiences, fantasies and obsessions.

"The Zahir"

I conclude this chapter with another one of the famous Borges congeries. The story entitled "The Zahir" begins thus,

> In Buenos Aires the Zahir is an ordinary coin worth twenty centavos. The letters N T and the number 2 are scratched as if with a razor-blade or penknife; 1929 is the date on the obverse. (In Guzerat, towards the end of the eighteenth century, the Zahir was a tiger; in Java, a blind man from the Mosque of Surakarta whom the Faithful pelted with stones; in Persia, an astrolabe which Nadir Shah caused to be sunk to the bottom of the sea; in the Mahdi's prisons, along about 1892, it was a little compass which Rudolf Cark von Slatin touched, tucked into the fold of a turban; in the Mosque of Cordova, according to Zotenberg, it was a vein in the marble of one of the twelve-hundred pillars; in the Tetuán ghetto, it was the bottom of a well.) [26]

In a theophanic mystic, the Zahir is the 'renowned', the 'visible'. According to the Koran, it is one of the ninety-nine names of God. It is "the First and the Last, the Visible and the Occult." For Borges the Zahir is a coin, a tiger, an astrolabe, a small compass, the marble lode, the bottom of a well. Any object, any fragment, person or animal, even the unthinkable, may be invested with divine powers. It depends only upon that unique magician and maker. This is the reason that Borges is able to state that every enumeration, even though it may seem chaotic, is cosmic. One must know the clue, break the code.

The code of this story is found, I believe, in the anagram remaining when N, T, and the number 2, mentioned in the description of the coin, are taken out. Then one reads *O-ce-avos*, which in Argentina sounds exactly as "o sea vos," Spanish for "that is to say, you"—that is to say, Borges. This indicates therefore who is the sinister man who possesses the Zahir. Further on another enumeration, half-fantastic, half-real, allows him to make reference to coins or symbols thereof, culled from the most exotic stories and the most diverse fables. "As if in a dream," writes Borges, "the thought that every piece of money entails such illustrious connotations as these, seemed to me of huge, though inexplicable, importance." [27] Such obsessive and exhibitionist drive occupies his mind, until, even as the younger sibling of Teodolina Villar, he finally loses his mind.

Is the Zahir an expression of an absolute deity or an uncanny torment? God or Satan? Thanks to his thematic and rhetorical resources, Borges reaches exceptional heights as a crafter of beauty who weaves the sublime with the uncanny.

The Uncanny

Corominas' etymological dictionary of the Spanish language relates the terms *"siniestro* (uncanny)" and *"ominoso* (ominous)," to the superstitious notions of unlucky omens, presages, and predictions of disaster. [28] Bad luck may originate in an incantation or a spell. Sometimes a certain look suffices: the "evil eye" is the distrustful look proper of envy. One of the most eloquent names of Satan is "The Envious One."

The German term *"unheimlich"* used by Freud, translated into English as "uncanny," means literally the "unfamiliar," since it is an antonym of "heimlich," the familiar, private, secret, domestic. Hence one may conclude that something is terrifying when it is not habitual or expected. Yet not all that is new or unusual turns out to be terrifying. According to E. Jentsch, the essential quality of the uncanny results from our feeling disconcerted, lost.

Studying the etymology of *"heimlich"* and *"unheimlich,"* Freud concludes that the former word, "among its different shades of meaning, exhibits one which is identical with its opposite, *'unheimlich'*; on the one hand it means what is familiar and agreeable, and on the other, what is concealed and kept out of sight."[29] We are dealing here with something that may have been familiar and has become strange and inhospitable, as the result of represssion suffered in the personal history of one's childhood or philogenetically, in the process of overcoming certain aspects of ancestral groups. Hence he also reaches the conclusion that "uncanny" is the quality of something which, having been revealed, must remain a secret, whether it had been familiar or not to begin with.

In literary fiction there is a peculiar quality to what is "terrifying" that differs from the corresponding real life experiences. Many things which would be ominous if they occurred in reality, are not so in literary creation; viceversa, in literature there exist manifold possibilities of creating uncanny effects which are not part of everyday, real life. Freud includes in the realm of the *"unheimlich"* the following: animism and magic; the themes of the Doppelgänger or "double" and mirrorlike relationships; the identification with others to the point of confusion and estrangement from one's own self; the omnipotence of desires; the connection with death; the "eternal return of the same" (Nietzsche) as in the recurrence of physical traits and names in the course of generations on account of an inexorable destiny. "The compulsion to repeat," he writes, "vanquishes the pleasure principle and bestows daemonic characteristics to some aspects of psychic life." In *Beyond the Pleasure Principle* he defines the compulsion to repeat as the underlying substratum of the death instinct.

The "*unheimlich*" experience is motivated by all that cannot be explained, dominated or controlled from the known and the conscious. It emerges as a return of the repressed, to which Freud assigns the essential connotation of castration anxiety. Sand in the eyes in Nathaniel's delirium or the dismemberment of the doll Olympia in Hoffmann's "The Sandman," a story Freud analyzes in his work entitled "The Uncanny" are examples of this peculiar and ultimate sense of the uncanny.

When in "The Zahir" Borges succeeds in getting rid of the coin, he is "distracted" from the task of composing a fantastic story. He writes,

> The narrator is an ascetic who has abjured the society of men and who lives in a kind of wilderness. (The name of this place is Gnitaheidr[30]). Because of the simplicity and candor of his life there are those who consider him an angel; but this is a pious exaggeration, for there is no man who is free of sin. As a matter of fact, he has cut his own father's throat, the old man having been a notorious wizard who by magic arts had got posession of a limitless treasure. To guard this treasure from the insane covetousness of human beings is the purpose to which our ascetic has dedicated his life: day and night he keeps watch over the hoard... In the end we understand that the ascetic is the serpent Fafnir,[31] that the treasure upon which he lies is the treasure of the Nibelungs. The appearance of Sigurd brings the story to an abrupt end.[32]

Taking the Nibelungen saga as a starting point, Borges succeeds in surprising us with the uncanny: the angel who has cut his father's throat is referred to with calculated cynicism, and he attempts to justify him, since the father was a wizard who had appropriated a limitless treasure.[33] Borges constructs his story, as he does most of his writings, somewhere in between the power of a reality of unsatisfied desires and the world of his profuse imagination. Thus, he fills with haunting creations, in cathartic sublimation, the blank spaces, the pain of the lack, the anger of impotence.

Zarathustra says, "One must truly carry chaos within in order to be able to engender a dancing star."

His creative hallucination is as disconcerting as it is unusual, but it opens paths of beauty. "Beauty lies in wait," states Borges in his lecture on poetry. This image has paranoid resonance and it seems to agree with the statement of the German poet, Rilke, "The beautiful is the beginning of the terrible that we humans are able to bear." It agrees also with the conclusions reached by Eugenio Trías in *Lo bello y lo siniestro* (*The Beautiful and the Uncanny*), "Beauty is always an (orderly) veil through which chaos must be sensed."[34] This author develops the theory that the uncanny is a condition and a boundary of the beautiful.

In conclusion, the presence of the ominous in Borges is self-evident. All the stimuli that produce such effect are manifest in his work. It would be redundant to cite again his most famous stories, his thematic reiteration, his artful style. It is a style that makes us shudder. Personally I am most impressed by the writer's indifference, his dispassionately cold handling of certain characters who kill or are killed as if they were puppets of an absurd and ruthless destiny. Borges's text betrays the fracture between a painful absence (that of love) and an implacable presence, that of Thanatos.

When the tigers, pistons, bison, mirrors, labyrinths, books, library, sword, knives, nightmares, give him some respite, Borges reflects, "And yet, and yet[35] ... To deny temporal succession, to deny the ego, to deny the astronomical universe, are apparent desperations and secret assuagements. Our destiny... is not horrible because of its unreality; it is horrible because it is irreversible and ironbound... The world, alas, is real; I, alas, am Borges."[36]

Notes

1. Umberto Eco, *The Name of the Rose* (*Il nome della rosa*), trans. William Weaver, (New York: Harcourt Brace Jovanovich, 1983).
2. Jorge Luis Borges, "Funes, the Memorious," *Ficciones*, trans. Anthony Kerrigan (New York: Grove Press, 1962), 115.
3. Ibid., 114.
4. Borges, "Epilogue," *Dreamtigers*, transl. Mildred Boyer and Harold Morland (New York: Dutton, 1964), 93.
5. Borges, "The Analytical Language of John Wilkins," *Other Inquisitions, 1937-1952*, trans. Ruth L. C. Simms (Austin: University of Texas Press, 1975), 103.
6. Ibid., 104.
7. Michel Foucault, *The Order of Things: an Archaeology of the Human Sciences*, trans. of *Les Mots et les Choses* (New York, 1970), xv. His references to Borges's text lead to the discussion of the project to write a history of madness since antiquity, a history of the similar—the Same—circumscribed by the history of the Other. The Other represents the different, and, according to cultural standards, madness. In his book *El otro, el mismo* (The Same, the Other), published in 1964, Borges uses these terms with a connotation different from Foucault's: the "same" is the identity that endures despite the time that elapses, bringing about the "other." Borges refers to that which recurs, and cannot fail to recur, in various manifestations.
8. Ibid., xvii-xviii.
9. Ibid., xviii.
10. Sigmund Freud, "A Metapsychological Supplement to the Theory of Dreams," SE 14, 219-35.
11. Freud, "The Unconscious", SE 14, 201.
12. Borges, "The Aleph," *The Aleph and Other Stories, 1933-1969*, ed. and transl. by Norman Thomas di Giovanni in collaboration with the author (New York: Dutton, 1970), 18.
13. G. K. Chesterton, cited by Borges in "The Analytical Language," *Other Inquisitions*.
14. Borges, "Doctor Brodie's Report," *Doctor Brodie's Report*, trans. Norman Thomas di Giovanni in collaboration with the author (New York: Dutton, 1972), 117.
15. Freud, "The Antithetical Meaning of Primal Words," SE 11, 155-61.
16. Borges, "*Alguien sueña* (Somebody Is Dreaming)," *Los conjurados* (Buenos Aires: Alianza, 1985), 44.
17. In Spanish "*Amor*" read in reverse, is "*Roma*" = Rome. Translator's note.
18. Gershom Scholem, *On the Kabbalah and Its symbolism*, trans. Ralph Manheim (New York: Schocken Books, 1965).
19. Borges, "The Aleph," 23.

20. A city and harbor of northern Scotland.
21. Pliny the Elder, a Roman writer (23-79), author of *Naturalis Historia*.
22. City in Mexico.
23. Borges, "The Aleph," 26-28.
24. *Malo* means in Spanish both "bad or evil" and "sick." [Translator's note.]
25. The author puns on the Spanish word for "spite," *des-pecho*, where the second element is identical to the Spanish for "breast," *pecho*. [Translator's note.]
26. Borges, "The Zahir," *Labyrinths: Selected Stories and Other Writings*, trans. Donald A. Yates and James E. Irby (New York: New Directions Publishing, 1964), 156.
27. Ibid., 160.
28. Joan Corominas, *Breve diccionario etimológico de la lengua castellana*, (Madrid: Gredos, 1973).
29. Freud, "The Uncanny," SE 17, 222-26.
30. Gnitaheidr is the place to which Fafnir is said to have removed the stolen treasure in the Norse saga Fafnismal.
31. Fafnir killed the divine Hridmar because he refused to yield to his children the part of the treasure to which they were entitled. (To read Borges one needs reference tools, just as one would need a bilingual dictionary to read in a foreign language. In English, the reader may consult Evelyn Fishburn and Psiche Hughes, *A Dictionary of Borges* (London: Duckworth, 1990). [Translator's note.]
32. Borges, "The Zahir," 160.
33. How can we help wondering about patricide, how can we fail to think that this limitless treasure is the mother?
34. Eugenio Trías, *Lo bello y lo siniestro* (The Beautiful and the Sinister), (Madrid: Seix Barral, 1984), 43.
35. In English in the original.
36. Borges,"The Analytical Language,"*Other Inquisitions,* 186-87.

Chapter 4

From Asterion to Oedipus

> In the facade of the palace was a warning:
> You were here before entering
> and when you leave you will not know that you are staying.
> Diderot relates the parable. It encompasses my days,
> my many days.
> Jorge Luis Borges[1]

The Enigma of Asterion

"The House of Asterion" is a brief yet admirable story where Borges deftly toys with us, allowing us to discover its sense only in the last two lines.[2] "This story stimulates our mind by creating and releasing tension, through concealments and revelations, questions and answers, problems and solutions. It has the form of a riddle," says Enrique Anderson Imbert.[3] I add: a riddle that once again tells of Borges and his personal pathos.

The epigraph of this story is a citation from *The Library*, a repository of myths attributed to Apollodorus of Athens (perhaps of the second century B.C.E.). It names the protagonist of Borges's story: "And the queen gave birth to a son who was called Asterion." I summarize Apollodorus's version of his myth. Minos, to prove that he had been fated by the gods to rule as king of Crete, begged Poseidon to send to him a bull from the bottom of the sea. He promised to sacrifice the animal to the god. But the white bull was so beautiful that Minos was unwilling to immolate him. Then Poseidon, angered, sparked in Pasiphae, Minos's wife, a burning passion for the beast. Asterion, known as the Minotaur, was born from the mating of the bull and Pasiphae. He had the head of a bull, yet the rest of his body was human. The Minotaur dwelled in a Labyrinth built by Daedalus. Later Minos imposed upon the Athenians a tribute: a group of seven boys and seven girls had to be periodically sent to Crete to be sacrificed to the Minotaur. Theseus was one of the third group of sacrificial victims. But Ariadne, daughter of Minos, fell in love with him and gave him a sword and a ball of thread. With the sword, Theseus slew the Minotaur; with the thread, that he had unrolled as he made his way into the Labyrinth, he could retrace his steps and find the exit.

Using the technique of riddles, Borges speaks about the "House" and "Asterion" rather than saying "Labyrinth" and "Minotaur." He relates the story in the first person. It is Asterion who tells of his life and his confinement, his misfortunes and his aspirations. The last surprising line, in the third person, offers the clue to the story.

A Reading

Borges desired to have, ever since he was a boy, a magnifying glass that would allow him to enter the drawing and discover the Minotaur. Perhaps this obsessive desire to identify was the same that led him to gaze at the Asiatic tiger in the zoo. It is a desire to look through a fissure, a net or a grill: the one outside seems eager to absorb, to fuse with the one inside.

The Minotaur in the labyrinth, like the caged tiger, like the images in mirrors, are images able to capture the onlooker; the spaces inside are realms one can enter but from which it is not possible to exit. Dissociation, doubling: outside and inside, ego and non-ego, good and bad, in continuous waves accompanied by diverse reflections, are always present in Borges's work. We are dealing here with fusions and separations from an Other that is real and an Other that is subjective. They are tantamount to a constant attempt to elaborate a traumatic situation, which by virtue of being traumatic returns again and again.

Borges explains in the postscript to *El Aleph* (Buenos Aires: Emecé, 1961) how the inspiration to write this story emerged: "I owe 'The House of Asterion' and the character of its wretched protagonist to an 1896 painting by Watts." Borges is likely to have seen the reproduction of the painting in G. K. Chesterton's biography of George F. Watts, published in London in 1904. He refers to it at least five times in *Other Inquisitions*. Chesterton speaks of the "stupid brutality" of Watt's Minotaur, which he interprets as a moral reaction, half Stoic and half Puritan, against the modern city's cruelty. Anderson Imbert reminds us that some biographers say that Watts painted the Minotaur in three hours, outraged because of the greed, the voracity of the materialistic cultures of his time. He adds, "One cannot tell whether Borges was able to discern how, in Watt's painting, the monster has crushed a bird with his huge hand, and seems to be looking out to the sea, expecting other beautiful victims."

I believe Borges observed the details of the painting, and that is why he sensed the Minotaur's poverty. Asterion is the tiger caged in the labyrinth, turning around and around until he is turned impotent by exhaustion. Greed empties him, capturing so many others makes him void of his own self. He is the "wretched protagonist" who, alone, plays with his imaginary double and anxiously awaits a redeemer: "I hope he will take me to a place with fewer galleries and fewer doors."[4] Asterion, a misogynous, arrogant, and mad misanthrope who feeds on human flesh, lives as an exhausted, terrified and terrifying prisoner. Borges comments on this story: "I wrote it in a single day. Because I was editor of a magazine, and there were three blank pages to be filled, there was no time.... I felt there might be something true in the idea of a monster wanting to be killed, needing to be killed, no? Knowing itself masterless, I mean, he knew all the time there was something awful about him, so he must have felt thankful to the hero who killed him."[5]

The Labyrinth

Many lines of interpretation have been proposed for the labyrinth. In early societies the image of the labyrinth had an attraction similar to images of an abyss, a water whirlpool, fire, and the like. Sanctuaries for rituals of initiation were given this shape. Archaeologists have found the ruins of mazes in a vast area of Asia and Europe. According to Mircéa Eliade the essential mission of the labyrinth is that of barring access to the center, that is to say to sacrality, to immortality, to an absolute reality. Attempting to penetrate the labyrinth was equated to doing battle against the Dragon. There are those who think that labyrinths were built in order to delude the evil daemons, making them enter the labyrinth only to be imprisoned in it. Others believe that knowledge of the labyrinth represents knowledge of how to enter the realm of the unknown, the realm of death.

> From south and east and west and north,
> Roads coming together have led me
> to my secret center.
> These roads were footsteps and echoes,
> women, men, agonies, rebirths,
> days and nights,
> Falling asleep and dreams,
> Each single moment of my yesterdays
> And of the world's yesterdays.
>
> Now I can forget them. I reach my center,
> My algebra and my key,
> My mirror.
> Soon I shall know who I am.[6]

Bewildered by so many galleries—longing, diverging, converging galleries—Borges aspires to the secret center where he will finally learn who he is. In the Greek myth of the Minotaur the labyrinth is related to the cult of the double axe, and it is derived from the Greek word for axe, "*labrys*." Both elements clearly were important in Minoan cult. In turn the double axe may be related to the symbol of the double horns, prominent in Cretan palace architecture and represented in the murals preserved. Sacred tauromachies are likely to have been celebrated in pre-hellenic times. Borges speaks about the Minotaur and refers to the worship of the bull and the double axe in *El libro de los seres imaginarios* (The Book of Imaginary Beings)." One interpretation of the double horns sees it as a symbol of the power wielded by the Minoan royal family at Cnossos.[7] Such a symbol would be one in essence, but double in its creative as well as its destructive potential. In a Cretan sarcophagous of Hagia Triada, there is a triple figure consisting of a cone, a double axe, and a bird. The cone perhaps represents the deity, the double axe, and like all doubles, it may be assimilated to the zodiacal sign of Gemini, and finally, the bird represents the image of the human soul.

However true the above correspondences may be in regard to Minoan religion, what matters is the associations that these and other similar symbols have acquired in the western world. Often these symbols come to signify clusters of meanings related to several systems of belief. One such association links the double horns to Gemini, "the Twins," the third sign of the Zodiac, generally symbolic of polar opposition (divine / mortal, white / black). Marius Schneider, who has studied the myth of the Gemini in prehistoric cultures, indicates its double nature: one white,.the other black; one creates, the other kills. Gemini is definitely the place of death and resurrection. While the "heavenly Gemini" presents the opposites fused, the "terrestrial Gemini " displays the gap, the split. The double axe also suggests the Roman Janus, a double-image god that symbolizes the conflict of opposites or at least their discordance. Janus is, in diverse metaphors, another frequent presence in Borges's work.

These are all paradigms of ambivalence and ambiguity, of the simultaneity of thesis and antithesis, paradise and hell, love and hate, peace and war, clarity and darkness. The awarenes of ambiguity explains Borges's contradictory adjectives, the abundance of his paradoxes, his frequent use of the oxymoron and of literary antinomies. The monstrous figure of the Minotaur poses duality. "Ovid in a line that is meant to be clever speaks of the *Semibovemque virum, semivirumque bovem* ('the man half bull, the bull half man'). Dante, who was familiar with the writings of the ancients but not with their coins or monuments, imagined the Minotaur with a man's head and a bull's body (Inferno, XII, 1-30)."[8]

Borges repeats this reflection in "The House of Asterion": "What will my redeemer be like?, I ask myself. Will he be a bull or a man? Will he perhaps be a bull with the face of a man? Or will he be like me?"[9] Having to choose between the body or the face of a bull, Asterion prefers the face. With regard to the split between body and mind, Borges has "the spirit of a bull" while his body, simply human, isn't worth much at all.

Freud, discussing infantile sexual theories, refers to the myth of the labyrinth in his "New Introductory Lectures on Psycho-Analysis": "... often light is thrown by the interpretation of dreams on mythological themes in particular. Thus, for instance, the legend of the labyrinth can be recognized as a representation of anal birth: the twisting paths are the bowels and Ariadne's thread is the umbilical cord."[10] Freud does not dwell on the details of the myth. If we consider it, however, from this angle, the labyrinth and the Minotaur turn out to be primitive versions of fantasies of origin. The labyrinth is the mother's body and the fetus is the small Minotaur. We see now the realm where mother and child encounter and are sheltered for nine months, in parasitic and cannibalistic interdependence.

In myth the Minotaur's birth is the result of the carnal union of bull and woman, and this brings us close to the fantasy of a primal scene which is an imago of the parents in a mating that has sadistic connotations. A monstrous primal scene conceived as a rape explains the origin or a monstrous being. Perhaps that is why Borges says, in the story on Ibn Hakkan al-Bokhari, "The Minotaur amply justifies its maze."[11]

It is well-known that Freud defines the earliest pregenital sexual organization as an oral cannibalistic stage.[12] Its source is the oral zone. Incorporation, intimately related to the nourishing mother, provides the model of this object relation. The child, engrossed in his world of fantasies, fixed on this early oral stage, may feel that his love is evil, that it destroys its object. Narcissistic personalities suffer the vicissitudes of an oral relatioship with these characteristics.

According to Melanie Klein, who has made an invaluable contribution to the psychoanalytic understanding of the early stages of development, the child's fantasies of voracity and intrusive emptying out may be explained by the mechanism of projective identification. In this perspective, Asterion clearly appears as the paranoid, melancholy cannibal who expects punishment and redemption. "There is genetic continuity from the persecutory fears of the infant, produced initially by cannibalistic impulses, through the ambivalence of the latency period (when the disapproving voice of the parents is internalized), to the tortured feeling of guilt and repentance of an adult who has failed to act according to his ideals."[13]

At this stage of early emotional development, love and hatred measure their forces, so to speak, in the sanctuary of the "double axe," a field of ambivalence. Primary frustrations, real or imaginary, set off the projective-introjective play of good and evil, love and hatred. For Melanie Klein in the first few months of life there is a schizo-paranoid position, accompanied by intense death anxiety, and characterized by a partial object relationship. Gradually, as integration progresses, a different relationship develops. Here guilty fantasies and reparatory wishes emerge. This is the depressive position. When a schizoid position such as the one described dominates and is persistent, we have an essentially tragic situation. It furnishes the themes of many great literary tragedies. Oscar Wilde expresses it eloquently in *The Ballad of Reading Gaol*, "Yet each man kills the thing he loves."[14]

These individuals find it difficult to give of themselves emotionally, since they can never totally elude the fear that their gifts may be deadly. Not only giving evokes this fear; receiving love from others does so too. And for this reason, like the troubadours, they may allow themselves to love and be loved only from a distance. They renounce social contacts, and sometimes they feel that passively distancing themselves is not enough, and so they often act in such a way as to alienate their objects from themselves. They mobilize all the recourses of their aggression against Others, and especially, against their libidinal objects. To this effect they substitute hatred for love, but they also endeavor to induce rejection.

Anderson Imbert, a writer not aligned with psychoanalysis, observes: "Borges imprisons his reader in a linguistic labyrinth and toys with him until he defeats him. With his aesthetic delight, however, is mingled a perceptible anguish. This is the anguish that emanates from his awareness of being unique, solitary, delirious, perplexed and lost inside a blind man. Borges is Asterion, the Minotaur." Thus Asterion is part of Borges. The Minotaur inhabits him. It is of this little monster of insatiable voracity that Borges is forever trying to rid himself. In this story he seeks that through the redeemer, Theseus. Asterion vacillates between the arrogance of the "unique" child of a queen and the image of the "wretched protagonist," between the omnipotent madness of feeling himself to be "perhaps, the creator of sun and stars," and the melancholy of the character. In an interplay of crossed and inverted identifications, every nine years he "liberates" his victims "from all evil," and he too awaits the redeemer who will save him through this death. In that space of magic identifications, the redeemer is also the redeemed monster. The father is the bull. Above shines the "intricate sun," and below is Asterion—or the other way around: he might be the creator of the sun and stars. The sun (a paternal symbol) occurs at the end, "gleaming" on the bronze sword of Theseus. "Would you believe it, Ariadne?" said Theseus. "The Minotaur scarcely defended himself."

Here is a dramatic, a moving revelation of the character and his desire. The sun metaphor glitters on the bronze sword of Theseus, who comes to kill Asterion, the boy-monster retained and imprisoned in the harsh labyrinth-uterus. The number nine suggests the period of gestation. Theseus is the redeemer who, killing him, saves him, "liberates him from all evil." Is this an intuitive allusion to the function of the father, as midwife of the symbiotic split, of the symbolic castration of a phallic mother? The split is necessary. This is the first death, one "we must go through from the moment we are born. The death of the marvelous/terrible child we have been in the dreams of those who have brought us to the world," as Leclaire writes.[15]

The task of killing the unconscious representative of "his majesty the baby," witness and testimony of primary narcissism, is inexhaustible. We all carry him; his bereavement is necessary so we may have access to life, to desire, to language. Only thus will Asterion really be, exist in the successive, human, and mortal time of Oedipus. Whoever does not achieve that goal will remain on the clouded shores of expectation, in the circularity of recurring time, devoid of illusion or hope.

"I am in a circular prison cell and the infinite wall closes in on me," says Borges again and again in different words, to finally attain the painful and lucid understanding: "My life has lacked life and death." When that early death is not achieved, the other one, definitive death, becomes a torturing threat. Death is an unavoidable presence in Borges's work, but nowhere as in this story are the angst of imprisonment and the yearning for liberation so paramount. Freud wrote, "The thorniest aspect of the narcissist system, that immortality of the Ego threatened by the force of reality, has found shelter in the child. Love for the parents, such a moving emotion but deep down such an infantile one, is nothing but revived narcissism."[16] In *"El inmortal"* (The Immortal), Borges wrote: "... I recognized them [the immortals]: they belonged to the bestial breed of the troglodytes, who infest the shores of the Arabian Gulf and the caverns of Ethiopia; I was not amazed to see that they could not speak and that they devoured serpents."[17]

Notes

1. Borges, "A Francia," *Historia de la noche* (Buenos Aires: Emecé, 1977), 111.
2. Borges, "The House of Asterion," *Labyrinths: Selected Stories and Other Writings*, trans. Donald A. Yates and James E. Irby (New York: New Directions Publishing, 1964), 138-147.
3. Enrique Anderson Imbert, *Revista Iberoamericana,* 25 (Jan-June 1960): 49.
4. Borges, *Labyrinths,* 140
5. Richard Burgin, *Conversations with Jorge Luis Borges* (New York: Holt, Rinehard and Winston, 1969), 41.
6. Borges, "*Elogio de la sombra*" (In Praise of Darkness)," *In Praise of Darkness,* trans. Norman Thomas di Giovanni. A Bilingual Edition (New York: Dutton, 1974), 124-127.
7. Juan Eduardo Cirlot, *Diccionario de símbolos* (Madrid: Labor, 1981).
8. Borges, "The Minotaur," *The Book of Imaginary Beings,* trans. Norman Thomas di Giovanni in collaboration with the author (New York: Dutton, 1970), 158-59.
9. Borges, *Labyrinths,* 140.
10. Sigmund Freud, "New Introductory Lectures on Psycho-Analysis," SE 22, 25.
11. Borges, "Ibn Hakkan al-Bokhari, Dead in His Labyrinth," *The Aleph and Other Stories. 1933-1969,*" ed. and tr. Norman Thomas di Giovanni in collaboration with the author (New York: Dutton, 1970), 123.
12. Freud, "Three Essays on the Theory of Sexuality," SE 7, 198.
13. Paula Helmann, "*Quelques Fonctions de l'Introjection et la Projection,*" *Développements sur la Psychanalyse* (Paris: P.U.F., 1966).
14. Oscar Wilde, *The Ballad of Reading Gaol* (New York: The Heritage Press, 1937), 3.
15. Serge Leclaire, *On tue un enfant. Un essai sur le narcissisme primaire et la pulsion de mort* (Paris: Ed. du Seuil, 1975). Spanish translation: *Matan a un niño* (Buenos Aires: Amorrortu, 1977), 21.
16. Freud, "On Narcissism: An Introduction," SE XIV, 67-102.
17. Borges, "The Immortal," *Labyrinths,* 108.

Chapter 5

Borges, the Man at the Pink Streetcorner[1]

This attempt to read Borges's creative work in a psychoanalytic perspective has taken us to visit the lonely, the autistic dweller of "The House of Asterion." Walking just another step further, we find the themes of *cuchilleros* (knife-wielding hoodlums) in "Man at the Streetcorner," "The Dead Man," and "The Intruder."[2]

Asterion did venture out into the street and into life, but in doing so he showed his peculiar self-centeredness, on occasion openly perverse. Borges peeps out of his intellectual labyrinth and comes close to the "pink streetcorner," that of the whorehouse and the *compadrito*.[3] There he stays, imprisoned in that other confused labyrinth, one of confrontations, of arrogant and compulsive acts of vengeance. *Compadritos* fulfill their inexorable destiny. They murder without hating, as if murder were a ritual response. Death is for them an atonement that both perpetrator and victim accept with resignation.

> Where are those who passed
> leaving behind a tale to epic,
> a fable to time, and who without hatred,
> greed or passion of love knifed one another?[4]

"The *Compadritos*," says Borges to Mario Mactas, "came into my life and my work with the hoodlums and the "*arrabales*,"[5] in part out of curiosity and in part because in the religion they had constructed—a religion of courage—I found things I was missing in my life: physical daring, bravery, all of that. My military ancestors had something to do as well with that nostalgia of sorts." [6]

The World of the *Compadrito*

In order to understand this type it is important to know something of the social reality in which such individuals lived; thus I start with a few testimonies offered by historians and students of Argentine mores. The turn of the nineteenth century saw the population of Buenos Aires, the so-called "Great Porteño Village" grow in a few years from 250,000 to almost two million.[7] A great immigrant wave, the most intense to occur in Argentina, shook the traditions and changed customs dating back to the time it had been a colony. Gone was the provincial prudery. Young people came to these shores from the whole world, fleeing wars and miseries. "They arrived," says José S. Tallón, "with flesh stormed by urgent appetites and with few moral scruples or none."[8] They were free to engage in dishonest behaviors because many came alone, leaving behind, in their own countries, families and allegiances. The "*conventillo*" was born and the poorer quarters of the city were soon populated by a unique fauna belonging to the street and to the night.[9] Decent working families suffered the invasion with resignation yet not without fear. Traditional families were motivated to reject these foreign "*gringos*." And yet together with these unsavory characters others came too, people ready to struggle for a living, people with clear class consciousness, influenced by the incipient socialist movements.

Thus, in the "indefinite *arrabal*" popped up whorehouses and *compadritos*, gangs of ruffians, murderous braggarts, bullies, and thieves in the most diverse varieties. The *arrabales* were urban boundaries inhabited also by the "gauchos" who, drawn by the attraction of the city, came as another immigratory wave, an internal one. Leopoldo Lugones defines the *compadrito* as "a triple hybrid of gaucho, gringo, and black."[10] According to Fernando Guibert "the unbelievable story of the *compadre* had these beginnings. Poverty was the faded portrait of the mother, getting increasingly frayed at the borders, as day after day she went about her tasks; the father often was a portrait stored and forgotten in a drawer."[11] The *compadrito* was no workaholic. When no *guapo*[12] job to carry out for the slum boss was forthcoming, he made a livelihood from gaming and a few small roberies.

Tallón states that "the musician and the tango dancer had an irresistible appeal for whores. The *compadrito* had to counteract them by being a *'guapo'*, that is to say, by his dagger." He continues, "The *compadritos* were excessive in every way, especially as regards attire and adornment. In those days they used to be dubbed as *relajados* (loose). They followed the fashion of the well-to-do and they dressed and embellished themselves with feminine narcissism, blatantly sexual and suspicious.... .Their typical gait, the swinging of the hips, was caused by the high heels; they made it rather fussy if not effeminate. From a distance they smelled like the whorehouse, like mental degeneration, hereditary alcoholism, and erotomania."[13]

Compadre, from the Latin *compater*

The etymology of the term *compadre* is quite suggestive. It comes from the Latin *compater*, and it denotes reciprocally both the father and the godfather of a child. Being a *"compadre"* is synonymous with sharing the father's commitment to his child. Thus, in the act of baptism or religious "confirmation" of a child, he joins the parents in promising to care for his *ahijado* (from *hijo*, son). The conterpart of this concept is that of *comadre* involving the mother and the godmother.

A derivative from *compadre* is the verb *compadrear*, quite common in Argentina and Uruguay, which means to show off, boast, brag. No one can explain this usage; perhaps it reveals the pride inherent in braggadocio. Thus we come to *compadrito*, defined in the *Diccionario de argentinismos* as "an individual who brags, lies, provokes and is a traitor, one who makes use of a particular language and has affected manners. Also known as *compadre and compadrón*; *compadrito* is, however, the term that educated people choose to denote this type."[14]

As we have seen, then, *compadrito*, a diminutive of *compadre*, is etymologically related to godfather and father. In the *"Historia de Rosendo Juárez* (History of Rosendo Juárez)" Borges has the titular character say: "It never entered my head to find out who my father was. Clementina Juárez—that was my mother—was a decent woman who earned a living doing laundry.... I grew up like a weed."[15]

We may infer from this passage how important the absence of a father figure was in these destitute homes, and how the woman-mother, who performed all the roles, was intensely idealized. In this story by Borges she is Clementina; in the story of another famous *guapo*, Ecuménico López, she is Natividad.[16] To brag or show off as being "big" (strong), must have served to fill painful gaps. "Growing up like a weed," with the street as school, sharing the vice, the idleness, and the criminal activity of older thugs, this son of promiscuity and indigence was forced to get "bigger." That is to say, he had to show off, boast, become a braggart. Naturally, this was compounded by the suspicion and resentment caused by early, chronic frustration.

Donald Winnicott speaks of a pseudo-self that can account for the psychological process in the development of this child-man who will later become a man-child. The pathology of sadomasochistic drives and of identification bonds, closely connected with the father's absence, also creates difficulties in his ability to relate to women. Since the imago of a woman-mother, idealized and forbidden, and that of a woman who can be "used" or "hired" have been dissociated, he approaches the whorehouses. Courage, like intercourse, is a difficult test of his masculinity. In the uncomplicated and indifferent satisfaction of pure orgastic drives he finds both release for his *guapo* tensions and a challenge. Under extreme circumstances, killing will be experienced without guilty feelings, because its goal is revenge. A melancholy, or a suicidal soul is hiding behind the absence of fear or behind the compulsion not to feel fear. Thus, some young men who were products of these conditions became ruffians or hired bullies, out of resentment and cockiness. They exhibited a maniacal rejection of all social norms.

Borges and the Milongas

Porteño barrios or neighborhoods inspired many milongas and tangos. This creative process, however, "was surrounded by real human horrors," says Horacio Ferrer.[17] Borges published in 1930 *Evaristo Carriego*. In its chapter "History of the tango" he defines the difference between milonga and tango.[18] The origin of the milonga lies in the *payadas* (improvised singing dialogues) performed around rural stoves, later around soldiers' stoves and in city suburbs. To reel off a milonga, the guitar's six strings are sufficient.

Milongas come to Borges almost of their own accord, "from my blood, as it were," he says. They seem to be dictated by his ancestors. "They are the ones who have written this, not I. The proof of it is that, though it may not be apparent, I usually edit repeatedly my writing. A sonnet, one of my sonnets... well, it is the final product of several generations of drafts. Not so with milongas."[19]

Tangos, on the other hand, were born in whorehouses. Borges substantiates this statement, mentioning "... the lasciviousness of the dance steps; the sexual connotations of certain titles, such as *"El choclo"* (The Corn Cob), *"El fierrazo"* (The Big Rod); the fact, which as a boy I myself observed in Palermo and years later in Chacarita and Boedo, that it was danced on street corners by male couples, because decent women would have no part of such a wanton dance." Further on he adds a suggestive comment: "The tango's sexual nature has often been noted, but not so its violent side. Both, it is true, are modes or manifestations of the same impulse. In all the languages I know the word 'manly' connotes sexual potentiality and a potential for bellicosity, and the word *virtus*, Latin for 'courage,' stems from *vir*, meaning "man." In the same way, an Afghan in the novel *Kim* can state—as if the two acts were essentialy one—'when I was fifteen, I had shot my man and begot my man.' "[20]

Borges's interpretation of this line from Rudyard Kipling is intriguing. Kipling's original reads: "When I was fifteen I killed *my* man and begot *my* man," expressing the change, the growth that takes place at that age. Borges translates: "... I had shot *a* man and begot *a* man." The association of the ideas of killing, sex, and procreation—"essentially one," says Borges—is often reiterated. It becomes a signifier to which I shall refer several times.

Once again Borges is emphasizing destiny as the force driving the *compadrito*, "for there are acts carrying such infinite responsibility (engendering or killing a man) that both repentance and boastful pride are nonsense." Because of "that awe bordering on perplexity that the instinctive arouses in a literary man" Borges looks out, from a library and a garden, toward the shores, the borders, searching for the margins of reality. No doubt his glance was a dissociated glance. "From his blood" he pointed to one aspect alone, one detail only, cutting one branch off, metonymycally as it were, from the tree. Those were difficult times: there were international and national economic crises; the fall of Yrigoyen's government marks the beginning, institutionally and politically,

of what would be a long period of institutional darkness. Borges does not seem to have registered those harsh realities. And yet in 1974, as he writes an epilogue for his *Obras Completas* and imagines a brief vita to be published in 2074, he tries to remedy his scotomization and attempts, once again, to justify himself: "It should in the first place be remembered that Borges's years were those of the country's decline. He belonged to a military family and he recalled with nostalgia the epic destiny of his ancestors. He believed that courage is one of the few virtues men are capable of, yet his cult drove him, as it did many others, to the thoughtless veneration of underground figures. Thus the most popular of his stories was "Man at the 'Streetcorner,' where the first-person narrator is a murderer."
This is precisely the story to which I now turn.

"Man at the (Pink) Streetcorner"

In an early version of this story (1927), a man from the Corrales or from Barracas, having heard of the famous Juan Muraña, a knife-wielding thug of Palermo he has never seen, comes to challenge him. They meet at a grocery store. The provocation made, they go out to fight, and they wound each other in the street. Muraña slashes him, saying: "I spare your life so you'll come back looking for me."
"That gratuitous duel left a mark in my memory," Borges comments. The title of his story was laconic: "Men Fighting." He signed it with his great-grandfather's name, Francisco Bustos. Years later he added to the story a feminine character, La Lujanera, and renamed it *"Hombre de la esquina rosada* (Man at the Pink Streetcorner)."[21]
The action takes place in the whorehouse of La Julia and its characters are Rosendo Juárez, the Slasher, and Francisco Real, the Butcher.[22] Rosendo's girlfriend, La Lujanera, who "had the others all beat by a mile," was a token and prize of courage. When the newcomer challenged everyone and her man did not respond, she slipped his knife out and gave it to Rosendo, saying, "Rosendo, I think you'll need this," whereupon Rosendo "flipped the knife behind him out of the window into the Maldonado stream." The frustrated Lujanera throws her arms around the Butcher's neck and out of her rage and in an attempt to temper the Butcher's rage, tells him, "Let the bastard alone… he tried to make us think he was a man!"

The narrator who relates this story to Borges is a young man who until now has been, like all the youths in the slum, an unconditional admirer of the *guapo*. "All of us younger guys," he says in the story, "used to ape him even to the way he spit." Disappointed and humiliated by the behavior of his idol, he reflects, "The more he gets beaten, the tougher he has to be." Yet the story does not end here. Taking advantage of the darkness, Rosendo goes out unnoticed to look for Francisco Real, who is probably "going at it in some ditch" with La Lujanera. He finds Real, challenges him to fight and wounds him mortally. No one will suspect who did it: "Nice and easy, I walked the two or three blocks back to my shack. A candle was burning in the window, then all at once went out." That night, which "he would never forget," La Lujanera was awaiting him.

Didier Anzieu sees in this story a revived version of Oedipus: "Just as the Sophoclean Oedipus fascinated and horrified the spectators enacting the realization of their unconscious desires, thus the narrator of Borges's story accomplishes in reality the double urge that the author could only accomplish in his imagination and his writing, namely the death of his rival and the possession of the unattainable woman."[23]

Mine is a different interpretation. Even though the scene is set on a manifest triangular pattern, it is the story of a challenge. What is at stake is not desire for a woman but, rather, saving the "honor" that has been stained, the wounded pride. The narrator, snubbed by Rosendo, who called him "dummy," saying that he was "always in the way," will demonstrate that he can do what the renowned Slasher could not. La Lujanera does not motivate the murder. Its real cause and purpose is saving the dark reputation of Villa Santa Rita, which was challenged by the troublemaker. The prize is a night with the best whore. An abyss separates duel and revenge, but Borges does not distinguish between them. In the former, a regulated contest of strength is apparent; in the second, narcissistic rage pushes a thug to treachery, deceit, surprise. Two codes are involved: one has to do with honor, the other with trickery. One relates to courage, the other to a perverse outburst. One takes place in the open, and in the other, one leaps upon the opponent from the back.

Thirty five years later, Borges tried to vindicate Rosendo Juárez. In a story with the title "*Historia de Rosendo Juárez* (Story of Rosendo Juárez)," published in a volume with the title *El informe de Brodie* (Dr. Brodie's Report), Borges has Brodie explain what caused his behavior: "The odd thing was that the two of us looked a lot alike. He was mulling over some trick ... he drew up to me and began praising me up and down...

. He wasn't letting the gin alone, either, maybe to work up his courage, and finally he came out and asked me to fight. Then something happened that nobody ever understood. In that big loudmouth I saw myself, the same as in a mirror, and it made me feel ashamed. I wasn't scared, maybe if I'd been scared I'd have fought with him."[24]

The mirror of prideful courage has become the mirror of shame. Borges, now seventy years old, reveals in a magnificent description the thanatic narcissism of these characters.

"The Dead Man"

"The Dead Man" is another realistic story, written in 1946 and published in *El Aleph*. Benjamín Otálora is "a strapping young man of nineteen... a man from the outlying slums of Buenos Aires... a sorry hoodlum with little else to his credit than a passion for recklessness." He flees to Uruguay because "a lucky blow with a knife has made clear to him that he is also brave."[25] He bears a letter of introduction from a crime lord of the district to one Azevedo Bandeira, cattle driver and smuggler.

Between these two there is a duel. Almost as if this were the narration of a death that has been anounced, Bandeira gradually gives Otálora, who is young, ambitious, and unscrupulous, opportunities to appropriate all he owns, namely a woman with red braids, a bay horse, and a sheepskin saddle blanket trimmed with a jaguar skin. But, finally, Bandeira gets it all back by murdering him. "Otálora realizes, before dying, that he has been betrayed from the start, that he has been sentenced to death—that love and command and triumph had been accorded him because his companions already thought of him as a dead man, because to Bandeira he already was a dead man."[26]

Didier Anzieu emphasizes again the Oedipal pattern, yet adds that the plot of "The Dead Man" makes it a "grotesque version of what was a pathetic one in "Man at the Streetcorner." Concerning the story's end and Otálora's death, he observes, "The vainglorious Oedipus becomes the ridiculous Oedipus."

Granted that "The Dead Man" lends itself, more readily than "Man at the Streetcorner," to such an interpretation; there remain, however, some difficulties. They arise in the process of distinguishing between what is manifest and what is latent in a literary work. One is wary of overinterpreting. It is noteworthy, however, that the boss, Azevedo, has the same surname as Borges's mother and that the companion who betrays

Otálora is called Suárez, the surname of his grandmother on the mother's side. These two names signal the trapping and killing of Benjamín Otálora in punishment for his undue ambition to possess all that belongs to the boss. Can this be interpreted as a negative Oedipal drive where the *compadrito* yearns for the possessions and the "riches" not of the father but of his mother?

From a different perspective, we could also consider that Otálora sounds very much like Norah, Borges's sister, who as we know from evidence concerning his childhood was more outgoing, more voluble than Borges. We should also note that she was the family's favorite child; that the encounter with Azevedo takes place at Paso de los Molinos, where the siblings used to spend their vacations; that Otálora is of about the same age as Emma Zunz, who avenges an embezzlement connected with primal scene fantasies (see chapter 6). Why not associate this story with a dream? Bandeira Azevedo—Borges Azevedo—kills the "dumb pet," the "foreigner" who came and deprived him of all that he owned.

I advance these possible interpretations in order to suggest that the apparently positive Oedipal plot may conceal latent elements of a negative Oedipal one, actually a pre-Oedipal, narcissistic, constellation.

Furthermore, the woman identified as a readhead is no more than an attribute, an adjective (her hair is red, just as the horse and the saddle blanket). From this viewpoint, should we speak of Oedipus? Fate seems to have a name, Bandeira. The victim is he who desires to be and to have as much as his boss, yet as pure property, where love counts for nothing. "To be a cattle driver is to be a servant; Otálora decides to work himself up to the level of smuggler."[27]

The Duel

> Two will stand out in any contest,
> one of our own and the other a foreigner.
> They've never set eyes on one another,
> They never will:
> They fight neither for goods
> Nor for a woman's favors.[28]

Borges's fascination with these themes comes from his lineage, and, just as the milongas themselves, "they are dictated to him." In "*El Sur* (The South)," "an ecstatic old man, a symbol of the South," puts in his hands a dagger to "heroically" face the infantile provocation of a drunkard who throws crumbs at him.

There is certainly a conflict in the "discord of his two lineages." He stands between cowardice and courage, impotence in action and omnipotence in thought. There is a duel between the two Borgeses: the one he is and the one "he would have wished for himself." There is no end to reiterations, because there is a duel in which Borges was not able to engage: one against his primary narcissistic representative. Borges carries out the unconscious desires of each one of these commands: courage becomes literature. As he will avow to Carrizo, "Epic is an elemental appetite."

"La intrusa (The Intruder)"

The book published in 1970, *El informe de Brodie* (Doctor Brodie's Report), includes several stories: *"Historia de Rosendo Juárez* (Rosendo's Tale)," *"El encuentro* (The Meting)," *"El otro duelo* (The Duel)," and *"La intrusa* (The Intruder)." The latter is a realistic story with a linear structure, resembling both in form and in content "Streetcorner Man." Borges says near the beginning:

> I set down the story now because I see in it, if I'm not mistaken, a brief and tragic mirror of the character of those hard-bitten men living on the edge of Buenos Aires before the turn of the century.
>
> ....
>
> The Nilsens liked carousing with women, but up until then their amorous escapades had always been carried out in darkened passageways or in whorehouses. There was no end of talk, then, when Cristián (the elder brother) brought Juliana Burgos to live with him. Admittedly, in this way he gained a servant, but it is also true that he took to squandering on her the most hideous junk jewelry and showing her off at parties.

The younger brother, Eduardo, falls in love with this woman. Thus one day Cristián says to his brother, "I'm on my way over to the Farías place, where they're throwing a party. Juliana stays here with you; if you want her, use her." So Juliana is shared. "Nobody will ever know the details of this strange partnership which outraged even the Costa Brava's sense of decency. The arrangement went well for several weeks, but it could not last. Between them the brothers never mentioned her name, not even to call her."

They argue. "Without knowing it, they were jealous of each other. In tough neighborhoods a man never admits to anyone—not even to himself—that a woman matters beyond lust and possession, but the two brothers were in love. This, in some way, made them feel ashamed." We read something similar in "Rosendo's Tale": "A man who thinks for all of five minutes about a woman is no man but a sissy." Is this a Borgean paradox or does it betray intense homosexual fantasies? Borges continues, "The woman attended both men's wants with an animal submission, but she was unable to keep hidden a certain preference, probably for the younger man." One day they agreed to sell her to a whorehouse. The money was split between the two brothers. Apparently they went back to their normal lives, but one day soon they met by accident as they were both waiting their turn to see her in the brothel.

"If we go on this way, we'll wear out the horses. We'd be better off keeping her close at hand." So they went right ahead and bought her again. "[Cristián]... drew a handful of coins out of his money belt, and they took the girl away. Juliana rode with Cristián. Eduardo dug his spurs into his horse, not wanting to see them together." They started cheating. "Cain was on the loose there, but the affection between the Nilsens was great—who knows what hard times and what dangers they may have faced together!—and they preferred taking their feelings out on others." Cain does not kill Abel, he kills Juliana, and he tells his brother these words:

> Let's get busy, brother. In a while the buzzards will take over. This afternoon I killed her. Let her stay here with all her trinkets, she won't cause us any more harm.
> They threw their arms around each other, on the verge of tears. One more link bound them now—the woman they had cruelly sacrificed and their common need to forget her.

A Reading

Two elements in "The Intruder" are intriguing. One is the enigma of its epigraph: II Kings 1.26. The other is that the last line in the story, referring to the murder of Juliana, was written by Borges's mother.

The epigraph is amazing because Kings only has 18 verses in the Bible. I thought it might be a typographical error until I discovered an essay by Norman Thomas Di Giovanni, who, in collaboration with Borges, translated several of his works into English. Di Giovanni avows having encountered the same difficulty.[29] Di Giovanni consulted Borges, who explained that he was referring to The Second Book of Samuel, which in some editions of the Bible is cited as "Kings." When Di Giovanni inquired the reason for this bewildering citation, the answer was, "Well, *Reyes* (Kings) is a far more beautiful word than Samuel, don't you think so?"[30]

Borges is once more up to his tricks, since he is discreetly concealing the following verse (II Samuel.1.26): "I am distressed for thee, my brother Jonathan: very pleasant hast thou been unto me: thy love to me was wonderful, passing the love of women." Even without its context, the citation synthesizes the story's content. But there is more: David, the speaker of the verse in The Second Book of Samuel, is not Jonathan's brother. His love for David results from his admiration of the latter's early heroic deed of killing the Phoenician giant with a stone. Doing this he aroused the envy of King Saul, the father of Jonathan, who tried to do away with David. Several times Jonathan took David's side and finally was able to save him. The verse is David's posthumous homage to Jonathan, who died in battle. This love then, comes close to brotherly affection in overt opposition against the father and king.

Borges himself describes what I find also a striking circumstance surrounding this story: "I was dictating [to his mother] a story with the title "The Intruder" and it hinged completely on the statement the elder brother makes informing the younger one that he has killed this woman. I could not find the words. My mother, who was taking the dictation uneasily, said, 'There you go, forever with your boors and knife-wielding hoodlums...' I replied: 'Here comes the climax, the whole story hinges on this. It depends on the words with which the elder brother tells the younger one that he has killed a woman whom both love.' My mother said: 'Let me think,' and then she added, in a wholly different voice, 'I know what he told him,' as if that had been a real event. She wrote the sentence and then read it to me: 'Let's get busy, brother. This afternoon I killed her.' She is the one who found this sentence, which was later highly praised. Without it the story would have collapsed. It was her sentence. Then she added, 'I hope this will be the last time you deal with these subjects.' Of course, she did not like them; she thought it was all absurd. What is more, she used to tell me that all boors are cowards, that my admiration for impostors was absurd.'[31]

Thus, despite her displeasure, Doña Leonor wrote the sentence that, according to her son, holds the story together. "The Intruder" was published in 1970, the year that Borges was estranged from the wife to whom he had been married (if it was a marriage) since 1967. "The Intruder" was no longer around. This is indeed a striking dialogue between a seventy-year-old man, blind and single, and his mother, with whom he has always lived, and who, now ninety years of age, rebukes him with statements and observations pertaining to times and standards gone by.

The entire story hinged upon one sentence, where the death of the intruder is announced. Anyone who cuts or interrupts a dyadic bond may be experienced as an intruder. This third person's presence interferes with a relationship between another two, leaving one—herein is the great terror involved—vulnerable and defenseless. "Cain was on the loose there..." Cain killed Abel out of jealousy and envy. In "The Intruder," the two brothers—"who knows what hard times and what dangers they may have faced together!" —engage in a discourse of endogamic faithfulness, in a symbiotic bond that they privilege and which prevents them from growing up and breaking away. Freud relates homosexuality to the difficulty in renouncing primary narcissism. In a homosexual relationship one seeks to be cared for by the other, just as one was once cared for by one's mother. Cristián, the elder brother, speaks and takes action, in an obvious authoritarian discourse of command. It is not the brother who is the intruder: jealousy is displaced and acted out upon Juliana.

The birth of a sibling is more or less traumatic, depending on circumstances and the elder child's age. It is more traumatic for a first-born child, especially if it happens when the latter is still very young, as was Borges's case. "Norah could have been a poet. My sister is a painter and a graphic artist, and she must have thought: 'If I publish my poetry, I will be invading a territory that does not belong to me; I will be an intruder.' She could have been an admirable poet, yet she has destroyed all her writings, simply in order not to be an intruder in the region she deems belongs to her husband and her brother."[32]

Lacan refers to a "Complex of Intrusion" with the subtitle "Jealousy: An Archetype of Social Feelings." "Surprised by the intruder in the distress of the weaning stage, jealousy is reactivated each time he sees the baby. The child then makes a regression which, depending on the parameters of the Ego, may be manifested as a schizophrenic psychosis or a hypocondriac neurosis. Other reactions may take the path of the imaginary destruction of the monster, and this in turn will create either perverse impulses or obsessive guilt." If the birth of a sibling occurs after the Oedipus complex, the situation is different. In this case the newborn is "adopted" by the elder child on the level of parental identifications, and the aggressive drives are sublimated into love or stern guidance. Lacan adds an important

observation: "the connections of paranoia with the fraternal complex become manifest in the frequent themes of filiation, usurping, and despoiling. Its narcissistic structure is revealed in the more paranoid themes of intrusion, the influence of doubling, of the double and all the delirious transmutations of the body."[33]
In "The Intruder" the woman has no voice. These lacks—her lack of speech, of desire—create the drama. Juliana Burgos is the intruder insofar as she masochistically subjects herself to the two brothers and tolerates the humiliation of total silence. When a father takes the attitude of Juliana Burgos vis-à-vis the mother-son dyad, or when the mother leaves him no other role, eventually the son turns out to be a phallic possession of the mother. The exogamic path beyond Oedipus has been blocked, and paranoia or other pathologies are not too far away. In my view, Borges displaced upon Doña Leonor the "killing" of the intruder because some of his unconscious had come to light (just as it did to Emma Zunz in the whorehouse). There would be no further interference, they could stay together: "Here we are both talking and *tout le rest est littérature*..."

Postscript I: Juliana Burgos

Her name evokes the name of Jorge Borges. One is also reminded of Jorge de Burgos, Umberto Eco's character in *The Name of the Rose*. I believe Juliana, just as Eduardo, the younger brother in the story, may impersonate the grimmer aspects of Georgie's relationship with his mother, his severely passive and masochistic subjection to her.

Just as Asterion, only death can liberate Juliana Burgos. Borges insightfully puts a weapon in the hands of the mother ("the Intruder") or of Theseus, whom I see as a persona of the father ("The House of Asterion"). In an interview with Burgin in Cambridge (1967), Borges said he considered "The Intruder" as "the best story I have ever written." And he adds: "There is absolutely nothing personal in it... It is not a story with a trick... What I was trying to tell is an inevitable story."

Postscript II

Having finished his B.A. in Geneva in 1919, Borges traveled to Spain with his family. In 1920 the tabloid *Ultra*—connected with the Ultraist movement of Vicente Huidobro and Rafael Cansinos Assens—published a little-known text by Borges, *"Estética del lupanar* (Aesthetics of the

Brothel). Because of its literary value and because it contains some observations related to my purpose in this book, I reproduce it below, setting out in italics the elements that stand out in a psychoanalytic reading. It was published in the newspaper *La Razón,* in Buenos Aires, on 10 October 1985.

The stone walls, standing in the sternest pose, petrify us. Drunken billboards jump out of the balconies. Yet next to a lighted rectangle that whispers CAFE *there are a hallway and a vehement flight of stairs*, plus a door opening as meekly as books that open on a first page groped at and exhausted by study. Then... comes the whorehouse.

It is a small, dirty room where a few decapitated hats bleed from the hangers on which they are perched. Several girls. A tropical spiraling of laughter. Our boredom yawns while clutching a lamp where the lie of a carnival of cards is multiplied. The women, the hopeful, even-tempered showcase of a provincial whorehouse, offer themselves with the tenacity of a delivery note that is too expensive.

An infantile ambiance of spontaneity prevails, the atmosphere of a playroom or of a patio with a fountain. Totally primitive, anti-Christian, anti-Pagan, anti-maximalistic and anti-pathetic.

All creeds fail here. The Judaic belief system fails, because the tree of Genesis has been pruned with phallic blows, while Adam and Eve are reduced here to their most pitiful performance as merchandise and customer. Hedonistic philosophy fails, since pleasure has been mutilated. On the one hand, it has been robbed of the romantic vision's prestigious tiaras; on the other, its tone of harsh fatalism has been enhanced.

The whole thing is trained, tamed, official. It remains primitive even after it has been fitted on rails, just as a horse that performs tricks or a *vidalita* where *dolor* and *amor* rhyme... And we await on the shore of midnight as if on the shore of a river.

The day lies down at our feet like a tired dog, and we pet it on the back. We comprehend sculpture—that gesticulating, majuscule thing— as we find delicious the easy curves of a wench, essential and sculpted like a Quevedo sentence. She accepts—no great pretence of surprise— the rusted counterfeit coin of our verbal displays.

Then... the carnal linking. These three words suffice for me, since no formula can encompass pleasure, something not stored in memory.

Of the sensory entanglement memory only stores auditive and visual threads. The others—pleasure, pain, temperature—persist only translated to the language of sight and sound. And deep down, *what do we care for the interjections and the changing fluency of the stages of coupling,* if these elements are just parallel to pleasure, which is the only essential thing, which no one will ever be able to capture in a web of art?

We go out. The square block of air that was oppressing our back sinks. The scaffolding of garlands made of honeyed arms and voices also fades away. The sky is now full of astronomy. A gasping star trembles over the market roofs. Our eyes pulsate many stars. The streets, like expert rails, push us to unknown destinations.

Our steps bounce against the steely silence of the city, *as if we were the scouting advance contingent of an army coming to take over a dismantled and bare city.* A lax hour falls stumbling from a clock. *The wind robs us of the lights or strangles them.* In the outskirts of the world the monstrous and feeble dawn goes around like a lie.

Notes

1. The story by Borges with the title "*El hombre de la esquina rosada*" has been translated into English as "Man at the Streetcorner." The title of this chapter is a literal translation of Borges's Spanish title. [Translator's note.]
2. All three in Borges, "The Aleph," in *The Aleph and Other Stories. 1933-1969*," ed. and trans. Norman Thomas di Giovanni in collaboration with the author. (New York: Dutton, 1970). ["*La intrusa*" is feminine. Translator's note.]
3. An Argentine term usually applied to a city swaggerer, a boaster, a show-off; also a low-life, a ruffian, a trouble-maker. (Evelyn Fishburn & Psiche Hughes, *A Dictionary of Borges*, London: Duckworth, 1990). [Translator's note.]
4. Borges, "*El tango*" From "*El otro, el mismo*," (Buenos Aires: Emecé, 1974), 888.
5. I do not translate "*arrabal*" as "*barrio*" because in Argentina the former refers to a poor quarter of a town or city, while the latter does not denote (as it does in U.S. English) an Hispanic or a poor neighborhood, but is a synonym of "neighborhood" or "suburb." [Translator's note.]
6. Mario Mactas, cited by Bracelli in the magazine *Gente*, 1971.
7. *Porteño*, literally "of the harbor" is an adjective applied to Buenos Aires and its inhabitants. [Translator's note.]
8. José Tallón, cited in Ernesto Sábato, *Tango, discusión y clase* (Buenos Aires: Losada, 1965).
9. "*Conventillo*" denotes in Buenos Aires a tenement in a neighborhood at the lowest socioeconomic level. Tenants could include asocial types.
10. Leopoldo Lugones, cited in Ernesto Sábato, *Tango*.
11. Fernando Guibert, *El compadrito y su alma* (Buenos Aires: Perrot, 1957), 17.
12. The "*guapo*" of a neighborhood would demand and obtain respect as a "tough one."
13. Tallón, cited in Sábato, *Tango*, 58.
14. Lisandro Segovia, *Diccionario de argentinismos (neologismos y barbarismos)* (Buenos Aires: Comisión Nacional del Centenario de Buenos Aires, 1911). Cited by M.A. Renard, *Borges* (Buenos Aires: Kapelusz), 102.
15. Borges, "The Aleph," 194.
16. Samuel Eichelbaum, *Un guapo del 900* (Buenos Aires: Kapelusz, 1976).
17. Horacio Ferrer, *Tangos*, cited in Ernesto Sábato, *Tango*.
18. Borges, *Evaristo Carriego. A Book about Old-time Buenos Aires*, trans. Norman T. Di Giovanni (New York: Dutton, 1984).
19. Antonio Carrizo, *Borges el memorioso* (Buenos Aires: Tierra Firme) 62.
20. Borges, "A History of the Tango (*Historia del tango), in Evaristo Carriego* (New York: Dutton, 1984), 134-35.
21. Borges, *The Aleph*, 33-42.

22. The feminine definite article, *"la,"* except when preceding, in Italian style, the name of a famous diva or ballerina, smacks of popular,uneducated, usage and, in the context of this story, it hints at the dubious reputation of the women thus named. [Translator's note.]
23. Didier Anzieu, *"Le corps et le code dans les contes de Borges," Le corps de l'oeuvre*, (Paris: Gallimard, 1981), 282.
24. Borges, "Rosendo's Tale," *Doctor Brodie's Report*, trans. Norman Thomas di Giovanni, (New York: Dutton, 1972), 59.
25. Borges, "The Dead Man," *The Aleph*, 93.
26. Ibid., 99.
27. Ibid, 96.
28. Borges, "Milonga del forastero," *Obra poética* (Buenos Aires: Emecé), 58.
29. Norman Thomas Di Giovanni, "Trabajando con Borges," *Asedio a Borges*, ed. Joaquín Marco, (Madrid: Ultramar, 1982), 214-15.
30. Ibid, 215.
31. Carrizo, *Borges*, 30.
32. Ibid., 74-75.
33. Jacques Lacan, *La Famille: Le Complexe, facteur concret de la psychologie familiale. Les complexes familiaux en pathologie* (Paris: Encyclopédie Française Larousse, 1938), vol. 8.

Chapter 6

Emma Zunz:
the Enigma of a Name

> It is surely possible to throw oneself into a line of thought and to follow it wherever it leads out of simple scientific curiosity, or, if the reader prefers, as an *advocatus diaboli*, who is not on that account himself sold to the devil.
>
> Sigmund Freud[1]

The story entitled "Emma Zunz" was very well received, just as "Man at the Streetcorner" had been earlier.[2] Films followed, both in Argentina and abroad. For this reason, before proceeding with its analysis, I shall consider some of Borges's answers to different interviewers and the diverse, even contradictory observations he offered to each.

In a conversation with Antonio Carrizo, Borges said: "This story was a gift of Cecilia Ingenieros. She gave me the plot, which I do not like because it is a revenge story, and I am skeptical of revenge. I believe revenge is useless; furthermore, the only real revenge, as I have said many times, is oblivion. That is also the only forgiveness. I dedicated it to Cecilia, ... rather than dedicate it, I should say that I returned it to Cecilia. She made up the plot." Then he adds, "The whole atmosphere of this story is atrocious. All of it is mediocre, even the name, you see, 'Emma Zunz.' I purposefully chose a Jewish surname so the reader would accept this story which is somewhat strange; so the reader might think, 'Well, these things might happen among Jews.' If I had named her López, the reader wouldn't have accepted the story. Nevertheless, if Emma Zunz is accepted, she is a bit distant."[3]

Another interview, this time with Richard Burgin, went like this:

> BORGES: That is the story of a living labyrinth. It's very strange, because in a story like "The Immortal" I did my best to be magnificent, while the story "Emma Zunz" is a very drab story, a very grey story, and even the name Emma was chosen because I thought it particularly ugly, but not strikingly ugly, no?
> BURGIN: But one still feels compassion for her. I mean, she is a kind of tool of destiny.
> BORGES: Yes, she's a tool of destiny, but I think there's something very mean in revenge, even in a just revenge, no? Something futile about it. I dislike revenge. I think that the only possible revenge is forgetfulness, oblivion. That's the only revenge. But, of course, oblivion makes for forgiving, no?[4]

These statements contradict those he makes in the Epilogue of "The Aleph": " 'Emma Zunz' is a splendid plot, much better than its fearful execution." Beyond his modesty, his vain self-deprecation, Borges takes a stance, by emphatically rejecting the feelings associated with revenge, which is in no way absent from his stories. "He preferred vengeance to pardon," Borges says of the poet William Blake. And in one of the few references to Freud one finds in his work, he continues: "... reasoning that every injured person wants to avenge himself, and if he does not, the unsatisfied desire—and this anticipates Freud—will sicken his soul."[5]

Summary of the Story

On January 14th, 1922, upon returning from the cloth manufacturing company Tarbuch and Loewenthal, Emma Zunz found a letter where, in nine or ten lines, she was being informed that Mr. Maier "had taken by mistake a large dose of veronal and had died." It was signed by a boarding-house friend of her father, one Fein or Fain.

> Emma dropped the paper. Her first impression was of a weak feeling in her stomach and in her knees, and then of blind guilt, of unreality, of coldness, of fear; then she wished that it were already the next day... she had already become the person she would be.

In the growing darkness, Emma wept until the end of that day for the suicide of Manuel Maier, who in the old happy days was Emmanuel Zunz. She remembered summer vacations at a little farm near Gualeguay, She remembered (tried to remember) her mother, she remembered the little house at Lanús which had been auctioned off, she remembered the yellow lozenges of a window, she remembered the warrant for her father's arrest, the ignominy, she remembered the poison-pen letters with the newspaper's account of "the cashier's embezzlement."

She had never forgotten the secret that her father had confided in her before his departure, six years earlier: he was not guilty. Aaron Loewenthal, formerly the manager of the factory and at the time one of the owners, had embezzled the money. Emma guarded this secret zealously, because "... perhaps she believed that the secret was a link between herself and her absent father."

Disturbed by the news, Emma planned to revenge her father. After work she joined her friends in their usual activities as if there were nothing out of the ordinary. The next day she read in the newspaper that the ship "Nordstrjärnan de Mälmo" would sail that evening from Pier 3. And so Emma Zunz, who at almost nineteen years of age still had an almost pathological fear of men, went to "the infamous Paseo 9 de Julio" and tried to attract the attention of some of the sailors of that ship.

One of them, very young, she feared might inspire some tenderness in her and she chose instead another, perhaps shorter than she and coarse, in order that the purity of the horror might not be mitigated.

One attribute of a hellish experience is unreality, an attribute that seems to allay its terrors and which aggravates them perhaps. How could one make credible an action which was scarcely believed in by the person who executed it, how to recover that brief chaos which today the memory of Emma Zunz repudiates and confuses?

The man, a Swede or Finn, did not speak Spanish... [he] led her to a door, then to a murky entrance hall and afterwards to a narrow stairway and then a vestibule (in which there was a window with lozenges identical to those in the house at Lanús) and then to a passageway and then to a door which was closed behind her.

... During that time outside of time, in that perplexing disorder of disconnected and atrocious sensations, did Emma Zunz think once about the dead man who motivated the sacrifice? It is my belief that she did think once, and in that moment she endangered her desperate undertaking. She thought (she had to think) that her father had done to her mother the hideous thing that was being done to her now. She thought of it with weak amazement and took refuge, quickly, in vertigo. The man ... was a tool for Emma, as she was for him, but she served him for pleasure whereas he served her for justice.

When she was alone, Emma did not open her eyes immediately. On the little night table was the money that the man had left. Emma sat up and tore it to pieces... Tearing money is an impiety, like throwing away bread. Emma repented the moment after she did it. An act of pride and on that day... Her fear was lost in the grief of her body, in her revulsion.

... Emma was able to leave without anyone seeing her; at the corner she got on a Lacroze streetcar... she selected... the seat farthest toward the front, so that her face would not be seen... Paradoxically her fatigue was turning out to be a strength, since it obligated her to concentrate on the details of the adventure and concealed from her the background and the objective.

Aaron Loewenthal was to all persons a serious man, to his intimate friends a miser... he feared thieves... money was his real passion.

Emma Zunz asked to speak with him to give him a confidential report on the strike that was crippling the factory at the time. Her lips were repeating in a low voice "the sentence which Mr. Loewenthal would hear before dying. Things did not happen as Emma Zunz had anticipated. Ever since the morning before she had imagined herself wielding the firm revolver, forcing the wretched creature to confess his wretched guilt and exposing the daring stratagem which would permit the Justice of God to triumph over human justice. (Not out of fear but because of being an instrument of Justice she did not want to be punished.) In Aaron Loewenthal's presence, more than the urgency of avenging her father, Emma felt the need of inflicting punishment for the outrage she had suffered. She had to kill him after that thorough dishonor." (She could not help killing him just as before she could not help thinking what her father had done to her mother.) The scene continues to be described in great detail:

> Seated, timid, she made excuses to Loewenthal, she invoked (as a privilege of the informer) the obligation of loyalty, uttered a few names, hinted at others and broke off as if fear had conquered her. She managed to have Loewenthal leave to get a glass of water for her. When he, unconvinced by such a fuss but indulgent, returned from the dining room, Emma had already taken the heavy revolver out of the drawer. She squeezed the trigger twice. The large body collapsed as if the reports

and the smoke had shattered it, the glass of water smashed, the face looked at her with amazement and anger, the mouth of the face swore at her in Spanish and Yiddish. The evil words did not slacken; Emma had to fire again. In the patio the chained dog broke out barking, and a gush of rude blood flowed from the obscene lips and soiled the beard and the clothing. Emma began the accusation she had prepared ('I have avenged my father and they will not be able to punish me... '), but she did not finish it, because Mr. Loewenthal had already died. She never knew if he managed to understand.

The tense barks reminded her that she could not, yet, rest. She disarranged the divan, unbuttoned the dead man's jacket, took off the bespattered glasses and left them on the filing cabinet. Then she picked up the telephone and repeated what she would repeat so many times again, with these and with other words: 'Something incredible has happened... Mr. Loewenthal had me come over on the pretext of the strike... He abused me, I killed him...

The story ends thus: "Actually, the story was incredible, but it impressed everyone because substantially it was true. True was Emma Zunz's tone, true was her shame, true was her hate. True also was the outrage she had suffered: only the circumstances were false, the time, and one or two proper names."[6]

First Approach: Revenge in the Pre-Oedipal Register

Three questions inevitably come to mind: why does Emma Zunz choose this method of revenge rather than another?, whom does she really want to revenge?, and why do love and care appear in minimal and timid references only? On a realistic level, Emma Zunz aspires to remedy an outrage, suffered by her father as he was unfairly accused of embezzlement. Her vengeful design unconsciously drives her to place herself in an inverted scene, a mirror-scene where she will be the one falling into a trap and submitting to outrages. In order to justify before society the murder of Loewenthal, she plots a prostitution scene and even though "she had an almost pathological fear of men" she is able to break her own resistance by way of this "daring stratagem" for the sake of her purpose, namely avenging her father. Yet right when the "rape" takes place—after a tortuous path of doors, entrance halls and stairways—she discovers with surprise an unexpected revelation, almost a hallucinating one: her father had done with her mother the same "hideous thing" the sailor was now doing to her. This is a new identifying mirror-situation, where from passive spectator she turns protagonist. It is a peculiar moment after which "her desperate purpose is at risk."

When she is penetrated by the sailor, the infantile experience which from the deepest level of her unconscious was directing her project, becomes evident to her. She finally wonders whether she desires to revenge her father, who was falsely accused of embezzlement, or to revenge herself for the "embezzlement" she felt the victim of, when he went to bed with her mother, the object of her love. This is a story about embezzling, which literally means taking for oneself an amount of which one is supposed to be a custodian.

After that moment, the father, rather than one being accused unjustly, becomes one who is justly accused; he is now the defrauder rather than one defrauded, the violator rather than the violated, the perpetrator rather than the victim. The father becomes the thief who violently took for himself part of the treasury (the mother) which Emma, in her narcissistic fantasy, had entrusted to him for custody only. Emma cannot control her murderous drive and in Loewenthal she actually kills the father "violator" (under the false charge of "sexual abuse"). Resentful, she condemns her mother to oblivion, a preferred form of revenge, according to Borges. It is actually the bond with the mother, suggestively accorded only a few words in the story ("she tried to remember her mother"), that propels her plan of revenge.

"What does the little girl require of her mother? What is the nature of her sexual aims during the time of exclusive attachment to her mother?" Freud wonders. "The girl's sexual aims in regard to the mother are active as well as passive and are determined by the libidinal phases through which the child passes… in every field of mental experience, not merely that of sexuality, when a child receives a passive impression it has a tendency to produce an active reaction. It tries to do itself what has just been done to it."[7]

In the same essay Freud notes that these instinctual drives can only be resignified later. They even appear as forms of expression connected to the father—not their actual origin—and thence they become difficult to understand. Given all that comes upon Emma at the time of her sexual intercourse, killing Loewenthal almost becomes a nonsensical act which cannot express the motivation of the murder, silently rehearsed by her. With the sailor, Emma came close to bringing to consciousness the traumatic situation, yet did not, perhaps because of the remaining intolerance and hatred; perhaps because at the time she felt she was betraying her mother as the mother had earlier betrayed her. Whatever the reason, she pursued her plan. The parents' sexual intercourse is felt as an attack on her self-esteem, an attack so intense as to justify hatred, humiliation, and criminal desires. For Emma Zunz (just as for Borges) sexuality invariably occurs in a context of violation and obscenity. On a pre-Oedipal register, one that is therefore perversely anal and sadistic, the father's suicide has compelled her to desire an outrage on herself that might justify the murder. In the brothel, she has a clear insight into the real, the irrational motivation of her murderous drive.

Second Approach: the Oedipal Register and Incest

The primal scene, that "horrible thing" lived by Emma Zunz as a trauma, is now fixed on account of the compulsion to repeat. Yet she controls it now as she sets the scenario placing herself no longer as an excluded witness who rages with jealousy and anger but as a protagonist. Now, with the sailor, she is the mother with whom the father has intercourse. She chooses "another, perhaps shorter... and coarse sailor because she fears a younger one might inspire some tenderness in her." Tenderness surely alludes to sexual excitement. During the encounter at the brothel she observes the lozenges, identical to those in the home of her childhood. Borges refers to lozenges as he evokes his own childhood memories of playing with his sister and his cousin, memories that lead to some unconscious associations with incest.

The story's plot prompts the following question: Why doesn't Emma incite Loewenthal to carry out sexual intercourse? The answer may be that the figure of Loewenthal, since he is Jewish as her father was, is in the position her father ought to have occupied, and is closer to her incestuous fantasies. Such fantasies appear to her as tremendously intolerable and sinful, and she kills Loewenthal, accusing him of a desire that is her own. Were she to accept that desire in connection with her father, that would be tantamount to the total realization of the Oedipal scene, with the consequent exclusion, the "murder" of the mother. That it is difficult to remember the mother, that she is condemned to oblivion, is somehow a configuration of her murder.

After the sexual act, "her fatigue was ... a strength, since it obligated her to concentrate on the details of the adventure and concealed from her the background and the objective." Through her conscious purpose, she prevents the real unconscious motivations from reappearing. What are then "the background and the objective"? This Oedipal register found in interpreting the plot of "Emma Zunz" needs to be considered in the analysis of other works by Borges. Sex and the primal scene as linked to reproduction are associated with revulsion in several of his stories. Thus in "The Masked Dry-Cleaner Hákim de Merv," first published in the newspaper *Crítica*, we read: "The world we live in is a mistake, a clumsy parody. Mirrors and fatherhood, because they multiply and confirm the parody, are abominations. Revulsion is the cardinal virtue."[8]

Once again alone after the encounter with the sailor, Emma Zunz's "fear was lost in the grief of her body, in her revulsion...." We know that the feeling of revulsion is related to incest. Shouldn't we apply it to the story of Emma Zunz?

Third Approach: Guilt and Crime

Did Emma Zunz commit the murder out of an unconscious feeling of guilt?

Freud studies this behavior in "Some Character-Types met with in Psycho-Analytic Work (1916)"[9] and again in "The Ego and the Id (1923)," where he says: "It was a surprise to find that an increase in this unconscious sense of guilt can turn people into criminals. It may sound paradoxical, yet it is undoubtedly a fact. In many criminals, especially youthful ones, it is possible to detect a very powerful sense of guilt which existed before the crime, and is therefore not its result but its motive. It is as if it was a relief to be able to fasten this unconscious sense of guilt on to something real and immediate."[10]

When she read the letter with the news about her father's death, Emma had "a weak feeling in the stomach and in her knees, and then of blind guilt, of unreality, of coldness, of fear; then she wished that it were already the next day." Blind guilt seems an excellent definition of the unconscious feeling of guilt. It is related as well to being "blind with fury, with hatred."[11] The father may have been condemned, exiled and killed by Emma Zunz from the very time when, as a young child, she was trapped in a situation that was traumatic for her, trapped by that "horrible thing" the father kept doing to the mother.

In the schizo-paranoid stage described by Melanie Klein, a period of maximal sadism, hatred is focused upon a combined parental figure, in the imagined or real intercourse of the parents: "The death wishes he feels against [his parents] during the primal scene or in his primal phantasies are associated with sadistic phantasies which are extraordinarily rich in content and which involve the sadistic destruction of his parents both singly and together."[12] On a factual level, Emma was upset by the news of her father's suicide and relived her hostile feelings at being abandoned by him when she was thirteen or even earlier (when he "left" her and preferred her mother), and may have reactivated regressively her unconscious feelings of guit. When she wished it were the next day so she might kill Loewenthal, upon whom the imago of the bad father had been displaced, was she perhaps seeking the relief of connecting those feelings with a fact, with something happening in reality?

Freud wonders,

> What is the origin of this obscure sense of guilt before the deed, and is it probable that this kind of causation plays any considerable part in human crime? An examination of the first question held out the promise of bringing us information about the source of mankind's sense of guilt in general. The invariable outcome of analytic work was to show that this obscure sense of guilt derived from the Oedipus complex and was a reaction to the two great criminal intentions of killing the father and having sexual relations with the mother. In comparison with these two, the crimes committed in order to fix the sense of guilt to something came as a relief to the sufferers. We must remember in this connection that parricide and incest with the mother are the two great human crimes, the only ones which, as such, are pursued and abhorred in primitive communities. And we must remember, too, how close other investigations have brought us to the hypothesis that the conscience of mankind, which now appears as an inherited mental force, was acquired in connection with the Oedipus complex.[13]

For Emma Zunz the Oedipal conflict has no solution. There is no mediation, no renouncing the father as an object of love, nor an identification with the mother that might allow her to assume a true dimension of femininity. Thence the deep pathology that, from resentment and through revenge, leads to self-debasement and crime. Thence the "blind guilt." Freud states with respect to the need for punishment: "With children it is easy to observe that they are often 'naughty' on purpose to provoke punishment, and are quiet and contented after they have been punished."[14]

Antonio Carrizo gives a remarkable version of his own, from an insightful and reasonable perspective: "I have always thought," he says in an interview of Borges, "that you had placed in this story hell and condemnation before the crime, because Emma's early actions are like a hell, a punishment." And he adds, "Because she plots that alibi, but it is really a way of punishing herself, condemning herself to something that is already a hell."

Fourth Approach: Inquiry from the Text

If the unconscious is structured like a language, it behooves me to explore now some aspects of the story "Emma Zunz" taking my point of departure from the signifier. I am aware that such an endeavor is risky. In the psychoanalysis of creative works one aims at discovering fantasy: one has to take care not to fantasize a discovery.... Borges's typical ambiguity, his constant game of erudite allusions in several languages, his Cabbalistic calculations, his poetic and even phonetic predilection for some words, give fodder to a search for unconscious discourse. Some of his statements are alternative or doubtful. The letter is signed by a certain Fain or Fein; the sailor is Swedish or Finnish; Lowenthal insults Emma in Spanish and Yiddish; Manuel Maire is Emma's father, and in happier days he was Emmanuel Zunz. Borges puts an end to the story with these words: "... only the circumstances, the time, and one or two proper names, were contrived."

Symbology of Letters and Numbers

The signs with which language is expressed tend to have symbolic meanings, sometimes both on the basis of their shape and their sound.[15] Thus the letters of the Hebrew alphabet have symbolic and semantic connotations, with two orders of meaning, standard and Caballistic, corresponding to the Tarot images. For instance, the letter Aleph is equivalent to the numeral value of 1 and it also represents will, man, the magician. In alchemy, Aleph is the beginning of everything.

Helena P. Blavatsky, a famous theosophist, points out that the holiest letter is M, masculine and feminine at once, since it symbolizes the great original abyss of water. M. Loeffler posits that among Semites as well as among Aryans, M tends to be the initial in words related to water and to the birth of beings and worlds.[16] Words denoting the mother also begin with M. N, on the other hand, is considered a sort of antithesis of M: in other words, if M corresponds to the regenerative aspect of primordial water, N belongs to its destructive aspect, the dissolution of forms.

Numbers in turn are more than merely quantitative: they are thought to be forces, each with special traits. One often symbolizes being, the manifestation of the essential. It is an active principle that becomes fragmented to create multiplicity, and it is also identified with the center, with a radiating point and the supreme power. It symbolizes as well spiritual unity, as the basis of the fusion of beings. René Guénon makes a distinction between Oneness and One, following the speculations of Islamic mysticism: Oneness is an absolute realm, closed upon itself, and it admits neither of Two nor of dualism. One is also identified with light.

Presocratic philosophers considered the idea of one as "the One" or "Primordial Oneness," as a property of all that is, of the universe as a whole. To a great extent, Parmenides' doctrine on Truth is founded upon the concept of "the One." What is One cannot be many, for the One is the opposite of the many, which is the realm of illusion. The One, in contrast, is pure identity, pure simplicity, and pure uniformity. Plato, in turn, said that what matters is not that a being be One, but that one ox be the ox One. Aristotle wrote "something is said to be One because it is indivisible, insofar as it has no parts; yet, on the other hand, something is said to be One because, even if it consists of parts, the sum of these constitutes the unity." Neoplatonists were concerned with this issue, how it is possible to conceive the One as absolute, without any plurality, and at the same time conceive that plurality emanates from the One. For Plotinus the One was the original hypostasis, that is to say the union of human nature with the Divine Word, which is the first and supreme reality.

Some view the One as Everything and Nothing (a title that Borges gives to one of his stories). Others disagree with the concept of unity as identity and adhere to a concept of unity as harmony. For Aquinas the One is God, as individual of infinite perfection. In Hegel, the One is always challenged by its opposite, in an antithetical duality and conflict that can only be resolved dialectically, with a new One emerging as a synthesis of the two opposite principles.

Two is represented by echo, reflection, conflict (sometimes in the pause that occurs when forces are equal). Two symbolizes the first of the material nuclei, nature opposite the creator, the moon compared to the sun. It also means shadow as a double, and the other gender, that is, sexuality introduced everywhere. There is dualism in the Gemini, the

Twins, who must be interpreted as the connection of immortal and mortal, the invariable and the changing. Three symbolizes spiritual synthesis. It crystallizes when a child is born. It implies the resolution of the conflict posed by dualism. Four is, of course, a doubling of twos. It does not signify the separation of two, but the ordering of what was separated. It represents therefore order in space and in, by analogy, any other structure or situation. Among other numbers, fourteen may symbolize fusion, justice, and temperance. For Borges, 14 equals the infinite. Generally speaking, numbers have a filiation: even numbers are negative and odd numbers are affirmative and active.

Names and Their Mystery

Proper names that occur in this story are: Manuel Maier, Emmanuel Zunz, Emma Zunz, Fein or Fain, Elsa Urstein, Perla Kronfuss, Milton Sills, Aaron Loewenthal, Gauss.[17] Emma has a consonant doublet between the vowels E and A. It is included in the father's name, Emmanuel, and its anagram is a Yiddish word for mother, Mame. Zunz is a quasi-palindrome, with "un" (Spanish for "one") between the two z's.[18]

Emmanuel, the name of Emma's father, means in the Bible "God is with us." He is the son of the Virgin. Isaiah 7.14 reads, "Behold, a virgin shall conceive, and bear a son, and shall call his name Immanuel. In the New Testament, this is Jesus Christ." "When his mother Mary was espoused to Joseph, before they came together, she was found with child of the Holy Ghost" (Matthew 1.18). in quoting the prophet, the name is explained: "... which was spoken by the prophet, saying 'Behold, a virgin shall be with child, and shall bring forth a son, and they shall call his name Immanuel, which being interpreted is, God with us' " (Matthew 1.22-23). Emma "had imagined herself ... exposing [to Loewenthal] the daring stratagem which would permit the Justice of God to triumph over human justice."[19]

Aaron, a name with geminated vowels, was that of Moses' elder brother. A mirror image of this name is almost identical to Norah, the name of Borges's sister. Manuel Maier: both name and surname begin with M. In Manuel there is "nu," an inverted *"un,"* (Spanish for "one"). Fein or Fain: in German and Yiddish, *ein/er* = one. *"Fein"* in German is also close in meaning to English "fine." Urstein has the German prefix *Ur-*, meaning "primordial." *"Stein"* means stone. It could be interpreted as primordial stone. But it also contains *ein* (= one). Elsa and Perla have two consonants between the same vowels as does Emma. Kronfuss ends with geminated s. Phonetically it evokes time (cf. Greek *kronos*) and "confusion." There is a geminated "s" in Gauss too. This name suggests the figure of Karl Gauss, the German mathematician who created complex numbers and the theory of algebraic numbers. Once again we find m̲ and n̲ in Milton, which must allude to John Milton, the English poet, theologian, and playwright of the seventeenth century. Borges writes about him in his *Introduction to English Literature*:

> Before writing a single line John Milton knew he was predestined to be a poet. He wanted to leave a book that future generations could not resign themselves to forget. He thought that to sing of heroic actions one must have a heroic soul, and for that reason, as a priest of poetry, despite his sensual temperament, he lived in chastity until the day he got married. He was blind when, in 1667, he published *Paradise Lost*. The sublime manner is typical of Milton, yet the reader soon notices how much there is in him that is mechanical, since he does not follow the promptings of passion. *Samson Agonistes*, written in 1671, may be Milton's masterpiece. Sampson is betrayed by his wife; surrounded by enemies and blind, he mirrors Milton.[20]

Borges, in turn, looks at himself in the same mirror. Traditionally Milton was seen as a typical Puritan, yet he is thought to have created a system bordering on pantheism, and Denis Saurat has even discovered in his work the influence of the Cabbala. Milton's surname in this story is Sills, and "ill" (meaning both sick and bad or wicked), is framed by two "s" sounds, just as Zunz. Emma Zunz hides the letter underneath the portrait of Milton Sills, and in him we can perceive the presence of Borges.

It is interesting to consider the meanings perhaps associated with these names, or their phonic analogues, in German: *Sünd* (fem; plural *Sünde*): sin. *Hässlich wie die Sünde*: hateful as mortal sin. *Wie die Sünde hassen*: to hate like mortal sin. *Sündebahn*: road of perdition. *Sühnen*: expiate, atone for a crime; *sühnbar*: expiable; *Unzucht*: impudence, prostitution, lasciviousness; *Löwe*: lion. Graphically, if not phonetically, Loewe[nthal] or Löwenthal might evoke English "love," as well as English "low," and the verb "lower" (with the meaning "humiliate"). Loewenthal may therefore be an anagram alluding to love that is brutal ("leonine"), ignoble, and humiliating.

Numbers and the Cabbala

Seeing how keen Borges was on the possibilities the Cabbala offered for his hermeneutic and cryptographic games, I cannot ascribe to pure chance the frequency with which he includes certain numbers in his writings. In "The Mirror of the Enigmas" he says,

> Bloy... did nothing but apply to the whole Creation the method that the Jewish Cabbalists applied to the Scripture. They thought that a work dictated by the Holy Spirit was an absolute text: a text where the collaboration of chance is calculable at zero. The portentous premise of a book that is impervious to contingency, a book that is a mechanism of infinite purposes, moved them to permute the scriptural words, to sum up the numerical value of the letters, to consider their form, to observe the small letters and the capital letters, to search for acrostics and anagrams; and it led them to other easily ridiculed exegetic rigors.[21]

Borges also summarizes the interpretation that the *Seoher Yetzrah* (Book of the Creation) gives of Genesis 1.2: ("And God said, Let there be light. And there was light"): "God Omnipotent created the universe by means of the cardinal numbers that go from one to ten and the twenty-two letters of the alphabet. That numbers may be instruments or elements of the Creation is the dogma of Pythagoras and Iamblichus; that letters also may be used in the Creation is a clear indication of the new cult of writing."[22]

Borges wonders, "... did Emma Zunz think once about the dead man who motivated the sacrifice? It is my belief that she did think once only, and in that moment she endangered her desperate undertaking."[23] "Once" is emphasized and repeated, and it appears to be important. One is born and one dies only once, and sexual initiation occurs just once. "In the *Summa Theologiae* it is said that God cannot unmake the past, but nothing is said of the complicated concatenation of causes and effects which is so vast and so intimate that perhaps it might prove impossible to annul a single remote fact, insignificant as it may seem, without invalidating the present. To modify the past is not to modify a single fact; it is to annul the consequences of that fact, which tend to be infinite."[24] Borges eloquently expresses a principle that is often restated in psychoanalysis.

The letter received by Emma Zunz is dated 14 January 1922. In "The House of Asterion," which, interestingly, follows "Emma Zunz" in the Spanish edition of *The Aleph*, Borges states that fourteen is a numeral equivalent to infinite. When the Cabbala is applied to this date it turns out to be symmetrical: 14-1-1922, because the digits of 1922, added up, total 14. So the number "1" is between 14 and 14, two equal and even numbers.[25] Nineteen is the age of Emma Zunz, repeated under different circumstances of Borges's stories. Benjamín Otálora, a character in "The Dead Man" is also 19 in 1891 (note that 91 is the inversion of 19). Otálora's destiny is to die for having appropriated his boss's girlfriend and his cattle. "Funes the Memorious" was 19 years old when he became a cripple.

Would it be too daring to suggest that all these "coincidences" may be echoes of Borges's own first sexual experience, when he was nineteen years old, in Geneva? Pursuing the numbers game further, we note that 2 apears duplicated in 1922, and 3 occurs only in two circumstances. First, it is the number of the pier from which the ship Nordstjärnan of Malmö departed. In Malmö a Spanish speaker may hear *"mal"* (bad) and/or *"mamó mal"* ("was nursed badly"). Emma seeks a man with whom she will have sexual intercourse among the sailors on that ship. She chooses one of two, the one who will violate her vagina, who will rob her of her virginity. There is a 3 also in the number of shots that kill Loewenthal, and the clarification is given that two follow one another closely and the third shot finishes him off.

Psychoanalytic Symbology

The One often resonates in Borges. He conceives of it now as the unity required to integrate the needs of multiple identification, now as the unity that will conciliate opposites. Other times it emphasizes the necessity of an event occurring only once, or it is tantamount to God, the prime element, or, like the Aleph, the beginning of a divine sequence. Actually from a psychoanalytic viewpoint, the One must be interpreted as "desire for the One." Green conceptualizes it as utopia questioned by the unconscious. The One can only be attained when the separation from the "dual unity" has been achieved. The psychological development begins from that "Two in One," which after the separation of birth and the loss of the object, creates the One, that is to say, the One of the Other, preceding the One Itself.[26]

In this numerical game of psychoanalytic symbology, three is the cipher of access to a level that structures the subject. Three are the characters of the Oedipus myth, Oedipus, Laius, and Jocasta, and his tale unfolds at the crossing of three roads. This is the tale of neuroses, of successive time, of life and of death. Before Oedipus, another scenario reigned, where the key is, precisely, "Two in One." It is a circular time-space, brought to a halt, "immortal." It pertains to narcissistic structures and to neuroses of destiny.

I believe that the name of Emma Zunz, because of its spelling as well as because of its phonetic associations in German, alludes to the primal scene, connected in turn to mortal sin, impudence, lasciviousness, prostitution, and hatred. (The element Zun- appears in the story "The Aleph" in the names of two contemptible characters: Zunino and Zungri, and again in Zunni, the protagonist's attorney.) When MM are joined, Emma is divided, dissociated into E and A. In Zunz, ZZ are separated by "un" (Spanish "one"), that is Emma. If we consider the consonants as a reference to the parents united and undifferentiated, we find the image of the combined parental couple that Melanie Klein speaks of. Because of its symbolism, M, as a simultaneously masculine and feminine letter, mingles man and woman into a single narcissistic and omnipotent figure, thus cancelling the representation of the couple.

The primal scene is terrifying not only in itself but because of its consequence: procreation. In "Tlön, Uqbar, Orbius, Tertius," Borges writes, "From the far end of the corridor, the mirror was watching us; and we discovered, with the inevitability of discoveries made late at night, that mirrors have something grotesque about them. Then Bioy Casares recalled that one of the heresiarchs of Uqbar had stated that mirrors and copulation are abominable, since they both multiply the numbers of man."[27] And further in the same story, a footnote reads: "All men, in the climactic instant of coitus, are the same man. All men who repeat one line of Shakespeare are William Shakespeare."[28] Fatherhood and differences are cancelled, creator and reader are fused.

To summarize my conclusions, considering Borges's surnames with geminate letters, others where the element Fein or Ein (i.e. One, outstanding) is present, the Cabbalistic play with 1/14/1922 (see above: in Spanish 14/1/1922 (1 + 9 + 2+ 2 = 14), we can observe that the numbers Two and One, or One between two Two's, are a play on the reality of the presence of both parents and child. The number One is extolled as good, choice, and Two as equal, undifferentiated, and confused. In "Emma Zunz" we see geminated M and Z. Perhaps there is a play between Two equals and One. The repeated Two, equal to itself, is transformed into One. What is unacceptable here is the Two of difference, therefore of procreation. In the story "*Los tigres azules* (Blue Tigers)," Borges intriguingly writes, "If 3 and 1 can be 2 or can be 14, reason is madness."[29] Actually 2 may be 3 and/or 1, that is to say, 4, as many as there were in his family nucleus. Also 14 is the number that functions as infinite. Symbolically the possibilities for procreation are infinite.

The characters of "Emma Zunz" are two men (Emmanuel and Aaron) and a woman (Emma). While in "The Intruder" two brothers end up killing the woman who interfered in their relationship, here Aaron is eliminated, manifestly, because he carried out an embezzlement of which Emma's father was wrongly accused. In the same mystery novel style of "Death and the Compass," Borges lets us discover that the name of Aaron includes as an anagram the name of "Noraa," that is Norah, in a palindromic reading.[30] It is surprising to find in "Emmanuel" the name of his daughter, and coincidentally in "Aaron" the name of Borges's sister. Such a peculiar symbiosis of names opens up another line of interpretation. Perhaps Emma Borges is revenging an "embezzlement" tightly connected with her parents' primal scene that produced the "thief" of the love she possessed. By killing Aaron-Norah she kills the intruder who prevents him from being the One and Only (like Asterion).

The inability to be Two, or the denial that Two can create One is evident in "The Circular Ruins" where Borges attempts to play with the omnipotent longing to achieve the creation of one other, by desiring him intensely. Confronted with that impossible reality, the magician who is the protagonist finally understands, when the son he has created in dreams is consumed by fire that consumes him, that he too is "a mere appearance, dreamt by another."[31]

In another context Borges refers to the word *luna* and compares it with its English translation, "moon," which he likes "because it forces the voice to dwell." These are suggestive words. Borges probably did not miss the fact that *luna* includes *-una* (femenine of One) and that "moon" includes phonetically the Spanish "*un*" (One). It should be mentioned that moon is a frequent metaphor in Borges in statements concerning women.

> I know that the moon or the word "moon"
> Is a letter that was created to share
> In the complex scripture of that rare
> Thing that we are, both manifold and one. [32]

One is the point and goal where everything converges. "Being one" is the expression of a chimeric yearning: "I who have been so many men in vain want to be one and myself," says the narrator's voice to God in "Everything and Nothing."[33] "Yet how costly this victory is—being only oneself!" writes André Green. "Rather than to the psychoanalysts we should resort to Borges, who has comprehended better than anybody how it hurts not to be able to be the Other."[34] The Aleph and the Zahir, the point and the coin, appear to be that "only thing" where there is room for all things, for the whole universe. To return to "Emma Zunz": these digressions lead us to the narcissist foundation upon which an Oedipal history is constructed.

Notes

1. Sigmund Freud, "Beyond the Pleasure Principle," SE 18: 59.
2. Jorge Luis Borges, "Ibn Hakkan al-Bokhari, Dead in His Labyrinth," *The Aleph and Other Stories. 1933-1969*," ed. and trans. Norman Thomas di Giovanni in collaboration with the author (New York: Dutton, 1970).
3. Antonio Carrizo, *Borges el memorioso* (Buenos Aires: Tierra Firme, 1982), 234.
4. Richard Burgin, *Conversations with Jorge Luis Borges* (New York/ Chicago/ San Francisco: Holt, Rinehart and Winston, 1968), 23.
5. Borges and María Esther Vázquez, *An Introduction to English Literature*, trans. L. Clark Keating and R. O. Evans (Lexington: The University Press of Kentucky, 1974), 48.
6. Borges, "Emma Zunz," *Labyrinths: Selected Stories and Other Writings*, trans. Donald A. Yates and James E. Irby (New York: New Directions Publishing, 1964), 132-37.
7. Freud, "Female Sexuality," SE 21: 235-36.
8. Borges, "The Masked Dry-Cleaner Hákim of Merv," *A Universal History of Infamy*," trans. Norman Thomas di Giovanni (New York: Dutton, 1972), 84.
9. Sigmund Freud, "Some Character-Types Met with in Psycho-Analytic Work," SE 14: 311-336.
10. Freud, "The Ego and the Id," SE 19: 52.
11. The script of the film "Días de odio" (1953-54), directed by Leopoldo Torre Nilson, is an adaptation of this story. What Borges says of Henry James in his *Introduction to English Literature* is also noteworthy: "In 1877 he published the novel *The American*. In the last chapter the protagonist renounces revenge, not on account of forgiveness or compassion, but because he feels that this act would be another bond tying him to those who injured him."
12. Melanie Klein, *The Psycho-Analysis of Children*, trans. Alix Strachey (London: Delacorte/Seymour Lawrence, 1975), 132.
13. Freud, "Character-Types," SE 14: 332-33.
14. Ibid., 333.
15. Juan Eduardo Cirlot, *Diccionario de símbolos* (Barcelona: Labor, 1981).
16. M. Loeffler, *Le symbolisme des contes de Fées* (Paris, 1949), cited by Cirlot, ibid.
17. Borges writes in "*Historia de los ecos de un nombre* (History of The Echoes of A Name)," "Otras Inquisiciones," *Obras completas* (Buenos Aires: Emecé, 1974), 750: "The Gnostics inherited or rediscovered this singular opinion. Thus a vast vocabulary of names was gathered, which Basilides (according to Irenaeus) reduced to the cacophonic or cyclic word Caulacau, a universal key of sorts of all the heavens."

In "*Una vindicación del falso Basílides* (A Vindication of Pseudo-Basilides," "*Discusiones*," *Obras completas*, 214, he writes: "The redeemer of this cosmogony is called Caulacau." Similarly, he considers his own name, Jorge Borges, as mirror-like and cacophonic for no purpose (See p. 193). In "Emma Zunz" Borges shows his craft at such minutiae; there he also cites Gualeguay (a city in the province of Entre Ríos, Argentina).

In *Literaturas germánicas medievales* we read: "Many poets (Vergil, Dante, Ronsard, Cervantes, Whitman, Browning, Lugones, Persian poets) have inserted their names in their compositions. Cynewolf, an Anglosaxon poet, probably born in the eighth century, availed himself of this literary device, which smacks of mystery novels. In his *Legend of Saint Julia* he put runes, i. e. Germanic letters permanently engraved on a knife, a crown, a horn, a bracelet, gravestones, and which can be read from right to left, as in Hebrew or Arabic. The name of each runic letter is that of an idea or an object. Thus the name of N is Nead, which sounds as English "need," suggesting "suffering"; U is called UR, evocative of English "our"; C suggests Enlgish "keen" or "brave." Cynewolf introduces runes in other poems to signify those words and he spells his name in like manner. We can observe that letters were thought to convey secret, holy meanings since antiquity. For instance, the Cabbalists thought that God may have created the world with the letters of the alphabet." Jorge Luis Borges and María Esther Vázquez, *Obras completas en colaboración*, (Buenos Aires: Emecé, 1979), 880.

Gerardo Goloboff, analyzing in this respect the *"Poema del cuarto elemento* (Poem of the fourth element)," notes how frequently the syllables in Jor-ge Bor-ges occur and states, "We may assume that the 'fourth element' in question is not just water, but as a 'reflection' of that, also *the composition of himself.*" (G. Goloboff, *Leer Borges* (Buenos Aires: Huemul, 1978), 339. In regard to the importance of vowels as compared to consonants, Borges writes, "The Germanic languages are rich in vowels, especially suitable to epic beauty, rather than the quiet sweetness of lyric." *Obras completas en colaboración* (Buenos Aires: Emecé, 1979), 861.
18. Borges himself says to Alina Diaconú (in an unpublished interview, see p. 117, fn. 9): "The name of Emma was chosen because I thought it was, if not horrible, particularly ugly. I remember a good friend called Emma who once said to me: 'Why did you give my name to that horrible girl?' Of course I couldn't tell her the truth, which was that when I wrote the name of Emma—with geminated 'm'—and Zunz—with geminated 'z'—I was trying to obtain an ugly name that was also without sheen, and I had totally forgotten that Emma was the name of one of my best friends. It seemed such a senseless, insignificant name! Doesn't it sound that way to you?"
19. Borges, "Emma Zuntz," 136.
20. Borges, *Obras completas*, 824-25.
21. Borges, "The Mirror of the Enigmas," in *Other Inquisitions, 1937-1952*, trans. Ruth L.C. Simms (New York: Simon and Schuster, 1968) 128.
22. Borges, "On the Cult of Books," *Other Inquisitions,* 119.

23. Borges, *Labyrinths*, 135.
24. Borges, "The Other Death," *The Aleph*, 110.
25. This reasoning is based on the convention for abbreviated dates used in Spanish: day-month-year.
26. André Green, *Narcissisme de vie-narcissisme de mort*, (Paris: Ed. de minuit, 1983), 55.
27. Borges, "Tlön, Uqbar, Orbis Tertius," trans. Alastair Reed, *Ficciones*, ed. Anthony Kerrigan (New York: Grove Press, 1962) 17.
28. Ibid., 27.
29. Borges, *El compás de oro* (Madrid: Swan, 1986).
30. In Spanish neither the presence of "h" in the spelling chosen for Norah's name, nor the geminated "a" in "Noraa" would make any perceptible difference in pronunciation. Translator's note
31. Borges, "The Circular Ruins," trans. James E. Irby, in *Labyrinths*, 50.
32. Borges, "*La luna* (The Moon)," *Dreamtigers*, trans. Mildred Boyer and Harold Morland (New York: Dutton, 1970), 66.
33. Borges, "Everything and Nothing," trans. James E. Irby, *Labyrinths*, 243.

Chapter 7

The Unspeakable: Primal Scene and Secret

In the previous chapter I have analyzed the primal scene made clearly explicit in "Emma Zunz." In this chapter, I detect its presence and delve into its psychoanalytic signification in two other stories, "*La secta del Fénix* (The Sect of the Phoenix)"[1] and "*Las ruinas circulares* (The Circular Ruins)."[2]

Freud refers to the primal scene sometimes as the original scene or protofantasy. Three fantasies, the primal scene, the scene of seduction, and the castration complex, are philogenetically present in human beings. The web of fantasies is constantly woven anew, and thus the so-called primordial fantasies become organizers that provide answers to crucial questions concerning origins. While the primal scene offers an explanation concerning the subject's origin, the scene of seduction is aimed at understanding the emergence of sexuality; the scene of castration, in turn, at explaining the difference between the sexes. Their statements are known as "childhood sexual theories."

Actually Freud proposes a twofold approach, since at the same time as this concept of protofantasies, he emphasizes the signification of real events experienced during childhood. In *The Interpretation of Dreams*

(1900), without specifically referring to a "primal scene," he underscores the importance of witnessing the parental intercourse as a generator of anxiety. In the *History of an Infantile Neurosis*, Freud refers to a patient who brought to light his experience of the primal scene as the father's agression within a sadomasochistic relationship; yet "the expression of enjoyment which he saw on his mother's face did not fit in with this; he was obliged to recognize that the experience was one of gratification."[3] Observation of the primal scene giving rise to the anxiety of castration. I focused on this anxiety and the defenses it mobilizes in the study of characters' names in "Emma Zunz."

A necessary trigger, however, for the construction of the complex of castration is the verification that there is an anatomical difference between the sexes: presence or absence of a penis. This experience comes to embody all the real or imagined threats the child has lived through. It has been claimed that the complex of castration stems from the anxiety of birth, the first detachment, and is activated later by the experience of weaning, by sphincter experiences, by object losses, and by diverse separations. Freud instead tends to underscore specifically the boy's anxiety relative to his sexual organ, heavily invested with narcissistic value and threatened by his incestuous desires for the mother. The girl, on the other hand, experiences the absence of a penis as a damage, which she attempts to deny, compensate for, or repair.

The castration fantasy is one of the complexes of intersubjective relationships from whence sexual desire originates. For this reason it is closely linked to the Oedipus complex in its nuclear and structuring role. Paradoxically, the castration complex serves as mediator allowing the boy to overcome the Oedipal stage and to identify with his father. Denying the differences means denying castration; hence the access to the triangular structure is difficult. Fixations or regressions to previous stages are obstacles that block development. Depending on their intensity and magnitude, the consequences may be neurosis, perversion, or psychosis.

According to the British School, such indifferentiation of the parental couple in coitus is interpreted as the conjunction of images of the parents collapsed together, constantly copulating and allied against the boy. His understanding of parental intercourse and the interest it arouses in him are supported by his own pre-Oedipal experiences with his mother, and by the desires resulting from such experiences. Each libidinal stage shapes with its own particular traits the staging of these fantasies. When oral impulses prevail, the experience of the parental intercourse is accompanied by fantasies of sucking, incorporating, biting, devouring, emptying. In the uretral-anal stage the fantasies are related to expelling, flooding, drowning, burning, and eventually controlling the object. As he assigns to his parents his own impulses (in a massive projection), the infant imagines that in the primal scene the mother *incorporates into herself* the father's penis and carries it hidden in her own body. He imagines that the father does the same with the mother's breast.

These fantasies, in conjunction with the early Oedipus complex, explain the intolerance the small child has vis-à-vis that union between his parents. Such intolerance is intensified when it coincides with weaning or on occasion of the mother getting pregnant again. To the intrinsically unfeasible desires of the child is added the frustration resulting, on the one hand, from the insatiable drive toward libidinous gratification, and on the other, from the destructive components of his impulses. Early ideas concerning the parents' physically intimate relationship become conscious only with growth and along time.

In *"Certaines fonctions de l'introjection et de la projection dans la première enfance,"* Paula Heimann states, "The concept of sexual relationship as a violation in which the woman is a victim of masculine violence, or as a mutually demeaning and destructive act, the idea of the woman-vampire who sucks her sexual mate until she kills him, monsters of folklore and myth that are part man, part human, or part human, part animal, are all examples attesting the horror caused by the deepest and earliest fantasies concerning parental intercourse."[4] This quotation brings us strikingly close to Borgean themes such as Asterion, the Minotaur in the labyrinth, and Emma Zunz terrified by sexuality and eager for revenge. Similar motifs reverberate in the Secret of the sectarians of the Phoenix. Borges combines in his characters—in an elusive and dispassionate way— hatred, resentment, revenge, belittlement, shame, and revulsion.

As he develops, the child gradually acquires more realistic perceptions. This involves overcoming pre-genital goals and the resulting distinction and recognition of the differences between diverse parts and functions of the body. Yet only with Oedipal elaboration will the total mother-father objects be consolidated and at the same time discriminated. The fantasy of a combined figure disappears, creating the conditions to allow their union as a couple. All of this takes place through a healing restitution which enables the child to imagine and to tolerate the parents' pleasure with each other and with him or her as a fruit of their union.

Guy Rosolato lucidly defines the primal scene as the touchstone of all mental structures. The primal scene contains and governs all fantasies of origin, since it includes a combination of sexuality, of origins, and of the Oedipal. According to Rosolato, it relates to the moment when the "object of perspective" is defined. He refers with this expression to the fantasy of the mother's penis, that is to say, the lack of sexual differentiation that will cause the formation of the fetish object. Thus the "object of perspective" commands castration. With reference to the primal scene, Rosolato states, "The unknown in it may result in the devastation and the horror of the unspeakable which is at the root of paranoia, or all to the contrary, it may be a source of life and the motivation of a fruitful curiosity."

Borges makes strikingly clear that this "unspeakable" is the "Secret" of the piece bearing the title "The Sect of the Phoenix," as he writes, "There are no temples specially dedicated to the celebration of this cult; a ruin, a cellar, an entrance way are considered propitious sites. The Secret is sacred, but it is also somewhat ridiculous. The practice of the mystery is furtive and even clandestine, and its adepts do not speak about it. There are no respectable words to describe it... "[5]

Devastation and horror are also conveyed by his poetry. Thus in *Fervor de Buenos Aires* he describes a "Butcher Shop":

> Meaner than a brothel
> The butcher shop defaces the street like an insult.[6]

It is significant for the approach taken in this book that Borges refers to sexual intercourse with expressions such as "elemental rite," "the habit," "that horrible thing," "the Secret," "they were doing it." When in "Tlön" he talks about "that vertiginous moment of coitus," I assume he does not mean coitus but orgasm.

The primal scene is related also to the "fissure" between looking and seeing involved in fetishist fantasies, according to Rosolato, who writes: "The most diverse reactions will occur: horror or phobia; fetishist constructions by denial; obsessive fixations or disquieting feelings of strangeness; deliriums; erotic excitement in their specific varieties and voyeurist enactments; finally, by way of inhibition and substitution, epistemologic inquiries." This "fissure" also brings to a focus the oppositions between without and within, the visible and the invisible, certain and uncertain, permitted and forbidden, familiar and ominous.

In creative literature, the primal scene may be represented in the metaphors of the Genesis, light and darkness, the day that is born and dies away, the vital waves of the sea and the debris that the sea deposits on the shore. These metaphors visualize the logic of nature, the dynamics of life and death.

Suggestively, Borges writes in "Tlön": "For one of those gnostics, the visible universe was an illusion or (more precisely) a sophism. Mirrors and fatherhood are abominable because they multiply and disseminate that universe"[7]

That Amazing Discovery

Reading an interview of Borges by Ronald Christ published in his book *The Narrow Act* one may see to what degree, and how, Borges is revealed in "Emma Zunz." Christ reports,

When Borges was in New York in 1968, I asked him if he ever revealed the answer to the riddle [in "The Sect of the Phoenix"]. "... Yes, sometimes... " Would he tell me? And I knew, at once, my error: he turned and looked at his wife for a moment [he was married at the time] and then said, "Not now, tomorrow. I'd like to keep you guessing for one more day." The following day at a reception I reminded him of his promise. He leaned over and whispered into my ear so that no one else could hear: "Well, the act is what Whitman says 'the divine husband knows, from the work of fatherhood.' When I first heard about this act, when I was a boy, I was shocked, shocked to think that my mother, my father had performed it. It is an amazing discovery, no? But then too it is an act of immortality, a rite of immortality, isn't it?"[8]

In Borges's words there is a reference to immortality in a metaphysical sense but in a way that relates to the infantile fantasy of the parental coitus as synonymous with procreation.[9] It is also possible to infer an aggressive component that may have accompanied Borges's early experience, when his sister was born. In "Leonardo Da Vinci and a Memory of his Childhood" Freud illustrates Leonardo's repudiation of sexuality, citing the following sentence of Leonardo: "The act of procreation and everything connected with it is so disgusting that mankind would soon die out if it were not an old-established custom and if there were not pretty faces and sensuous natures."[10] On this basis he states that it is highly doubtful that Leonardo ever embraced a woman.

"The Sect of the Phoenix"

This story-essay by Borges, originally published in *Artificios* (1944) deserves to be considered in detail. In a postscriptum to the 1956 edition, Borges wrote: "In the allegory of the Phoenix I set myself the task of suggesting a common event—the Secret—in a hesitating and gradual way that would lead to an unequivocal end. I don't know how felicitous it turned out to be." Borges cryptically alludes to sexual intercourse and the primal scene "in a hesitating way," just as, in his own words, he developed the plot of Emma Zunz "fearfully." The story begins thus:

Those who write that the sect of the Phoenix had its origin in Heliopolis and derive it from the religious restoration following upon the death of the reformer Amenophis IV, cite texts from Herodotus, Tacitus and the monuments of Egypt, but they ignore, or prefer to ignore, that the designation "Phoenix" does not date before Hrabanus Maurus and that the oldest sources (the Saturnales of Flavius Josephus, let us say) speak only of the People of the Custom or of the People of the Secret.

Further on he says an author compares these sectarians of the Phoenix with the gypsies, while Urmann sees the Phoenix as a derivation of Israel:

> One thing alone—the Secret—unites them and will unite them until the end of time. Once, in addition to the Secret, there was a legend (and perhaps a cosmogonic myth), but the shallow men of the Phoenix have forgotten it and now only retain the obscure tradition of a punishment. Of a punishment, of a pact or of a privilege, for the versions differ and scarcely allow us to glimpse the verdict of a God who granted eternity to a lineage if its members, generation after generation, would perform a rite... The rite constitutes the Secret. This Secret, as I have already indicated, is transmitted from generation to generation, but good usage prefers that mothers should not teach it to their children, nor that priests should; initiation into the mystery is the task of the lowest individuals. A slave, a leper or a beggar serve as mystagogues. Also one child may indoctrinate another. The act in itself is trivial, momentary, and it requires no description. The materials are cork, wax or gum arabic. (In the liturgy, mud is mentioned; this is often used as well.) There are no temples especially dedicated to the celebration of this cult, but certain ruins, a cellar or an entrance hall are considered propitious places. The Secret is sacred but is always somewhat ridiculous; its performance is furtive and even clandestine and the adept do not speak of it. There are no decent words to name it, but it is understood that all words name it

or, rather, inevitably allude to it, and thus, in a conversation I say something or other and the adept smile or become uncomfortable, for they realize I have touched upon the Secret... A kind of sacred horror prevents some faithful believers from performing this very simple rite; the others despise them, but they despise themselves even more. Considerable credit is enjoyed, however, by those who deliberately renounce the custom and attain direct contact with the divinity; these sectarians, in order to express this contact, do so with figures taken from the liturgy. Thus John of the Rood wrote:

> May the Seven Firmaments know that God
> Is as delectable as the Cork and the Slime.

I have attained on three continents the friendship of many devotés of the Phoenix; I know that the Secret, at first, seemed to them banal, embarrassing, vulgar and (what is even stranger) incredible. They could not bring themselves to admit their parents had stooped to such manipulations. What is odd is that the Secret was not lost long ago; in spite of the vicissitudes of the Universe, in spite of wars and exoduses, it reaches, awesomely, all the faithful. Someone has not hesitated to affirm that it is now instinctive.[11]

Ironic at times, at times pious, Borges describes a sect to which he does not belong. The Secret is a clue; the rite is what the sectarians of the Phoenix have in common. It is not known whether it is a punishment, a privilege, or simply a pact; but it is known that it guarantees eternity. This is a cult founded on its ritual, displayed in an obsessively woven plot, like a regulated habit, like a frozen, mechanically patterned ceremony: "... fulfillment of the rite is the only religious practice observed by the sectarians (Ibid, 102)." There is no trace of love, passion, desire or even need. "A kind of sacred horror prevents some faithful believers from performing this very simple rite; the others despise them, but they despise themselves even more (103)." This sacred horror, to which he also refers in "Emma Zunz," painfully forbids to him this "very simple rite."

On occasion, the other Borges laments what he was not able to do:

> I think of things that might have been and were not
> . . . .
> The love we do not share
> . . . .
> The son I did not have.[12]

Borges finds it difficult to describe the act itself, trivial and brief. A Superego nourished by the prejudices of an aristocratic, high-born family of the beginning of the century has marked it as dangerously clandestine. For that reason sexual initiation is the task of lepers and beggars. Granted, he adds with a certain tenderness, that a child may also indoctrinate another child. Wavering between acceptance and rejection, between spite and self-deprecation, he speaks of what is dirty and of the revulsion caused by the materials used in liturgy, the slime that is silt, sludge, sticky mud, gum arabic, wax (which is similar when melted), and cork. It is an intriguing catalogue. These substances resemble semen and are such that, once they have dried, they harden or set, as does gum arabic, or else leave traces on the sheets, as does ejaculation.

Another group of members of the sect "deliberately renounce the custom." We recognize the unspeakable. These individuals enjoy credit and prestige because they have attained "direct contact with the divinity" through other rites. Among them is John of the Rood, who writes, "God is as delectable as the Cork and the Slime." Thus Borges alludes, typically in a roundabout, riddling way, to the vote of abstinence and chastity that God-Father demands of the "chosen." John of the Rood is actually a reference to San Juan de la Cruz, the Spanish mystic and poet (1542-1591) who wrote, among other works, *Cántico espiritual* (*Canticle of St. John of the Cross*) and *Llama de amor viva* (*Living Flame of Love*). He is, with Santa Teresa de Jesús, one of the two greatest authors of Spanish mystic poetry. San Juan de la Cruz avails himself of the language of profane love to express the "infinite love" of God, puzzling the reader, who may sense that he is reading a love poem. His style exhales the voluptuous mood of the *Song of Songs*.

"I know that the Secret, at first, seemed to them banal, embarrasing, vulgar and (what is even stranger) incredible. They could not bring themselves to admit their parents had stooped to such manipulations." Toying with revelation, pain, and suppression, Borges shows all of this as mysterious, banal, and above all, incredible. Mystery, stealth, secrecy, cipher, clue, arcane are the terms that mark the phobias and terrors of most of his literary works.

I cite a few lines from " Juan, I, 14" (John I:14)[13]

. . . .
Who plays with a child plays with something
near and mysterious;

wanting once to play with My children
I stood among them with awe and tenderness.
I was born from a womb
by an act of magic.
I lived under a spell, imprisoned in a body,
in the humbleness of a soul.
. . . .
I was loved, understood, praised, and hung from a cross.
I drank My cup to the dregs.

John I.14 reads: "And the word was made flesh, and dwelt among us (and we beheld his glory, the glory as of the only begotten of the Father), full of grace and truth." And the preceding verse (I.13): "Which were born not of blood, nor of the will of the flesh, nor of the will of man, but of God." These references bespeak once again the negation, the rejection of the primal scene ("By some magic means I was born from a womb.") But they also suggest that Borges probably suffered because he was not "the only begotten," an only child.

The Phoenix

Why does Borges associate the Secret with the mythical phoenix? I find some clues in other writings. In Egyptian mythology, the phoenix was a sacred bird shown in temple iconography. The myth that this bird was reborn from its ashes became a Christian allegory of the resurrection of the body and the eternal life of the soul. In *An Introduction to English Literature*, written by Borges in collaboration with María Esther Vázquez, we read:

This Anglosaxon poem paraphrases the Latin *Carmen de Phoenice*. Tacitus and Pliny refer to the Phoenix. This bird dwells in the deserts of Arabia, and in the sacred city of Heliopolis it dies periodically in the fire but is reborn from its ashes. The Latin poem is full of paradoxical expressions. It states, for instance, that death is Venus for the Phoenix, which finds delight only in death; that it yearns to die in order to be born; that it is its own father and its own son.[14]

There is another note concerning the Egyptian myths of the phoenix in *El libro de los seres imaginarios* (*The Book of Imaginary Beings*). Here Borges refers to a famous passage (Herodotus. *Histories* 2.73) where the Greek historian states that the phoenix is a sacred bird that comes seldom into Egypt, actually only when his father dies (every five hundred years). Suggestively, he brings from Arabia his father's body in a peculiar manner: "First he moulds an egg of myrrh as heavy as he can carry, and when he has proved its weight by lifting it he then hollows out the egg and puts his father in it, covering over with more myrrh the hollow in which the body lies; so the egg being with his father in it of the same weight as before, the phoenix, after enclosing him, carries him to the temple of the Sun in Egypt."[15] Borges also mentions that Pliny's version of the tale speaks of a maggot rather than an egg, and that Claudian, at the end of the fourth century celebrates "an immortal bird that rises out of its own ashes, an heir to itself and a witness of the ages.[16]

Woman appears in this myth only in the reference to Venus, the goddess of beauty, love, and fertility, who becomes a goddess of death. Thus the phoenix is simultaneously its own father and its own son, "an heir of himself," immortal, reborn from his ashes, witnessing the passing of time. I see here a narcissistic and thanatic fantasy of self-conception that denies paternity, woman, sexual intercourse and procreation. As a matter of fact, all of this contradicts the content of the story. In the manner of a *lapsus linguae*, the title, while attempting to speak of intercourse, actually reveals narcissism. Man and woman do not figure, clearly defined, in this story. Searching for the identity of the sectarians, Borges finds Gypsies and Jews, without gender identification, and in words such as "followers" or "sectarians" the sexes are not distinguished either. This oxymoronic title may be interpreted as the expression of a cancelling mechanism with obsessive connotations.

Borges associates pregnancy with sexual intercourse as a child tends to do and transforms what is universally biological into the rituals of a sect. The sect of the Phoenix is perpetuated thanks to this "elemental rite." Full of orgasmic pleasure (which Borges does not mention) the sect survives despite world vicissitudes, wars and exoduses. Instinct and its vital force are forever reiterated, in spite of it all, in spite of Borges himself, and to his distress—the painful distress of not belonging to it.

> He was not born from a mother, he had no ancestors.
> The case of Adam, that of Quijano, are identical.[17]
> He is made of chance. Immediate or near,
> He is ruled by the shiftings of variable readers.

> He is chaste, knows nothing of love, has not loved.
> This viril man has renounced the art of loving.
> In Baker Street, where he lives, alone and isolated,
> That other art, oblivion, is alien to him as well.[18]

"The Circular Ruins"

I find similar thought patterns in "*Las ruinas circulares* (The Circular Ruins)" to those in "The Sect of the Phoenix." Rather than the mythical phoenix this story represents the impossible dreams of a demiurge, a wizard who yearns to create a man. The "Secret" is farther still from reality here, since it is found in the supernatural desire inspiring a magic, delirious project. Borges wrote this remarkable story in 1941, in the course of a week of hallucinated concentration.[19]

A gray, silent man disembarked in the "unanimous night," kissed the sacred mud, and, coming up to the bank, "he dragged himself, nauseous and bloodstained, to the circular enclosure crowned by a stone tiger or horse, which once was the color of fire and now was that of ashes. This circle was a temple, long ago devoured by fire, which the malarial jungle had profaned and whose god no longer received the homage of men."[20]

There the creator installed himself, in a place that evokes the fetal space, since he knew that "this temple was the place required by his invincible purpose." Once inside that matrix, he "felt the chill of fear and sought out a burial niche in the dilapidated wall… " Just as in "The Immortal" and in "The Sect of the Phoenix," the path goes from death to life, in the desire to rekindle fire from the ashes. "He wanted to dream a man: he wanted to dream him with minute integrity and insert him into reality. This magical project had exhausted the entire content of his soul; if someone had asked him his own name or any trait of his previous life, he would not have been able to answer (46)." His purpose was "the most arduous task a man can undertake." After persistent unsuccessful attempts, one day he realized that he had not really dreamt. When he started again, without premeditation, he finally dreamt of a beating heart: "… with minute love he dreamt it, for fourteen lucid nights. Each night he perceived it with greater clarity," he says, with words that might have been those of a pregnant woman. "On the fourteenth night he touched the pulmonary artery with his finger, and then the whole heart, inside and out… the innumerable hair was perhaps the most difficult task." Finally, he achieved his purpose: "He dreamt a complete man, a youth, but his youth could not rise nor did he speak nor could he open his eyes." Then, after supplicating the numina of the earth and the river, "he threw himself down at the feet of the effigy which was perhaps a tiger and perhaps a horse, but both these vehement creatures at once and also a bull, a rose, a tempest. This multiple god revealed to him that its earthly name was Fire, that in the circular temple (and in others of its kind) people had rendered it sacrifices and cult and that it would magically give life to the sleeping phantom."

Cult and ritual speak once more of the "Secret." To give life to this, his son, his Golem, in the solitude of his oneiric fascination, Borges the creator implores the sensual, vehement tiger, the fiery and passionate colt. But the erotic charges are frozen in symbolic effigies and from an abstract intercourse emerges, ominously, an "atrocious mongrel." This creature is, furthermore, a spurious conjunction of a bull, symbol of generative virility; a tenuous, fragile, feminine rose; a tempest, uncontrolled passion. "Gradually, he accustomed the boy to reality. ... That night he kissed him for the first time and sent him to [an]other temple. ... The man's victory and peace were dimmed by weariness. ... He would prostrate himself before the stone figure, imagining perhaps that his unreal child was practicing the same rites in other circular ruins... ."

To the very extent of the Dantesque configuration of tiger and colt, bull, and rose, of tempest and fire, the magician could not help but freeze his effigies. The fire that was in his son's name and root revealed to him his own identity. The fire that does not "burn his flesh" is self-consuming fire. It is fire that symbolizes life yet also destruction, if it is not contained but unleashed. Hence the relief as well as the pain of realizing it is all only a dream. The demiurge recognizes himself to be "a mere appearance, dreamt by another," the son of a scene of "identical rites."

"The Circular Ruins" is a marvelous tale of suffering, presided by the primal scene through monstruous fantasies. When pulsive charges reach such intensity, in pathological cases the Ego cannot help but give way to schizoid and paranoid conditions. In the sublimation that his poetic talent allowed him, Borges was able to create imaginary beings to dwell in his desolate landscape. Didier Anzieu remarks that an imaginary phallus is a response to imaginary castration.[21] His awesome imagination, like a Moebius band, travels through the unconscious and reemerges in his creative talent.

"We should not forget," writes Bachelard, "that alchemy is a science of men, single men, men without women, initiates excluded from human communion for the purposes of a masculine society."[22] What Bachelard says of alchemy applies also to codes and signs of systems of belief such as the Cabbala, different forms of magic and symbologies that enriched Borges's own store of symbols, which was that of a reclusive, shy man of genius. Sheltering himself in the enigmatic codes he uses, he fascinates us while he conceals his sophisticated distress.

The epigraph of this story reads: "And if he left off dreaming about you...." It is a quotation from Chapter 6 of Lewis Carrol's *Through the Looking Glass*. I sense that this epigraph may be a dedication to Borges's late father, who was in turn a dream of Francisco Borges, the colonel who in the battle of La Verde, wounded in his pride, sought death as he walked, raising his arms in the figure of the Cross, toward the spot where fire was most intense. "Not to be a man, to be the projection of another man's dream, what a feeling of humiliation, of vertigo! All fathers are interested in the children they have procreated (they have permitted to exist) in mere confusion or pleasure; it was natural that the magician should fear for the future of that son, created in thought, limb by limb and feature by feature, in a thousand and one secret nights." The father of "The Circular Ruins" is not totally conscious of his paternal role. He only "allows" the existence of a son, yielding because he is, in turn, another's dream.

There are multiple possible interpretations of "The Circular Ruins." The analysis I choose offers corroboration of the desires or dreams of parents and ancestors as they are unconsciously registered by each son. For the purposes of this psychoanalytic study of Borges's creative work, I interpret it as a veritable narcissistic delirium.

Postcript
The Secret as an Object of Study in Psychoanalysis

An issue of the *Nouvelle Revue de Psychanalyse* devoted to this topic included an article authored by J. Puget and L. Wender.[23] A translation was published in an issue of *Revista de Psicoanálisis* that the Asociación Psicoanalítica Argentina dedicated to Freud.[24] These authors, obviously independently from Borges, also capitalize the word Secret. According to them the secret is reviewed at every stage of the psychosexual development. "The Secret of the primal scene is the pleasure that unites the parents in a particular and unalterable manner. It is a fusion-union that excludes the son." Reactions range from scoptophilia to epistemophilia. In some persons these "secrets" may become fixed, permanent, as they become "traumatic nuclei laden with sadomasochistic charges which will be the source symptoms, lapsus, etc."—or, I might add, the source of a literary style.

The Spanish word *"secreto,"* like English "secret," are derived from Latin *secretus*, separate, isolated, remote. It is the past participle of *secernere*, to separate, isolate, which is in turn a compound of *cernere*, to distinguish, sift.

Serge Leclaire says,

> I can at this point articulate the motivation that drives me to be a psychoanalyst as an interest in the origin of language (castration, primal scene, death drive). Ever since I committed myself to the psychoanalytic experience I find again and again, always intense, the universal infantile "curiosity" concerning origin. Only as an analyst, while I listen to my patient, in that space through which language and the space of desire are generated over and over again, can the syncopated voice of the subject be heard. Only then is it possible to speak of the singularity of the patient's original scene and its origin, that is to say, the particular modes in which they are captured in the order of words, the singular order of its narration in relation to the silence of the first objects.[25]

These words of Leclaire move me, for while they express eloquently my own motivation for being a psychoanalyst, they also validate the objectives of this study.

Notes

1. Jorge Luis Borges, "The Sect of the Phoenix," *Labyrinths: Selected Stories and Other Writings,* trans. Donald A. Yates and James E. Irby (New York: New Directions Publishing, 1964), 101-104.
2. Borges, "The Circular Ruins," *Ficciones*, trans. James E. Irby (New York: Grove Press, 1962), 57-63.
3. Sigmund Freud, "History of an Infantile Neurosis," SE 17: 45
4. Paula Heimann, "*Certaines fonctions de l'introjection et de la projection dans la première enfance*," *Développements de la Psychanalyse* (Paris: P.U.F., 1966), 156-57.
5. Borges, "The Sect," 103.
6. H.R. Hays (ed. and transl.), *12 Spanish American Poets. An Anthology* (New Haven: Yale, 1944), 121.
7. Borges, "Tlön, Uqbar, Orbis Tertius," *Labyrinths*, 4.
8. Ronald J. Christ, *The Narrow Act. Borges' Art of Allusion*, (New York: New York University Press, 1969), 190, fn 18.
9. Alina Diaconú (in an unpublished interview) asked Borges this question: "A book is in a way like an imaginary son one has, right?" Borges replied, "No, because one continues to think about a son but forgets a book. Do you think writing a book and a sexual act are similar? No, no, no! They are two totally different things... . What is the goal of the sexual act, procreation? No, it is a very beautiful moment, of tender love, of whatever it is, but one does not think about the consequences... I believe. That's why I think they have nothing in common."
10. Freud, "Leonardo Da Vinci and a Memory of his Childhood," SE XI: 69.
11. Borges, "The Sect," 101-104.
12. Borges, "Things That Might Have Been" (English title in the original), *Borges, J.L. A Reader*, ed. Emir Rodríguez Monegal and Alastair Reid (New Yori: Dutton, 1988), 327. I have noticed that poems and stories with English titles tend to convey intimate confessions.
13. Borges, "John I:14," *In Praise of Darkness* (A bilingual edition), trans. Norman Thomas di Giovanni (New York: Dutton, 1974) 15-16.
14. Borges, J.L. and María Esther Vázquez, *An Introduction to English Literature,* trans. L. Clark Keating and R. O. Evans (Lexington: The University Press of Kentucky, 1974).
15. Borges, *The Book of Imaginary Beings*, trans. Norman Thomas di Giovanni in collaboration with the author (New York: Dutton, 1970), 185-86.
16. Ibid., 186-87.
17. "Quijano" is the character in Cervantes' novel who names himself "Don Quixote."

18. Borges, "Sherlock Holmes," *Los conjurados* (Buenos Aires: Alianza, 1985), 49.

19. María Esther Vázquez reports Borges's description of this week: "Something happened to me with "Las ruinas circulares" that had never occurred before. It happened only once in my life that in the course of the week that it took me to write it (which in my case does not mean laziness but rather fast writing) I was as it were obsessed with that idea of the dreamed dreamer. (...) I carried on my usual routine and at the same time I felt that it was all unreal, that what was real was the story I was imagining and writing. So if I can speak of inspiration I refer to that week, because I have never had a similar experience with anything else." (*Borges, imágenes, memorias, diálogos* (Buenos Aires: Monte Avila, 1977), 47-48.)

20. Borges, "The Circular Ruins," 57.

21. Anzieu Didier, *Psychanalyse du génie créateur,* ed. D. Anzieu et al. (Paris / Bruxelles / Montreal: Bunod, 1974).

22. Gaston Bachelard, *La Psychanalyse du Feu* (Paris: Gallimard, 1949) 109.

23. J. Puget and L. Wender, *Nouvelle Revue de Psychanalyse* (Paris: Gallimard, 1976), 14.

24. *Revista de Psicoanálisis*, vol. II (1980).

25. Leclaire, Serge. *On tue un enfant. Un essai sur le narcissisme primaire et la pulsion de mort* (Paris: Ed. du Seuil, 1975).

Chapter 8

Endymion in Buenos Aires

In the literary work of Borges, a chaste and celibate ascetic, sensuality, tenderness, and love are constrained by severe limitations. In this chapter I study this set of problems through Borges's own opinions as well as through the analysis of Ulrike and other feminine characters in his stories. I focus on the so-called Jocasta complex studied by Matthew Besdine, and I refer to María Kodama and to the poet Borges, loved by the moon.

I begin by transcribing part of an interview to Borges by María Esther Vázquez.

> **VÁZQUEZ**: Which virtues do you most appreciate in a woman?
> **BORGES**: I believe we seek in her kindness and tenderness, but above all, kindness.
> **VÁZQUEZ**: Yet you would not talk with a kind yet stupid woman.
> **BORGES**: No, I wouldn't. My sister, for example, would: she likes stupid people.
> . . . .
> **VÁZQUEZ**: Are you jealous?
> **BORGES**: Yes. I try not to be, but I am. I grant that it is a fault.
> **VÁZQUEZ**: Which are your faults?
> **BORGES**: I believe excessive conceit.
> **VÁZQUEZ**: You don't seem conceited.

BORGES: Yes, I am conceited, but with some shrewdness. I wish I were a man of action, such as my ancestors were. Unfortunately I must confess to not having died in 1879 at the battle of La Verde, nor having defeated Rosas' *Montoneros*, as did my great-grandfather Suárez. Too bad I was born a man, not a tiger! As a teenager I always envied Norah, because she once happened to be in the middle of a political confrontation and had to cross the Adrogué park running amidst bullets.[1]

Woman, virtue, kindness, stupidity, sister, excessive conceit, unsatisfied yearning to be a tiger, envy, Norah, shooting. These form a suggestive string of associations.

I don't know why some say I have no feelings, or that my life has been denied certain fundamental experiences. I suppose they mean love. Those who think I have not known love are wrong. I can assert that I have lived always in love. The first (certainly ideal) love of my life was an actress, Ava Gardner. I used to see her films twice a day. As soon as the show was over, I could not wait until the next day, when I'd see her again. Love requires proofs, supernatural proofs.[2]

I assume that Borges, weary of hearing the same questions in interview after interview, speaks about his early years tongue-in-cheek.

"*Ulrica* (Ulrike)"

In 1970 Borges published "*El informe de Brodie* (Dr. Brodie's Report)"; in 1975, "*El libro de arena* (The Book of Sand)." Critics did not acclaim these two books as they earlier had *Ficciones* and *The Aleph*. In the Preface to *Dr. Brodie's Report* Borges declares that it has been his intention to write "straightforward stories." If he achieved this purpose at all, he did it only from a formal point of view. Just as in *Dr. Brodie's Report*, there is great complexity and rich symbolic fantasy in the piece I analyze here, "Ulrike."

In the Afterword of *The Book of Sand* Borges writes: "The theme of love is quite common in my poems but not in my prose, which offers no other example than 'Ulrike'." In "Ulrike" at first glance one does not see the sinister, sometimes perverse quality of other works I have analyzed here, for instance "Emma Zunz," "The Intruder," or "The Dead Man."

Thus Gene H. Bel-Villada has written: "... for the first time in Borges's career with fiction, he depicts in positive terms (without erstwhile associations of danger or destructiveness) the experience of physical love between man and woman. 'Ulrike' builds up to nothing less than an erotic scene in a darkened, red-wallpapered hotel bedroom; it is a romantic anecdote, the story of a South American professor's casual encounter and night of sweet love with a lady from Norway..."³

"Ulrike" tells the story of the encounter in New York City of the narrator, Javier Otálora, a young Colombian college student, with a beautiful Norwegian young woman. They talk on their way to Thorgate, a few miles down the river. "The narrative," Borges declares in the first paragraph, "will encompass one night and a morning." Ulrike might be an Ibsenian character, a liberated woman for whom this episode could just be "one of many." She allows herself to enjoy, and by contrast she makes manifest Javier's inhibitions and passive attitude. She is a feminist "moved by a few poor swords of York Minster more than by the great ships in the Oslo museum." Otálora is "a bachelor well along in years," to whom "love is a gift no longer expected."

That evening Ulrike would continue her journey to London, while Javier would go to Edinburgh: "... their paths had crossed.." They departed together, and Otálora knew then that he was in love with Ulrike. Right after this reference to love, Borges writes, "...all at once, I heard the distant howling of a wolf. " Voracity and the terror it creates interfere with erotic desire. "'In Oxford Street,' she told me, 'I shall follow De Quincey's footsteps in search of his Ann, lost amid the crowds of London.' 'De Quincey stopped looking for her,' I replied. 'All my life, I never have.' 'Maybe you've found her,' Ulrike said, her voice low."

He kissed her, but "she drew away firmly but gently, " declaring, "I'll be yours in the inn at Thorgate. Until then, I ask you not to touch me. It is better that way." Remembering how love was in the past denied to him, Javier resigned himself: "The miracle has a right to impose conditions."

Hand in hand they talk as they make their way through the moors, since the woods are dangerous. "All this is like a dream..." says Javier. An allusion to the Volsung saga could not be missed here: she says she will call him Sigurd, he should call her Brunhild. "Brunhild," says Otálora, "you're walking as if you wished a sword lay between us in bed," says Sigurd, without realizing that they are now at the entrance of the inn.

She goes in first and calls down to him from the top of the stairs:

Did you hear the wolf? There are no longer any wolves in England. Hurry. (...) The walls were papered in a deep red. (...) The awaited bed was duplicated in a dim mirror, and the polished mahogany reminded me of the looking glass of Scriptures. Ulrike had already undressed. She called me by my real name—Javier. I felt that the snow was falling faster. Now there were no longer any mirrors or furniture. There was no sword between us. Time passed like the sands. In the darkness, centuries old, love flowed, and for the first and last time I possessed Ulrike's image.[4]

"Ulrike," Queen of Wolves

Borges himself explains, in *Literaturas germánicas medievales* (*Medieval German Literatures*) written in collaboration with María E. Vázquez, that Ulrike suggests German *Wulf* (wolf), and "rica" is a feminine Latinized form of the Saxon "rich," meaning ruler or king. When Javier Otálora and Ulrike are about to leave The Northern Inn, where they met, Javier says he heard "the distant howling of a wolf." Later, in the inn at Thorgate, also called The Northern Inn (Otálora was not surprised, which leads us to assume that the narrator-protagonist has never left the first inn) Ulrike asked from the top of the stairs if he too had heard the wolf. That wolves were a bane in England before the eighteenth century helps us to understand the symbolism of the wolf here: certain persecutory voices of the past, even after they have disappeared in reality, persist in the world of fantasies.

Ulrike and Otálora go upstairs to the room in the inn and there Borges describes the decoration: "The walls were papered in the style of William Morris, in a deep red... " Morris is the nineteenth century writer among whose works are *The Story of Sigurd, The Volsung*, and several other narratives of sagas. The Volsung Saga resonates throughout "Ulrike." The epigraph is a quotation from it: "He took the sword Gram and laid it naked between them." The "naked sword" figures also in *A Thousand Nights and One*: Aladdin, with the goblin's help and using his magic lamp, prevents the Great Vizier from enjoying the first night with his new bride, the princess Badroul-Badour (whom he loves). Aladdin manages to spirit her away, and, to demonstrate that he has no bad intentions, lays a naked sword between them, signifying that he would rather kill himself than touch her. Richard Burton, the most famous translator of *A Thousand*

Nights and One, understands—according to Borges— that the sword in those circumstances represents the hero's honor.

The sword may be interpreted as a symbol of man's renunciation of his desire of woman. But in the context of "Ulrike" we may infer that it is the male who is protected from the imagined voracity of the female. The image of the sword is in the epigraph and further references reinforce it. Only at the end does it disappear—after the disappearance of the furniture, the mahogany of the great mirrors that terrified Borges as a child, and the mortal sins of the sacred scriptures read again and again by his grandmother.

In his study of the *"Kenningar, Menciones enigmáticas de la poesía de Islandia* (Enigmatic References in the Poetry of Islandia)," Borges tells us that a sword is "the wolf of wounds"; fire, "the wolf of the temples"; the gallows, "a tree of wolves," and blood, " a stream of wolves."[5] The wolf is also a "sign of the enemy" in the English translation of the Volsung Saga, where all of Sigurd's cousins are devoured by giant wolves. Sigmund, Sigurd's father, has escaped this fate by means of an extraordinary and complicated trick: Sigmund finally forces the she-wolf to put her tongue into his mouth and then he manages to pull it out, causing the animal's death. Guttormthe killer of Sigurd, is called "Wolf-cub" and, before carrying out his crime, drinks a potion containing, among other ingredients, wolf's blood.[6]

"Ulrike" is a dream. It was included in *Libro de sueños (Book of Dreams)*, published by Borges in 1976. The analysis of "Ulrike" has shown that voracious/castrating connotations and the accompanying anxiety are located in this feminine character more clearly and more sharply than in any other. The symbology connected with the wolf, "sign of the enemy," explains the difficulty in approaching woman and love. The enigma of the dream has been revealed. The mask has fallen and Ulrike apears, in this other image of the wolf-woman, an archetypal character representing the author's suffering.

Ulrike in other stories

This name appears also in other works by Borges: *"Examen de la obra de Herbert Quain* (An Examination of the Work of Herbert Quain)" and *"La otra muerte* (The Other Death)."[7] In the former, she is a character in the only dramatic work of Quain, an imaginary author, a "heroic comedy" in two acts entitled (in English) *The Secret Mirror*. The action takes place in the country house of General Thrale, C.I.E. It tells of the unrequited love of a playwright, Wilfred Quarles, for the general's eldest daughter, Ulrica. She is "an arrogant Amazon" around whom the whole plot revolves, even though she never appears on stage. Contradictory notices are published in the newspaper concerning her engagement to the Duke of Rutland. This surname is significant, since it suggests the English connotation of "rut" applied to animals "in heat."

In an intriguing reference to Freud and to Julien Green, the story's narrator says:

> The texture of the acts is parallel, but in the second everything becomes slightly horrible, everything is postponed or frustrated. When *The Secret Mirror* opened, the critics pronounced the names of Freud and Julien Green. The mention of the first strikes me as totally unjustified. Rumor had it that *The Secret Mirror* was a Freudian comedy; this propitious (and fallacious) interpretation determined its success.[8]

Horror, delay, frustration, are frequent themes in Borges's work. Yet here he again also expresses his ambivalence vis-à-vis psychoanalysis.

In "The Other Death," Ulrike Von Kühlmann is only mentioned. As part of a supernatural conjecture she makes concerning the destiny of Pedro Damián, she says that God "cannot unmake the past but can affect its images..." The etymology of the surname "Kühlmann" in German leads us to "*kühl*" (with *Umlaut*, as Borges spells it), meaning "cool" and "Mann" meaning "man," whereas with a slight change in spelling and pronunciation we find the noun "Kuhle," with the meaning "deep hole" or "pit." This third Ulrike, who has a surname, is also disqualified. "We do not know," Osvaldo Sabino says, "with what level of awareness Borges has offered us his three Ulricas, but it seems that around this peculiar name the Borgean imagination has woven a constellation of ideas." Osvaldo Sabino perceives in Ulrike an image of love and death.[9] Indeed, Javier Otálora reminds us of Benjamín Otálora in "The Dead Man." Just as that character laments his fate, which is predetermined, Borges laments his own in so far as it regards woman and love. In "The Other Death" we read, "... war, like women, served as a test of men... (105)." Love is for the brave. Sexuality, also, is a hard test for males.

In examining these stories we realize that the love that Borges does not mention elsewhere in his prose has led us once more to the sinister: Ulrike turns out to be the woman-symbol where love is entwined with horror.

Other Feminine Characters

Other feminine characters in the work of Borges are generally socially despised figures. They are objects to be used, transferable. As Alicia Jurado puts it, they are "hens in the coop," polygamous females, now totally passive, now revengeful and murderous.[10] There are no stations between fear of man and prostitution. Borges identifies them with names that are traditional and yet pejorative: Juliana in "The Intruder," a story "that no woman can read without indignation and horror," as A. Jurado says; the *Serviliana* (cf. "servile") whom Cardoso brings to his shack and then throws out, "finding her in the way" in the cruel story of "*El otro duelo* (The End of the Duel)"[11], and Casilda in "*Historia de Rosendo Juárez* (Rosendo's Tale)." La Lujanera in "Streetcorner Man" abandons her man and gives herself to another hoodlum who is more courageous; Juan Muraña's widow kills with a knife to revenge her husband in "Juan Muraña" where the narrator says at the end: "The dagger was Muraña— it was the dead man she had gone on worshipping." [12]

"*El duelo* (The Duel)," contrary to the expectations the title creates, tells the story of two women who are passionate rivals as painters. Their competition conceals a latent homosexual relationship.[13] "Clara Glencairn painted against Marta and in a sense for Marta." Clara died, and "Marta realized that her life now lacked a meaning (41)." These two women, just as the two brothers of "The Intruder," are embroiled in a combination of rivalry and subjection.

As it is treated in Borges's stories, sexuality never includes the theme of love. It is rather geared to ideas of violence and death. In "*La noche de los dones* (The Night of the Gifts)," a thirteen-year-old boy both has his first sexual experience with La Cautiva, a prostitute of the brothel, and witnesses how a police sergeant murders a *criollo* who in the story is called Juan Moreira.[14] Borges prefaces the narration of this episode by saying that he heard it once when he was sitting at a coffee house with men who were debating the problem of knowledge.[15] Someone invoked the Platonic notion that "... to know is to know again. My father, I believe, said that Bacon had written that if to learn is to remember, not to know is in fact to have forgotten." Someone else in the group, speaking "slowly and deliberately," says he does not understand those Platonic archetypes. "Nobody remembers the first time he saw the color yellow or black, or the first time he tasted a certain fruit—maybe because he was small then and had no way of knowing he was initiating a very long series."

Of course, there are other first times that no one forgets." Here begins the story of what that April thirtieth night "gave" him.

Once, when he was spending the summer holidays "at the ranch of some cousins, not far from Lobos," a cowhand by the name of Rufino trained him in certain farm tasks. He was thirteen years old. On Friday, Rufino suggested that they go the next night to town "to have a little fun. I warned him I didn't know how to dance. Dancing was easy to learn, he said."

Rufino came, dressed up and with a silver knife in his belt. "I had a little knife like it, but I didn't bring mine for fear of being laughed at." When they arrived at Lobos, they dismounted "at a street corner where there was a house painted sky-blue or pink, with a sign saying *La Estrella* (The Star). At the end of the long entranceway was a large room with wooden benches on either side and a number of dark doors. "... half a dozen or so women dressed in floral dressing gowns came and went." Rufino said to the madam, " 'I've brought a new friend, but he's not much of a rider.' 'He'll learn soon enough," she replied. He felt ashamed.

One of the women, whom the others addressed as La Cautiva (The Captive), was different. While she was telling her sad story of having been seized in an Indian raid, some local toughs barged in drunk. Among them was Juan Moreira.[16] Scared, the boy ran to a dark room to hide. The Captive came and spoke to him *in a whisper*. " 'I'm here to serve—but to serve peaceable people,' " she said. "" 'Come closer, I'm not going to hurt you.' (...) She had taken off her dressing gown. I lay beside her and felt for her face with my hands. I have no idea how much time passed. We exchanged neither a word nor a kiss. I untied her braid, and my hands played with her hair, which was very straight, and then they played with her. We did not see each other again after that, and I never learned her real name." Moreira was killed by a policeman with a bayonet. "In the bare space of a few hours I had known love and had looked on death."

La Cautiva is a different character, a tender woman who initiates him in that important sequence of acts that are a prelude to love. Interestingly, the name of the place where the action occurs, *Lobos* (Wolves) reminds us of the allusions to wolves in "Ulrike."

Beatriz and Teodelina[17]

Two other female characters are also intriguing, namely Beatriz Viterbo and Teodelina Villar. They differ from the previously discussed women since they are socialites, and Borges seems to have entertained some special relationship with them.

Beatriz Elena Viterbo lends unity to the story of "The Aleph." We may imagine that Borges wrote this story as he says Dante wrote *The Divine Comedy*, "in order to intersperse the work with a few encounters with the irrecuperable Beatrice." Perhaps she represents someone snatched from Borges first by life and then by death. Desperate and resentful, he finds her in the small cosmic circle of the basement. Seemingly unconnected memories call up diverse images, and among other things, obscene, unbelievable, precise letters revealing the incestuous relations of Beatriz with his first cousin.[18]

Borges has an oddly ambivalent relationship with Carlos Argentino Daneri (an anagram for Dante Alighieri), whom he visits on every "melancholy and vainly erotic anniversary" of the late Beatriz's birthday. In an increasingly morbid progression of curiosity, the figure of Beatriz, in contrast to Dante, is gradually debased as his alienated curiosity and resentment grow. Teodelina Villar in "The Zahir" represents another frustrated relationship. The narrator-protagonist feels Platonic love for her and after her death worships her—not without a certain disdain. It is a somewhat ironic, spiteful cult: "... on the sixth of June, Teodelina Villar committed the solecism of dying in the very middle of the *Barrio Sur*. Shall I confess that I—moved by that most sincere of Argentinian passions, snobbery—was enamored of her, and that her death moved me to tears?[19] Probably the reader has already suspected as much." In these two stories Borges appears to be resentfuly and cynically spiting two women who may actually be one and the same.

"*Vi*," the first syllable of both Viterbo and Villar, is intriguing.[20] Because it is associated with sight, it may be important for Borges, not just because of his real progressive blindness, but also on account of some difficulties that he candidly complained about on occasion, for example in an interview with María Esther Gilio.[21]

> **GILIO**: In the story about Homer, the hero discovers that he no longer reads. You say, "he felt as if he recognized a melody or a voice,

and later that "he had reacted with fear, yet also with joy, hope, and curiosity."

BORGES: No, not with happiness. But I never lived in a visual world. For example… (After he said this, he remained silent for so long that I thought he had forgotten me.)

GILIO: What do you mean by saying that you never lived in a visual world?

BORGES: For instance, I know that I have two ties, because my mother, who never misleads me, has told me so. At other times I've had more, but I never knew how many.

GILIO: It seems to me this is related to other traits of your personality. You say you never lived in a visual or tactile world. You don't know how many ties you have, simply because you are not interested in ties.

BORGES: I don't know the color of the clothes I wear. For example, it has happened that I was in love with a woman, very much in love… and… and… I could not manage very well to imagine her.

GILIO: Explain to me exactly what you mean.

BORGES: I imagine her environment, the happiness of being with her. That I do imagine. But if someone should ask me about the color of her eyes, the shape of her nose or her mouth, I wouldn't know what answer to give.

In this conversation, with its stretches of prolonged and anguished silence, Borges refers to his mother's never misleading him or telling him that he has two ties and thereby implies that his inability to see affects him mainly in regards to limitations resulting from dependency. His loss of sight is not compensated by the increased sharpness of the other senses, as is normally the case in blindness. As he embarks on this moving and obviously painful confession, he says he can only envision a vague amorous encounter, the environment, and the place, but not the image and the special traits of the beloved's face. His suffering transpires elsewhere in his writings. In "Dreamtigers," he says: "I … cannot rightly recall the brow or the smile of a woman."[22]

In the story "Shakespeare's Memory," he writes: "… I still hold two memories… or rather, two memories hold me.[23] There is a region where they overlap. There is a woman's face but I don't know to which century I should assign it." In another passage of the same story, he says: "I would remember Anne Hathaway just as I remember that mature woman who taught me love in a Lübeck apartment so many years ago. (I tried to remember her but I could only recall the yellow wallpaper and the light shining through the window. This first failure ought to have warned me there would be others.)"[24] Anne Hathaway was in reality the wife of Shakespeare. Borges mentions her name once again in connection with sexual initiation in "Everything and Nothing."[25]

One might be tempted to blame his blindness for these problems, yet we must not forget that it was progressive and only became a serious handicap around 1955. When María Esther Vázquez asked him what were his early recollections of his sister Norah, he replied: "To the right, the Buenos Aires side, I can think of red-tiled courtyards, a garden with a palm-tree and *ceibos*, in a middle-class neighborhood... "

What is the reason for this harsh and unusual handicap suffered by someone with such a prodigious memory? It seems as if a serious process of repression, fragmenting and disconnecting certain visual objects, creates dark zones, oblivion. Shame, or the fear of looking, appears to make him shun aspects of the erotic body. He can evoke details of the environment associated with them, but only at a remove from his emotions. This unconscious operation, a phobic impairment, cuts off what he perceives and, sadly for him, affects especially the present face of women. Such a process may have begun with the first face that a human being sees, the mirrored face. Perhaps it implies some traumatic situation linked to the early stages of emotional development.

In another interview that resembles a free-association test, Carlos Peralta proposed to Borges certain words and asked him to respond to them one by one.[26] Responding to the word "woman," Borges says, "I realize with great sadness that I have spent all my life thinking about one woman or another; I thought I was seeing countries or cities, but there was always a woman shielding objects from me. I might wish it were not so; I might wish to have devoted myself entirely to the joy of metaphysics, or linguistics, or other disciplines."

Replying as he does, Borges reveals with great sadness and even with resentment that women had a role in his life that hindered his thought processes like a "shield" between objects and himself. He is not sure but he suspects he might have preferred a different pursuit, perhaps devoting himself entirely (more intensely even than he did?) to intellectual enjoyment. Borges recognizes regretfully the ties, the imprisonment, the interference imposed upon him, especially in his childhood, by those whom Didier Anzieu calls "abusive women." Borges could only see through his mother's eyes.

Where was the father? Where was the father for the mother?

The Jocasta Complex

The theme of women and love obviously leads us to a first woman and a first love. A photograph registers the presence of Borges and his mother: she is of a slight build, youthful and vivacious; he is tall, serious; he is looking far ahead. He was sometimes thought to be the father of doña Leonor.

Alicia Jurado, a long-time friend of the Borges, portrays the mother:

> She was an inseparable companion of every moment. Her energy and eficiency allowed him to carry out a large part of his work after his doctors forbade him reading. Until her great old age finally prostrated her, she was dynamic and lively and had a lucid mind. She read to her son the texts he needed to prepare lectures and classes, took dictation from him, took care of his correspondence, dealt with editors, handled bureaucratic matters and resolved domestic problems without ever forgetting anything. She retained the energy and the determination she had as a young woman, remained curious about everything around her, and knew everything and was concerned with everything. The best collaborator Jorge Luis Borges might have had, she went along in his travels, reminded him of his appointments, and lent to him her own eyes for numberless tasks... .[27]

Psychoanalysis has always emphasized, from different angles, the importance of the early bond between mother and son, the basic nucleus and foundation of a human being's healthy development. The mother also can make room for the father and facilitate his performance of the paternal role, no less structuring and organizing than her own. It is a matter of general consensus that the potentially pathogenic factor of a strong, domineering mother plus an absent or weak father, favors the continuance of symbiosis and hinders the process of separation and individuation. Many authors have observed such circumstances as the basis for homosexuality, schizophrenia, toxicomanias, and some psychosomatic diseases. Matthew Besdine discusses the particular type of maternalization that he dubs "Jocastian," occurring in individuals of genius.[28]

When Freud studied the famous Sophoclean tragedy he focused (because of his own limitations) on the case of Oedipus: he scotomized the sexuality of the mother. Yet Jocasta too becomes the wife of Oedipus "unwittingly," and together they have four children. In a contemporary interpretation of the Greek myth we may imagine Jocasta tormented by the same fears that Laius has of being killed by the first-born as predicted by the oracle. Furthermore, the oracle amounted to a prohibition imposed upon Laius of sexual intercourse with his wife. Laius, however, drunk, put an end to a long period of abstinence. This, we may imagine, would have satisfied Jocasta who fervently desired to have children. A male infant, Oedipus, was born, and she was separated abruptly from him when Laius ordered that he be carried away and exposed.

According to Besdine, the origin of the Jocastian maternalization is manifest in the myth: the yearning to have a son, the painful frustration when he is lost, the absence of a normal spousal relationship, and the husband's absence. These origins explain the traits of this type of maternalization, namely, seduction, intimacy, overprotection, excessive indulgence, adoration, infantilization, dominanceand symbiosis.

Here it is appropriate to cite what María Kodama said of Borges in 1985: "I notice that he is more open to people's problems, more understanding. He acts as if he were allowing himself for the first time liberties that were forbidden to him as a child, perhaps by excessive love or care, either because of poor eyesight, or because he was weaker or his parents thought him weaker than he really is."[29]

Besdine studies Michelangelo as a prototype of the genius and observes in him the following traits: "an unresolved Oedipal complex, the fear of love, an underlying feeling of guilt, strong masochistic tendencies, paranoid propensity, a clearly defined homosexual component, a remarkably self-centered personality, an exceptional need to be recognized and remarkable narcissism." Such pathognomic traits seem to manifest themselves, with variants, in Shakespeare, Freud, Goethe, Heine, Balzac, Proust, Dostoievski, and Sartre. Marcel Proust is an eloquent example. He was the eldest son of a Jewish mother, a beautiful and sensitive woman, and Catholic father, a professor in a school of medicine who was often travelling. When he was ten, he suffered an asthma attack, and his mother moved to his room to take care of him.

Jean-Paul Sartre describes his relationship with his mother. He was an only son. His father, a young Navy officer, died soon after Jean-Paul's birth. In The Words, he writes, "I had an older sister, my mother... Even today [1963], this is the only family bond that I am moved by." In a footnote, he adds, "What was seductive in this relationship was not so much the erotic temptation, but rather that making love was forbidden: fire and ice, delight and frustration mingled, incest pleased me as long as it remained Platonic."[30] Sartre believes his mother would have preferred to have a daughter: "Since God had not granted that, she compromised: I would be the gender of angels, ambiguous yet feminine at the edges.'"[31]

Freud writes, "[I]f a man has been his mother's undisputed darling he retains throughout life tje triumphant feeling, the confidence in success, which not seldom brings actual success along with it. And Goethe might well have given some such heading to his autobiography as: 'My strength has its roots in my relation to my mother.' "[32]

The mother's Oedipal relationship with her son is a transferential expression of her bond with her own father. In addition to this, she may be immature or have an older, absent, or weak husband, or a difficult marriage. If that is the case, it is not difficult to understand her exclusive, sublimatory dedication to her son. The traits emphasized by Besdine as common denominators in men of genius who exhibit a Jocastian maternalization seem manifest in Borges. We may add his name to Besdine's roster, only, however as a hypothesis. While this type of maternalization appears as a trait of personalities endowed with exceptional talents, it certainly cannot be their sine qua non.

María Kodama

María Kodama devoted herself for years to the care of a famous, aged, and blind Borges. She is the daughter of a Japanese chemist,

Yosabuko Kodama, who came to Argentina as an adult, and of María Antonia Schweitzer. The mother had hoped to become a pianist; at seventeen she married Kodama, who was then thirty years old. María Kodama once said: "My father could have been my grandfather. He was a Shintoist and free-thinker; he was engaged in living. My grandmother, on the other hand, was very strict. She had wanted to become a nun. I grew up like this, divided."[33]

Clearly María was raised among "grandparents" by a very young mother. "When I met Borges, I met for the first time someone other than my father with whom I could share my father's aesthetic and ethical principles. My world was always adult and sublimated. When Leonor, his mother, died, we started traveling together. We went around the world. We would not part again. Our relationship was very complex, so much so that I myself cannot possibly define it."

María reflects: "When I was a little girl, I had no friends. I enjoyed studying, and on the other hand I was not allowed to play much with other children. I could not relate to other children... I never felt that being a woman set limits. I owe that also to my father, who used to say that being a man or a woman made no difference: 'You are a human being with the same duties and the same rights.' I could never use the weapon of seduction to obtain things; that doesn't work for me. My father treated me like a man, and I responded like a man." In spite of her words it is easy to notice that María is quite seductive. "Borges had been always interested in the Eastern world, ever since he was a child, so that too brought us together. It is as if my childhood, perhaps seen nostalgically, were not gone forever... We never exchanged confidences. He does not talk about intimate affairs; that never goes through my mind. We also don't discuss feelings, emotions."

María Kodama describes Borges as "a Victorian gentleman, a modest gentleman. Since I was raised by my father, also a gentleman from another century, we can be friends. He is timid, selfish as anybody else, testy, contradictory, very stubborn, and much more cheerful and positive than I am.... Poor Borges, everyone pigeonholes him as the Borges of mirrors, tigers, labyrinths" ... "but he is very funny!" This quality, his humor, is commented upon by those who knew him well. "He doesn't just laugh about others, he is able to be ironic also about himself."

In 1977, Borges dedicated to María Kodama his book of poems, Historia de la noche (The History of Night), thus: "For the blue seas of atlases and the great seas of the world."[34] The dedication is protracted into a typically long string that ends: "For the memory of Leonor Acevedo; Venice, made of crystal and sunset; the one you will be; the one I will perhaps fail to understand; all these diverse things which may be, as in Spinoza's premonition, mere figurations and facets of one single infinite thing, I dedicate this book to you, María Kodama."

Seven years later, in 1985, he wrote in *Los conjurados* (The Conspirators): "This book is yours, María Kodama. I must tell you this inscription includes sunsets, the deer of Nana, the lonely night and crowded mornings, shared islands, seas, deserts and gardens, what oblivion loses and what memory transforms, the sharp voice of the muezzin, Hawkwood's death, books, and their illustrations. We can only give what we have given before. We can only give what already belongs to the other. This book contains those things that have always been yours. What mystery is contained in a dedication, a giving of symbols!"[35] Unexpectedly, on the twenty-sixth of April, the marriage of Jorge Luis Borges, eighty-seven years old and very ill, and María Kodama, forty-one, was announced. On June fourteen, 1986, Borges died, far from his country and his people. His friend and collaborator, Adolfo Bioy Casares, tells how in the last few days of the year 1985, Borges called him to make his farewell. María Esther Vázquez reports the dialogue that ensued:

> **BIOY CASARES**: I hope you do very well!
> **BORGES**: I will not do well, I am very ill. My doctor has given up hope of my recovering. I will die somewhere, I don't know where.
> **BIOY CASARES**: Then, why are you leaving?
> **BORGES**: María does not want to leave alone. She is taking me. And then, any place is good to die!
> Bioy Casares thought: "How sad. My poor friend!"[36]

Daedalus, Labyrinth, Enigma, Oedipus

Borges offers us, in "A Poet of the Thirteenth Century," a glimpse of the path leading from Asterion to Oedipus, from the labyrinth and minotaur to the enigma of Oedipus:

Think of him laboring in the Tuscan halls
On the first sonnet (that word still unsaid),
The undistinguished pages, filled with sad
Triplets and quatrains, without heads or tails.

Slowly he shapes it; yet the impulse fails.
He stops, perhaps at a strange slight music shed
From time coming and its holy dread,
A murmuring of far-off nightingales.

Did he sense that others were to follow,
That the arcane, incredible Apollo
Had revealed an archetypal thing

A whirlpool mirror that would draw and hold
All that night could hide or day unfold:
Daedalus, labyrinth, riddle, Oedipus King?[37]

The sinful tercets show him (does the poem's title suggest a thirteen-year-old boy?) the path he chose when he faced the "holy dread" of sexuality. Prudent and moderate, he identified himself with Apollo, the beautiful and powerful god of music, poetry, and art. The archetype of Apollo gives him answers: the god defeats female monsters such as the Delphian dragon whom he had to conquer in order to inherit Mother Earth's oracle; he punishes, with his sister Artemis, the giant Tityus who attempted to rape their mother Leto; he often has unhappy amorous adventures.

The "holy dread" (fear of castration?) imposes a holy sublimation on him who is like Apollo.[38] Apollo's twin sister Artemis was sometimes identified with the Moon, and Borges, the man loved by the moon, writes:

> I slept on the peak and my body,
> now worn out by the years, was beautiful.
> . . . .
> Diana, goddess who is also the Moon,
> Saw me sleeping on the mountain,
> Slowly she descended into my arms
> And gold and Love in the night ablazed.
> I pressed my mortal eyelids
> To blot out her lovely face
> My lips of dust profaned.

> I breathed in the fragrance of the moon
> And her infinite voice said my name.
> Ah, pure cheeks that are sought,
> Ah, rivers of love and of night,
> Ah, the human kiss and the bow strung tight.
> . . . .
> People shun me. They are frightened
> By the man loved by the Moon.
> . . . .
> My solitude wanders the common ways
> Of the earth, but I constantly seek
> In the ancient night of the numminous
> The daughter of Zeus, indifferent Moon.[39]

Endymion's genealogy varies in different versions; he is generally said to be the son of Aethlios (descendant in turn of Helios, the Sun-god) and the nymph Kalyke; in other texts he is the son of Zeus and Kalyke. While he was sleeping one night in a cave on Mount Latmos, the Moon (generally called Selene), saw him for the first time and fell in love with him. She descended to make love to him night after night until Zeus made him sleep forever. Was if because he wished to be immortal and ageless, or at Selene's request? Or was he perhaps punished because he had fallen in love with Hera?[40]

"Someone asked why," said Borges to Alina Diaconú in an unpublished interview, "I had chosen a theme that was so cold and so mythological, and I replied that it is not a mythological poem. It relates to the experience that every man has, that we all have, of having been loved, of having been very happy, and then that is over, and it seems incredible. I really believe that we have all been loved by the moon, or by a woman who was for us the moon. If you read it carefullly you will see that in this poem I am almost saying: once a woman loved me... I was very happy... now, after so many years, it seems incredible. And that is what the poem means. But to say with modesty, or to be able to say it without being too romantic, well... I have used the Greek legend... "[41]

Borges speaks enigmatically concerning this poem, and it is intriguing. How does he explain that people shun him, because a man loved by the moon frigthens them? Some drawings by Norah

Borges, especially "Virgin and child," suggest a maternal relation that shuns contact with and avoids the eroticization of the body.

> Slandered with infamy, why would they not love you?
> We seek our own shadow in the shadow of the other;
> Our reciprocal crystal, in the other's crystal.[42]

Borges writes a poem dedicated to María Kodama and entitles it "The Moon":

> There is so much solitude in that gold.
> The moon of the nights is not the moon
> Seen by the first Adam. Long centuries
> Of human vigil have replenished it
> With ancient tears. Look at it. It is your mirror.[43]

The lunar shape suggests the Spanish oval "moon mirror" and time. Shining at night, the moon is an ambivalent symbol, at onceprotective and dangerous. Like Janus, it has two faces.

Federico García Lorca has his own moons. In "La luna y la muerte" (The Moon and Death), he says, "The moon has ivory teeth,"[44] and in another poem of the same collection he writes,

> White turtle,
> Sleeping moon,
> How slowly
> You walk!
> Closing an eyelid
> Of shadow, you stare
> Like some archaeological pupil.
> It might be...
> (Satan is one-eyed)
> A relic.[45]

García Lorca draws the moon as crescent and gives it a sinister, disturbingly watchful eye. In another drawing where handwriting is an aesthetic and ideographic element he toys with the combination of two words, "*luna*" (moon) and "*puta*" (whore), with a red-colored animal, and a waning moon painted black. The four elements are linked by an arabesque of thin continuous lines that creates a circular association around them. Two curly lines emerge from the word "luna" and connect it with the word "puta." García Lorca puns on the words changing the vowels: pota, pita, peta, pata.

Not having studied the psychopathology of García Lorca, and knowing only some aspects of his life, I can only surmise that, on the basis of these poems and drawings, there may be some parallels with the Borgean moon. There is in narcissistic neuroses a resistance that only allows us to "cast an inquisitive glance over the top of the wall and spy out what is going on on the other side of it.[46]

Love

> A man who is all soul
> is a prisoner of his body.
> Lope de Vega

Freud writes,

> The nucleus of what we mean by love naturally consists (and this is what is commonly called love, and what the poets sing of) in sexual love with sexual union as its aim. But we do not separate from this—what in any case has a share in the name 'love'—on the one hand, self-love, and on the other, love for parents or children, friendship and love for humanity in general, and also devotion to concrete objects or to abstract ideas.[47]

Psychoanalytic research shows that all these aspirations are instinctive expressions. Sometimes these drives are forced to deviate from their sexual goal and inhibition or displacement occurs, yet their original nature can almost always be discovered.

One of the most esteemed figures of Borges's obsessive lexeme, the tiger, inspires him the following:

> He walked to and fro, delicate and fatal, charged with infinite energy, behind the firm bars; we all stood watching him. He was the tiger of that morning in Palermo, and was also the tiger of the Orient, and Blake's tiger, and Hugo's, and Shere Khan's, and was the tigers that were and will be, was the archetypal tiger, since in his case the individual is the entire species. We thought he was bloodthirsty and beautiful. Norah, a little girl, said: "he is made for love."[48]

Cruelty and sexual drive are tightly related. The aggression mingled with sexual instinct is for Freud a true remnant of cannibalistic appetites involving the instinct to possess: in every deviation from "normal" sexual activity, it is possible to discern a significant quotient of inhibition, or of the defusing or dissociation.of instincts. Sadism, therefore, harks back to an aggressive component of the sexual drive, and Freud, after 1920, in his theory of Eros and Thanatos, links aggression and sexuality.

Rather than elaborate here at length on all the possible paths that instincts may follow, I will just mention a few theoretical possibilities: they may turn into their opposite, they may turn against the subject, or undergo repression or sublimation. The power of the Superego that opposes sexual pleasure is preceded by the prohibition of the enjoyment of seeing, smelling, touching, tasting. Revulsion and shame are signs of repression.

Alicia Jurado writes: "I have always been surprised to see Borges's almost total disdain for sensual pleasures. It is true that he perceives imperfectly visual images, but he shows equal indifference for other sensations. Smells, tastes, sounds seem to mean nothing to him, except on account of a possible association with ideas. I wonder if this natural asceticism partly explains his difficulties in understanding the sensuality of others, translated into a remarkably puritan judgement of literary works."[49]

The theme of love is more often found in Borges's poetry than in his prose. He deals with it, I would say, in an infantile way, with fear and shame,—appearing clumsy, naive, resentful, and distressed when disillusioned.

In his first book, written when he was twenty four, he included the poem "*Sábados* (Saturdays)":

> You have no love
> Yet your beauty
> Lavishes its miracle through time.
> . . . .
> Night makes the bars more grievous.
> In the stern sitting room
> Our two solitudes seek one another like the blind.
> The glorious whiteness of your flesh
> Survives the evening.
> There is a pain in our love
> That resembles the soul.

The Saturdays of seclusion, loneliness and suffering are reiterated in Borges's work. Two years later, in a poem with the title "Mi vida entera (My Whole Life)," he recounts:

> I have known many lands; I have seen one woman
> and two or three men.
> I have loved a girl who was fair and proud,
> with a Spanish quietness.
> . . . .
> I have relished many words.[50]

The taste of words is always the only one, always the same. I owe to María Adela Renard a brief text that has as a title an unusual word in the Borgean vocabulary: "El juego (Play)":

> They did not look at each other. In the shared twilight they were both silent and earnest.
> He kept holding her left hand and putting on her fingers the ivory ring and the silver ring, and then removing them.
> Then he held her right hand and put the two silver rings and the gold ring with hard stones on her fingers and then removed them.
> She held out one hand at first and then the other.
> This went on for a while. Gradually they intertwined fingers and joined their palms.
> They did this with a delicate deliberation, as if afraid to err.
> They did not know that play was necessary so that a particular thing could follow later in a particular region.[51]

The Threatened Man

At the 1987 Book Fair in Buenos Aires, a conference was devoted to Jorge Luis Borges. One of the participants, José E. Clemente, who had been a friend of the poet, recounted the following anecdote: "Borges had a girlfriend in Villa Urquiza—who didn't, in those days? They had agreed to meet at 7 p.m. After lunch Borges started walking slowly in the direction of his rendezvous. Asked why he had started so early, he answered: 'I am now who I will be, I am with her I will be with.' He was so anxious waiting for the time of the appointment to come that he could do nothing else."

> If we are to enter the desert,
> I already am in the desert.
> If I must enter solitude
> I am now alone.[52]

Another friend of Borges, the writer and journalist Manuel Peyrou, told his La Prensa colleague Carlos Baudry that, in the 1920s or 30s, when Borges went with him and others to a house of prostitution, "Borges did not like the prostitutes; he never did. I think he came with us out of friendship, so as to be one of the group, not because he was interested. He was always quite discreet. Not even his best friends knew what he did or preferred in the way of women."[53]

A poem published in 1972 with the title "El centinela (The Watcher)" includes the following lines:

> One or another woman has rejected him, and I must share his anguish.
> He dictates to me now this poem, which I do not like.
> . . . .
> He is in my footsteps, in my voice.
> Down to the last detail, I abhor him.
> I am gratified to remark that he can hardly see.
> I am in a circular cell and the infinite wall is closing in.[54]

Another poem in the same book has the title "*El amenazado* (The Threatened One)." It was included in the *Obras Completas* (Emecé 1974) but omitted in the volume, *Obra poética*, published in 1977.

A *Clarín* reporter obtained this explanation from Borges on September 3rd, 1981:

> **REPORTER**: Have you ever refrained from publishing something you had written because you felt that it bared your soul too much?
> **BORGES**: "Yes, there is a poem, I believe the title was 'The Threatened One,' which I crossed out from my books because it was too intimate."
> **REPORTER**: Is it a love poem?
> **BORGES**: "Yes, that's why. I thought it was too personal, too immediate, so I eliminated it. It has been omitted, and I shouldn't have mentioned it tonight, but anyway... . Poetry requires something mythical, some ambiguity, which that poem lacked. It

was like an interjection, which I could not allow myself to use publicly.

This poem is indeed full of pathos and tenderness; it is a moving and painful *cri du coeur*. "The Threatened One" is a touching love confession and a dramatic confession of panic. It expresses a "impossible burning desire, a muffled cry of despair."

It is love. I will have to hide or flee.
Its prison walls grow larger, as in a fearful dream. The alluring mask has changed, but as usual it is the only one. What use now are my talismans, my touchstones: the practice of literature, vague learning, an apprenticeship to the language used by the flinty Northland to sing of its seas and its swords, the serenity of friendship, the galleries of the Library, ordinary things, habits, the young love of my mother, the soldierly shadow cast by my dead ancestors, the timeless night, the flavor of sleep and dream?
Being with you or without you is how I measure my time.
Now the water jug shatters above the spring, now the man rises to the sound of birds, now those who look through the windows are indistinguishable, but the darkness has not brought peace.
It is love, I know it; the anxiety and relief at hearing your voice, the hope and the memory, the horror at living in succession.
It is love with its own mythology, its minor and pointless magic.
There is a street corner I do not dare to pass.
Now the armies surround me, the rabble.
(This room is unreal. She has not seen it.)
A woman's name has me in thrall.
A woman's being afflicts my whole body.[55]

Notes

1. María Esther Vázquez, *Borges, imágenes, memorias, diálogos* (Buenos Aires: Monte Ávila, 1977).
2. Vázquez, *Borges, sus días y su tiempo* (Buenos Aires: Vergara, 1986).
3. Gene H. Bel-Villada, *Borges and His Fiction: A Guide to His Mind and Art* (Chapel Hill: University of North Carolina Press, 1981), 255.
4. The preceding citations are culled from Jorge Luis Borges, "Ulrica (Ulrike)," *The Book of Sand*, trans. Norman Thomas Di Giovanni (New York: Dutton, 1977), 21-25.
5. Borges, "Las Kenningar," *Obras completas* (Buenos Aires: Emecé, 1974), 368-71.
6. In this long and tragic story, Brunhild, feeling she has been betrayed, instigates the murder of Sigurd. After the latter's death Brunhild discovers that she cannot outlive him. She stabs herself, making a last request: "I wish to lie on the same pyre as Sigurd, with the naked sword again between us, just as it was in those days when we lay together on the same bed. Now we will truly be husband and wife and the door will not be shut after him when I follow him."
7. In *Ficciones* and *The Aleph and Other Stories*, respectively.
8. Borges, "An Examination of the Work of Herbert Quain," *Ficciones*, ed. by Anthony Kerrigan (New York: Grove Press, 1962), 77-78.
9. Osvaldo Sabino, *Borges, una imagen del amor y la muerte* (Buenos Airees: Corregidor, 1987).
10. Alicia Jurado, *Genio y figura de Jorge Luis Borges* (Buenos Aires: Eudeba, 1980).
11. Borges, "Doctor Brodie's Report," *Doctor Brodie's Report*, trans. Norman Thomas di Giovanni in collaboration with the author (New York: Dutton, 1972), 40-41.
12. Borges, "Juan Muraña," ibid., 86
13. Borges, "The Duel," ibid., 35-41.
14. Borges, *The Book of Sand*, 67-73.
15. The verb "to know" is sometimes used in the Bible to convey the thought of connection or union between man and woman, e.g. Matt. 1:25; Luke 1:34.
16. A famous gaucho who became a legendary romantic hero. He was said to have been victimized and finally killed by the police.
17. "Teodelina" is the name of this character in the Spanish original version of "The Zahir." I use it here even though in the English translation of this

story by Dudley Fitts (*Labyrinths*, 156) she was renamed "Clementina."[Translator's note.]

18. Several texts lead us to associating these fantasies with a certain naivety about sexuality, with polymorphous perverse connotations. The remaining guilt and Superego elements may relate to his own infantile /childhood with his sister and his Uruguayan cousin Haedo. Antonio Carrizo records this conversation with Borges in a published intervew with the writer: "Did you fall in love a lot as a teenager, Borges?" "Yes, I kept doing that. I remember... I was very young. I was in love with a cousin. I was about twelve, and she was in her twenties..."

19. Those who lived in this fashionable Buenos Aires neighborhood were looked at as snobs. Translator's note.

20. "*Vi*" in Spanish means "I saw." Translator's note.

21. María Esther Gilio, interview published in *Borges* (Buenos Aires: Letra Abierta, Mangrullo, 1976).

22. Borges, Jorge Luis, "*El hacedor* (The Maker)," *Dreamtigers*, transl. Mildred Boyer and Harold Morland (New York: Dutton,1964), 24.

23. Borges, "*La memoria de Shakespeare* (Shakespeare's Memory)," *Clarín* (Buenos Aires), 15 May 1980.

24. Is Borges referring here to actual later failures?

25. Borges, "Everything and Nothing," trans. James E. Irby, *Labyrinths*, 242.

26. Carlos Peralta, interview published in *Borges*, Letra Abierta (Buenos Aires: Mangrullo, 1976), 34.

27. Jurado, *Genio*.

28. Matthew Besdine, "*Complexe de Jocaste, maternage et génie*," *Psychanalyse du génie créateur* (Paris: Dunod, 1974), 168-208.

29. All of María Kodama's statements in this chapter are culled from Alberto Amato, "Interview with María Kodama," *La Semana*, 15 May 1985. .

30. Jean-Paul Sartre, *Les Mots* (Paris: Gallimard, 1988), 48.

31. Ibid., 88.

32. Sigmund Freud, "A Childhood Recollection from *Dichtung und Wahrheit*," SE 17: 147.

33. Amato, "Interview."

34. Borges, *Historia de la noche* (Adrogué: private edition, 1977), 44

35. Borges, "*Inscripción*," *Los conjurados*, *Obras completas*, v 2 (Buenos Aires: Emecé), 453.

36. Vázquez, *Borges, esplendor y derrota* (Barcelona: Tusquets, 1996), 326.

37. Borges, *Selected Poems 1923-1967*, ed. by Norman Thomas Di Giovanni (Delacorte/Seymour Lawrence, 1972), 99. Transl. William Ferguson.

38. Borges probably did not know that Apollo has been recognized in recent scholarship as a god of initiation, both in myth and in cult. He is likely however to have been familiar with the numerous literary allusions to this god and versions of the Greek myths where Apollo's amorous adventures end in frustration.

39. Borges, "*Endimión en Latmos,*" "*Historia de la noche,*" *Obra poética* (Buenos Aires: Emecé, 1977), 518. As he perpetuated the unorthodox identification of the moon with a daughter of Zeus, Borges is likely to have had in mind the lines by Keats (*Endymion* IV.380): "There came a dream, showing him how a young man... / would at high Jove's empyreal footstool win / an immortality, and how espouse / Jove's daughter." Neither Phoebe, "the Shining," identified sometimes with the Moon, nor Selene, could be in the ancient mythological genealogy a daughter of Zeus (Jove). Both were Titannesses, therefore of a generation earlier than Zeus. The Moon figures in the myth of Endymion in antiquity as Selene, not Phoebe.

40. Pierre Grimal, *The Dictionary of Classical Mythology*, trans. A. R. Mazwell-Hyslop (Oxford: Blackwell, 1986).

41. I owe these lines to the writer Alina Diaconú.

42. Borges, "*La moneda de hierro* (The Iron Coin)," *Obra poética,* 501.

43. Borges, "*La luna*" (The Moon), "*La moneda,*" 481.

44. Federico García Lorca, *Canciones para la luna* (Songs for the Moon),(Buenos Aires: Losada, 1940), 110.

45. Ibid., 60.

46. Freud, "Introductory Lectures on Psycho-analysis," Lecture XXVI, SE 16: 423

47. Freud, "Group Psychology and the Analysis of the Ego," SE 18: 90.

48. Borges, "El tigre," "*Historia de la noche,*" *Obras completas 1975-1985* (Buenos Aires: Emecé, 1989), vol 2, 173.

49. Jurado, *Genio*, 26-27.

50. Borges, *Selected Poems.* Trans. W. S. Merwin,

51. Borges, "*El juego,*" "*Historia de la noche,*" *Obras completas.*

52. Borges, "*El desierto,*" "*La cifra,*" *Obra poética*, 640.

53. Carlos Baudry, special edition of *La Semana*, 16 May, 1986.

54. Borges, "*El centinela* (The Watcher)," *The Gold of the Tigers,* trans. Alastair Reid (New York: Dutton, 1977), 28-29.

55. Borges, "*El amenazado* (The Threatened One)," *The Gold*, 22-23.

Chapter 9

The Man Resembled the Voice

> In my brief experience as a writer of narrative, I have learned that knowing how a character speaks means knowing who he is; to discover an intonation, a voice, a peculiar syntax, means to have discovered a destiny.
>
> Jorge Luis Borges[1]

The act of speech has been conceptualized as a bond between two, a transitional space where the relationship of subject and world is played out. It is a bridge between symbiosis and individuation, between the Ego and the object, helping to identify and elaborate the basic anxieties of the human being.

Spoken language, when natural and spontaneous, conveys shades of emotion and feelings that the written word, which undergoes elaboration and editing, is not able to express.

"He looked exactly like his voice," says Borges in "Streetcorner Man." Thus he confirms what Didier Anzieu and R. Gori state: "Words are the surface upon which the image of the body is projected and constructed."[2]

The pale youth that Gómez de la Serna describes as sensitive, quiet, timid, unsociable, distant, and non-conformist, was affected by inhibitions and certain speech impediments.[3]

Doña Leonor, his mother, remembers him as follows:

> At first he could not speak in public, but now he has overcome that impediment or perhaps has changed. When Perón had him fired as Director of the National Library, he wrote a speech for the formal dinner in his honor, but Pedro Henríquez Ureña had to deliver it. And, when the foundation of Buenos Aires was commemorated in 1936, he wasn't able to read a text he had prepared for only the radio microphone and once again had to ask Henríquez Ureña to come to the rescue. Many people commented that Borges's voice sounded very strange!.... His first lecture, given when he was twenty-three or twenty-four, was called *El idioma de los argentinos* (The Language of the Argentinians). Of course he avoided reading it, with the excuse that he could not see well. Rojas Sylveira read it for him. Georgie didn't even want to be present, out of timidity, but at the last minute changed his mind, as he later explained, so as not to pain me... "

She continues: "I was sure that he would be a writer. When he was six years old he wrote a little story, in Old Spanish, with the title "*La visera fatal*" (The Fatidic Eyeshade), four or five pages long. When he was very young his language was remarkably unusual. Perhaps he was not hearing well? He totally disfigured many words."[4]

Listening again and again to many recordings of Borges's interviews and lectures, I was able to perceive in detail what Borges himself called his "stuttering" and his "mumblings." His difficulties closely resemble a vocal tic, perhaps caused by some phonorespiratory spasms that force him to interrupt his speech, as if he could not find the words and had to resort to tags such as ... *eh... eh... este... este... y... y*. It is possible to hear before he speaks something that sounds like a breathing: "ah... ah..." At times of anxiety and acceleration, this symptom becomes more noticeable.

His tics in his lectures are less frequent than in interviews, where his diction flows more smoothly, though sometimes he seems to choke with ideas: "My memory is swifter than my words...." Sometimes he speaks so quickly that one only hears a mumbling. This occurs in a recorded conversation with the writer Jorge B. Rivera. He speaks very fast and almost inaudibly of a particular incident he witnessed as a child. He saw a man being killed at the boundary between Uruguay and Brazil. It is a particular and traumatic experience that can be recognized in his stories where the action is located in that far-away region.

In the same interview, he talks to Rivera about his panic before a lecture: "Well, it continues to terrify me, yet after a few minutes, when I hear the sound of my own voice... well, stuttering... yet saying things that are rather... well, concrete, I calm down."

The pauses in his speech are sometimes arbitrary, yet they remind me of his poetic punctuation rather than of prose. So he says: "Each word is a... poetic... work...." Compare the pauses in a lecture concerning nightmares: "... then... no doubt... when we tell... dreams...." This may also indicate an irregular respiratory rhythm, a product of phobic anxiety.

Stuttering

Although Freud wrote very little concerning stuttering, he explains it in the case of Emmy Von N., as caused by the presence of an "antithetical representation." In *Psychopathology of Everyday Life*, Freud makes a distinction between *"lapsus linguae"* and other speech problems related to the rhythm and delivery of a statement rather than to single words. As examples, he mentions stuttering and mumbling caused, he says, by internal conflicts that are revealed in such speech disorders.

The complex structure of fantasies regarding speech connect it, in its origins, with sphincter contraction. According to Otto Fenichel, these fantasies result exclusively from anal fixation; other authors believe that it may be oral or phallic as well. M. Klein argues that in schizo-paranoid situations and in function of fantasies of persecution, words are experienced as objects charged with aggression. Therefore, speaking may be risky. These very hostile fantasies, projected upon those who hear the words, intensify the fear of persecution. Oedipal guilt is positioned over pregenital anxieties with their oral and anal sadistic content. The speaker is exposed to castration fantasies located in all his libidinal zones, particularly in the mouth.

Annie Anzieu, who has studied in depth the problem of stuttering in children, says: "Numerous anamneses have shown that the baby who will later stutter is subjected to a mother who is as greedy as the child and who, furthermore, is intent on maintaining the complete dependence of the child to herself. By a formal and perhaps also essential hesitation, stuttering children hide all those desires that may be objectionable. The stutterer knows that he is intensely greedy and hides behind his stuttering."[5] Such anxiety, in this case of incorporation, would therefore explain the poor articulation, the hesitation, and the "tics" of a thought process that rushes the words.

David Liberman conducted research on the speech of a psychoanalytic patient.[6] His observations are also related to style (see pp. 43-44). Applying Liberman's terminology, I stated that while Borges's dominant style is reflexive, his narrative style serves as an important expression of obsessive and phobic fantasies. I can understand Borges's phobia of the public in his first attempts as a speaker. The stern Superego criticism by which he was surrounded as a child becomes manifest in his own demands of perfection and the care he gives to minimal details, in this case the choice of the appropriate word.

To sum up, I believe that on the basis of an early schizoid dissociation, Borges seeks defenses in reactive formations, in other words, his isolation, cautionary acts, magic, and meticulous attention to details, all of which are typical of obsessive neuroses.

He "Disfigured" Words as a Child

Borges's mother wondered why he "totally disfigured many words," and she hypothesized that the reason might be that he was not hearing well. Without further data to resolve the issue, I will advance a few hypotheses.

One explanation of this trait might be to consider it as the almost autistic game of a precocious child raised among adults. Another way to explain it would see it as his way of rebelling against an intrusive and demanding environment, as Freud suggests is the case when he speaks about the pleasure that children find in talking nonsense. To "shun the burden of critical reason" and save psychic energy, they invert syllables, disfigure words and create new ones, without paying attention to meaning or the coherence of sentences. These expressions of rebellion, occuring in adolescents and young adults, become one of the pillars of the psychogenesis of humor and the ability to fantasize. In Borges, this attitude persists when he takes pleasure in absurd enumerations (seeChapter 3)or in games of made-up bibliographies, or imaginative and absurd references. Ricardo Piglia comments on the parodic quality of some of Borges's stories.[7]

A third hypothesis (converging with the first two) focuses on the dislalic or dislexic difficulties that often arise as a result of learning two languages simultaneously: "English was spoken at home by my English grandmother and Spanish by the rest of the family. I knew that I had to speak with my maternal grandmother, Leonor Acevedo Suárez, one way, and another way with my paternal grandmother, Frances Haslam Arnettm who was Protestant, and the two ways were different. I read in both languages, but possibly more in English, because my father's library was English."[8]

Occasionally He Spoke Too Much...

Borges was afraid of speaking. He tended to hesitate and vacillate; he became flustered, stuttered: he avoided large groups. Perhaps because his blindness gave him the illusion of "not being seen" as in the games that children play, he ventured as an old man to open up. But sometimes he spoke too much.... As if the barriers of containment fell so that he no longer weighed what he was sayingor who his audience was, he made racist statements, praised Pinochet, and expressed skepticism about democracy, "that abuse of statistics." He disparagingly criticized poets such as Federico García Lorca, Alfonsina Storni, Pablo Neruda, and others.

Rodolfo Braceli, in a tender and passionate book, *Don Borges, saque su cuchillo porque he venido a matarlo* (Mister Borges, take out your knife because I've come to kill you) speaks of "a catalogue of outrageous statements of the third Borges." He writes, "I wish to get to the bottom of it and find out why the intelligent and sensitive Borges takes a step back, yields his space and authorizes this other, fictionally barbaric Borges, to offer unfailingly a daily show of the inhuman."[9]

"This mild-mannered man," said Pablo Neruda, "reveals through his reactionary statements some of his old English school narcissism." Because this unfortunate aspect of his personality drove Borges to speak too much (unless it was "his bloodline" that spoke through him), the Nobel Prize Committee never awarded him the literature prize.

Notes

1. Borges, Jorge Luis, "Martín Fierro," *Obras completas en colaboración* (Buenos Aires: Emecé, 1979), 517.
2. Didier Anzieu et al., *Psychanalyse et langage* (Paris: Dunod, 1987), 81. Didier Anzieu has emphasized the existence, before the stage of the mirror, of a sonic mirror or an auditive-phonic "skin" which condition the acquisition by the psyche of the ability to signify and symbolize. (Didier Anzieu, "*L'enveloppe sonore du soi,*" *Nouvelle Revue de Psychanalyse* 13 (1976). Edelheit says: "Language, more than any other function, characterizes the Ego as an unity." He adds : "The Ego would thus be a vocal-auditive organization." *Revista Uruguaya de Psicoanálisis*, Montevideo, 3.12 (1970).
3. Cited by Alicia Jurado, *Genio y figura de Jorge Luis Borges* (Buenos Aires: Eudeba, 1980), 182.
4. Leonor Acevedo de Borges, "Propos de Mme. Leonor Acevedo de Borges," *L'Herne* 4 (1964), 10.
5. Annie Anzieu, "*De la chair au verbe: mutisme et bégaiement*" in *Psychanalyse et langage* 13, 118-19.
6. David Liberman, *Lingüística, interacción comunicativa y proceso psicoanalítico*, vol, 1 (Buenos Aires: Nueva Visión, 1971), 89. Interestingly, he refers to speech as "verbal mimic."
7. Ricardo Piglia, *Crítica y ficción. Cuaderno de extensión universitaria* N° 8, (Rosario: Universidad Nacional del Litoral, 1986).
8. María Esther Vázquez, *Borges, sus días y su tiempo* (Buenos Aires: Vergara, 1986), 40.
9. Rodolfo Braceli, *Don Borges, saque su cuchillo porque he venido a matarlo* (Mister Borges, take out your knife because I've come to kill you) (Buenos Aires: Galerna, 1979), 39.

Chapter 10

Dreams and Nightmares in Borges: José, the Dreamer

> Rosaura: Is not that feeble exhalation there
> A light? That pallid star whose fainting tremors,
> Pulsing a doubtful warmth of glimmering rays,
> Make even darker with its spectral glow
> That gloomy habitation? Yes! because
> By its reflection (though so far away)
> I recognise a prison, grim and sombre,
> The sepulchre of some poor living carcase.
> And, more to wonder at, a man lies there
> Clothed in the hides of savage beasts, with limbs
> Loaded with fetters, and a single lamp
> For company. So, since we cannot flee,
> Let us stay here and listen to his plaint
> And what his sorrows are.[1]

Borges says in "*El guardián de los libros* (The Keeper of the Books)":

> The secret and eternal laws;
> the harmony of the world.
> These things or their memory are here in books
> that I watch over in my tower... .[2]

That Borges dreamed, reflected, and wrote about dreams is, of course, no surprise. Imprisoned in a narcissistic and paranoid enclosure, through dreams he was able to experience, see, and overcome the harsh humiliation, the "magnificent irony of God who gave him both books and the night." As a writer, he could find in dreams a wealth of materials for his creative work.

> In this city of books he made these eyes
> The sightless rulers who can only read
> In libraries of dreams... [3]

Dreams, memories, books, mirrors, labyrinths, mummified time and space—only by writing of these can Borges give life to death.

There are many signs of Borges's keen interest in dreams. Borges lectured on dreams and devoted a book to this topic, *Libro de los sueños* (*The Book of Dreams*), a compilation of other writers' dreams and his own.[4] In what was almost a morning ritual, Doña Leonor and Borges used to tell to each other their dreams of the previous night. In his literary work, he often includes dreams, playing with the potential overlappings of the real and the imaginary. With these combinations, in his unique style, he achieves effects sometimes fantastic, sometimes sinister. He weaves disturbing heterotopies, connecting diverse constellations of personal events, genuine or apocryphal bibliographic citations, and mythological motifs, either classical or Norse.

In a lecture on nightmares, Borges pointed out that in some cultures dreams are deemed to be episodes occurring during wakefulness.[5] He writes in "The Zahir," "According to the teaching of the Idealists, the words 'live' and 'dream' are rigorously synonymous..."[6] In the prologue to "*El informe de Brodie*" we read: "Furthermore, literature is nothing but a guided dream."[7]

As is well known, Freud considered dreams the "royal path" of access to the unconscious. Together with the lapsus, they reveal the surprise of the encounter with the supressed Other. Evading censorship, unconscious fantasies, representing impulses and desires, may return in dreams; hence they are disguised, with words transformed into images and projected onto any space or time. When the subject is asleep, stimuli follow a regressive path and instead of being directed toward motor responses are redirected toward sensory ones. Dreams, on the other hand, always involve a past history, either earliest experiences or traumatic events in the subject's life. The process of elaboration in dreams includes condensation and displacement, the main tools of the dream's staging. For Lacan, the unconscious is structured like language; and according to Petronius, "When the body does not weigh it down, the soul plays" So the elements of dream's free play are those of aesthetic creation. Freud makes no distinction between dream and nightmare; indeed, he never specifically addresses the topic of nightmares, though he speaks about anxiety dreams, dreams of punishment, of masochism, humiliation, and torture. These themes are easier to understand on the basis of the theories that Freud sets out in *Beyond the Pleasure Principle*, where many elements of nightmares are explained as resulting from a compulsion to repeat. He analyzes traumatic dreams and the incessant return of some painful behaviors in neuroses of destiny. Freud says about this compulsion to repeat (which he considers akin to the death drive): "... But we come now to a new and remarkable fact, namely that the compulsion to repeat also recalls from the past experiences which include no proximity of pleasure, and which can never, even long ago, have brought satisfaction even to instinctual impulses which have since been repressed."[8]

J. Laplanche and J. B. Pontalis define the compulsion to repeat as an irresistible urge with an unconscious origin.[9] The subject actively places himself in painful situations, repeating early experiences without remembering their origin. He strongly believes that the compulsion is fully motivated by the present circumstances. In this, one can recognize clearly that compulsions aim at repeating what is a characteristic quality of all drives, i.e. their conservative nature.

For J. E. Gedo Beyond, every behavior is controlled by a compulsion to repeat, whether it produces pleasure or displeasure.[10] In contrast, C. Hollande and M. Soulé point out that "clinically a pure compulsion of repetition never occurs without pleasure; play, character neuroses, transference, and neuroses of destiny are manifestations of the compulsion to repeat but pleasure and domination are also present..."[11]

Applying Freud's reflections on traumatic dreams in *Beyond the Pleasure Principle*, Angel Garma points to an infantile traumatic situation at the origin of all dreams. For Garma, it is not the satisfaction of desires that has an essential function in the genesis of dreams but rather the emergence of traumatic psychic elements that, before becoming conscious, become hallucinatory and undergo masking processes.

A nightmare is a mare of the night. The Spanish word for it, "*pesadilla*" (a derivative of Latin *pessumdo*), implies that a ghost or spirit "sends to the bottom" or "destroys" the sleeper. Victor Hugo referred to a nightmare as "*le cheval noir de la nuit.*" The German word for nightmare, *Alpdrücken,* means an "oppressing elf." The ancient Greeks imagined Ephialtes (nightmare) as a ghost or spirit that throttles the sleeper.

Ernest Jones carried out a psychoanalytic study of nightmares, and for him the nightmare is a variety of anxiety dream, with five aspects closely linked to superstitions such as the belief in incubi (demons in male form that had sexual intercourse with sleeping women) or succubi (the female demon counterparts of the incubi), vampires, werewolves, the devil, and witches.[12] These superstitions can be said to be phobias whose latent content represents some repressed component of the psychosexual instinct. Jones states that "the nightmare is a form of anxiety attack, that it is essentially due to an intense mental conflict centering around [the] reactivation of the normal incest wishes of infancy."[13]

Intense fear is the most remarkable feature of nightmares and anxiety dreams. Other common traits are the swift transformation of a person into another person or an animal, the alternating between intense attraction and extreme repulsion cause by some object, the person being simultaneously in two different places, a flying or riding through the skies, a feeling that one abruptly falls, and sexual relationships felt as acts of hostility and torture. Incubi exhibit "every possible gradation... between the pleasurable excitement of voluptuousness and extreme terror and repulsion."[14] Medieval literature speaks about incubi harassing widows, virgins, and nuns rather than married women. Convents were assiduously frequented by incubi.

In the nightmare, as J. J. von Goerres describes it, "Sometimes there is the anxiety of suffocation, sometimes rather a violent sexual excitement with the sensation that the muscle system becomes loose, something like the vertigo caused by speed."[15]

In a lecture on the nightmare delivered in 1977, Borges cited expressions used by Shakespeare, such as "the mare of the night," and "the mare of the night and her nine colts." Borges reflects, "There is something terrible in the notion of a 'mare of the night'," and describes "The Nightmare," a painting by Fuseli, a Swiss painter of the eighteenth century: "We have here a young woman waking up in bed, is terrified to see a small, black, evil monster lying on her belly. That monster is the nightmare."

In Ernest Jones' book there is a black-and-white reproduction of this painting and even here it is clear that a woman is lying down with her head hanging over the edge of the bed. Borges does not mention that, nor does he point out that the young woman's breasts rise in that position and that the little monster sits on them. With pointed ears and a sardonic smile, he gazes at her, so it seems, full of desire. The young woman has long, beautiful hair, and her countenance does not indicate any fear. The painting, on the contrary, is clearly and evocatively erotic. Borges also fails to mention that in the back of the painted scene, looking out from behind dark draperies, there is a beautiful head of a white horse, with ears similar to those of the little demon. The horse watches the scene with amazement. On a night table there is a vase with a single flower. In referring to this painting, Borges obviously emphasized its demonic rather than its erotic aspects. "There is the notion that a demon causes nightmares," said Borges in his lecture. "I believe there may be some truth in the concept—and I'm speaking candidly and sincerely...."

This avowal on his part is not surprising. He points to the magic and persecutory elements in nightmares. The demon that causes his own nightmares is the chaotic "disorganizer" of his drives that takes advantage of the silence of the night while he, the obsessive organizer of the world into axioms, is sleeping. That force may seduce him or punish him, even as it did to Faust.

Borges says: "[I]f we are anxious, we create or dream a sphinx that oppresses our chest. If we fear to provoke a tiger, we imagine a tiger... What is more, if a tiger were to enter this hall, we would all be afraid, yet if we are afraid, we invent the tiger...."

Hugo Bleichmar expresses from a psychoanalytic viewpoint what Borges intuitively senses. For Bleichmar, the products of the psyche that bring about nightmares run counter to the tendency that sleep has to diminish anxiety. In a persecutory series each situation may be replaced by another situation,—which demonstrates that none is essential, that they are just variants of a productive structure vaster than each one of them. For example, the belief that one will be inexorably murdered for some past action or desire, stages as in a play the dream of a verdict decided a priori and able to select elements that will support that notion of doom. Marshalled from the unconscious, fantasies of transgression and punishment, desires for death, and threats of revenge, organize the manifest content of the dream and support the persistent feeling of persecution.

Bleichmar postulates a "matrix belief" expressing unconscious fantasies which are closely related to the relationship of the child with his parents. The early bond between them and its vicissitudes are the seeds of traumatic situations, narcissistic wounds, and scars that, like foreign bodies, will determine by repression or denial the compulsions to repeat, the fetishes, the sense of the sinister, and the neuroses of destiny.

Closely related to nightmares is the insomnia of which Borges suffered painful periods. In an interview with Richard Burgin, the following dialogue took place:

> **BURGIN**: The story 'Funes the Memorious' is, among other things, about insomnia.
> **BORGES**: About insomnia, yes, A kind of metaphor.
> **BURGIN**: I take it, then, you've had insomnia.
> **BORGES**: Oh yes.
> **BURGIN**: So have I.
> **BORGES**: Do you have insomnia?
> **BURGIN**: I don't any more, but I've had it in the past. It's a terrible thing, isn't it?
> **BORGES**: Yes, I think there's something awful about sleeplessness.
> **BURGIN**: Because you think it will never end.
> **BORGES**: Yes, but you also think, or rather you feel, that it's not merely a case of being sleepless, but that somebody's *doing* that to you.
> **BURGIN**: A kind of cosmic paranoia.
> **BORGES**: Cosmic paranoia, or some fiendish foe, no? You don't feel it's an accident.
> You feel that somebody is trying to kill you in a sense, or to hurt you, no?[16]

Piera Aulagnier emphasizes that the basic postulate of the primary organizing process of fantasyis that the suffering of the subject is caused by a desire of the Other.[17] Clearly for a subject believing that the Other wants to make him suffer and that such desire is omnipotent, no amount of effort will eliminate the persecutor in the manifest content of the nightmare.

In the prologue to *El libro de los sueños*, Borges says, "There is not a single form in the universe that cannot be contaminated with horror—hence, perhaps, the peculiar flavor of the nightmare, different from fright and from the frights that reality can inflict upon us. The Germanic nations seem to have been more sensitive to this vague threat of the evil than the Latin; let us remember the untranslatable words "weird," uncanny," "*unheimlich.*" Each language produces what it needs."[18] This is *how* Borges recognizes the sinister in nightmares.

"I have two nightmares," he said further, "two nightmares that might get confused: the nightmare of the labyrinth and the nightmare of the mirrors." The first one emerges from a situation that would not appear traumatic but which we may interpret as linked to guilty feelings caused by the child's curiosity. Borges remembers himself as a child, facing a drawing of the Cretan labyrinth, like a steep amphitheater, ominously closed, yet showing cracks. He wished for a manifying glass powerful enough to go through those cracks and discover the Minotaur in the mysterious and terrible center of the labyrinth. The second nightmare, of the mirrors, refers, as we know, to a nightly childhood terror of seeing his own image disfigured in the three mirrors of the antique mahogany wardrobe in the old family house.

A more general question arises here. Is this curiosity, this wish to penetrate the mother's body to see what is inside, traumatic in itself? Or does it become traumatic according to each child's experience? The obsessive desire of Borges to gain entrance into the labyrinth to know appears repetitively in his dreams and must be considered traumatic. His curiosity was unusual, special, almost a fascination: as a child, he stayed at the zoo for hours, watching the tiger with the omnipotent desire to introject it, to "devour" it with his eyes so that he might perhaps become that tiger. The magnifying glass invites another conjecture. Was this dream possibly a premonition of his blindness, suggested by the blindness of his grandfather and his father? He needed to see, with a magnifying glass if necessary, but he had to see.

In the nightmare of mirrors disfiguring his image "another vision appears, another terror of my nights: the entry of masked people. Masks always frightened me. No doubt I felt that if someone were wearing a mask, he was hiding something horrible. Sometimes in my dreams— these are the most terrible nightmares—I see in a mirror my reflection wearing a mask, and I am afraid to take it off because I am afraid to see my real face which is atrocious. There may be hidden there leprosy, or evil, or something more terrible than anything I could imagine." What were the terrifying, chaotic experiences of the young Georgie? Are these the expressions of his internal world, full of drives, rage, evil, insatiability? Is this what he calls "leprosy"? "A curious trait of my nightmares," Borges continued, "which perhaps you share with me, is that they have a precise topography. For instance, I always dream about specific streetcorners in Buenos Aires. I know where I am and that I must go to a rather distant place. In the dream it could be mountain passes, swamps, or jungles. You see, I try to find my way..."

Just as a psychoanalyst can use the associations a patient provides of persons or events related to particular streetcorners, so, with Borges's dreams, we can use the street names related to battles, patriotic heroes, or heroic ancestors: Laprida, Soler, Arenales, and others.

María Esther Vásquez relates this conversation she once had with Borges:

> **VÁSQUEZ:** Do you think there is a single childhood event that has marked you or your literature in some way?
> **BORGES:** Many things. My grandfather's swords, for example.
> **VÁSQUEZ:** How so?
> **BORGES:** They stimulated my fantasy. The portrait of my great-grandfather, Colonel Suárez, also impressed me greatly. He won the battle of Junín and he departed from Buenos Aires with San Martín when he was sixteen. Returning home, at twenty-seven, his family did not recognize him. And my grandfather Borges started his military career when he was fourteen years old defending the park of Montevideo that the *Blancos de Oribe* were besieging. At sixteen he was at the battle of Caseros, in César Díaz's Oriental Division. Afterwards he had a long military career, with two years in the Paraguay war, the companies with....
> **VÁSQUEZ:** Do you have a lot of nostalgia for those things? Would you have liked it?
> **BORGES:** Yes, yes, yes, but I don't know if I'd have been good enough. You see, I try to find my way. [19]

Borges is trapped in a situation that can perhaps be described as the pathology of the double message: he wants to be like his ancestors but cannot; he wants to be like them but also be himself. Imprisoned, as he is, in the labyrinth that his forefathers and his parents have dreamed for him, he tries to find his way. To do so he will have to traverse mountain passes, swamps, and jungles. He will have to dream his nightmares.

Dream in Edinburgh

Borges tells the following nightmare in *"Los conjurados"* (The Conspirators).

> Before dawn, I had a nightmare that left me overwhelmed. I will try to tell it in order.
> Your elders engender you. In a far frontier of deserts, there are dusty classrooms, or may be dusty warehouses. In those classrooms or warehouses, there are parallel rows of blackboards, whose length is measured in miles or hundreds of miles, where someone has drawn letters and numbers with chalk. It is not known how many blackboards there are *in toto*, but it is assumed there are many, some crammed with writing, some almost blank. The walls have Japanese sliding doors, made of some metal, which is rusty. The entire building is circular and so huge that the circularity cannot be perceivedfrom outside. It is seen as a straight line. The crammed blackboards are taller than a man and they reach up to the gypsum ceiling, whitish or gray. On the left side of the blackboard words precede numbers, and are listed in columns as in a dictionary. The first word is Aar, a river in Berna. This is followed by Arabic numerals indefinite though certainly not infinite. These indicate the exact number of times you will see that river, the exact number of times you will discover it on the map, the exact number of times you will dream about it. The last word, which is very distant, may be Zwingli. On another oversize blackboard, the word "Neverness" is written, and next to that strange word there is a number. The entire course of your life is in those signs.
> There is not a second that is not gnawing at a series.
> You will exhaust the cipher corresponding to the taste of ginger and you will continue living. You will exhaust the cipher corresponding to the smoothness of crystal and you will continue living, for a few days. You will exhaust the cipher of the heartbeats set for you, and then you will have died.[20]

Arnaldo Rascovsky studied this dream in an unpublished paper entitled, "Analysis of a Dream of Borges: The Perception of Philogenetic Language." I summarize here his observations, some of which confirm my own hypotheses. We do not, however, always draw the same conclusions. He says, "We can see in Borges two central elements. One is the terrible concern of a paranoid nature, which can be gleaned from his cruel and bloody stories of knife-wielding men. Underneath that, however, there is something deeper, which I believe is his real achievement: a total immersion into the psyche of the unborn."

Rascovsky interprets the theme of the labyrinth and the grim vision of mirrors as a persistent desire to return to an enclosure (the maternal uterus) and restore a symbiotic bond. Indeed, Borges's life justifies this observation. His bond with his mother lasted many years and, for that very reason, must have contained intensely aggressive components. Following this line of thought, the dream would mean that the mother who was with him and helped him all his life also forced him to live within her.

Rascovsky says with respect to innate knowledge, quoting Arnold Gesell, who says that when a child is born, he is an old man bringing with him all the wisdom of the species. Rascovsky also paraphrases Coleridge who said that sixty or seventy years of life are insignificant compared to the nine months in the maternal realm.

For Rascovsky, Borges is like the prophet Teiresias, a blind man immersed in the world of self-knowledge.[21] Ancient seers and poets, thought to have great wisdom, were said to be blind. This mystic knowledge drawn from the archaic psyche by one who seems to be surrounded by a hostile external world suggests to Rascovsky the pathological parallel of autism, which he applies to Borges. He mentions Pascal and Mozart as individuals who had a similar innate knowledge. In mathematics and music, he adds, which are specific languages, there may be exceptional achievement without the mediation of learning. Thus Einstein was a genius who did not speak until he was four years old, was not successful in school, and lived isolated from the conventional aspects of everyday life. Knowledge of numbers is universal and primary, preceding the mother tongue which needs to be learned. Rascovsky states: "The psyche of the unborn was suppressed by Freud on account of his own personal history. He said that the greatest trauma for a very young child is the mother's new pregnancy."

Rascovsky points out how Borges's dream from the beginning alludes to procreation: "Your elders engender you." "A far frontier of deserts" may suggest the remote knowledge we may have of prenatal life. The circular shape of the entire building could represent the anatomic shape of the uterus.

A Reading

I concur with Rascovsky in his assessment of the extraordinary regressive and creative ability Borges possessed. I think he is right in qualifying Borges's introversion as nearly autistic, and in pointing to the intense, symbiotic, and ambivalent relationship of long standing with his mother. Equally remarkable is the relationship with his father, a Maecenas toward the son he hoped would be what he himself had not been able to become.

For Rascovsky, the Edinburgh dream conveys a sense of predestination. Once again, I agree but wish to add that the predestination originates in the desires of parents and forebears. I subscribe to the opinion that the early birth of a sibling can be traumatic. Borges was born in the eighth month of his mother's pregnancy, and Norah was born when Georgie was eighteen months, though in a striking mistake Borges said in an interview that his sister was three or four years younger.

I recognize in Borges's unique mental processes what one might call a genius's madness, and there is no doubt that his memory was prodigious. Yet I find it difficult to explain his precociousness as innate knowledge. I cannot consider this dream as an expression of philogenetic language, learned before birth. This image is one that I can only envisage symbolically, as the vision of a Borges who was a prisoner, chained to a destiny he could not rebel against or change. The interpretation propsed by Rascovsky may actually be more persuasive in the case of other stories such as "The House of Asterion," "The Circular Ruins," and even "Dr. Brodie's Report."

Though the Edinburgh dream suggests more than one possible reading, I read it as the parable of a cruel destiny. From "your elders engender you" to "You will exhaust the cipher of the heartbeats set for you, and then you will have died," an entire life is predetermined. The dreamer is totally passive, his destiny marked by genes. Borges does not even contemplate the thought of rectifying or changing this destiny. There is in the dream a repeated alternance between opposites: frontiers and great lengths (hundreds of miles), classrooms and warehouses, curves and straight lines, crammed and blank blackboards, never and always, everything and nothing. Are these classrooms with blackboards or dusty warehouses? Of what are they full and empty? The Spanish word for "crammed," *abarrotado*, suggests *barrotes*, bars of a jail. Borges disbelieved the existence of free will. He liked to cite Carlyle's reference to universal history as a book we are compelled to incessantly read and write, and where we are also being written.

Everything in this nightmare is beyond measure, in space and time. The parallel blackboards do not have any point of contact, and, gigantically tall, they divide, close, and imprison like a labyrinth. On the left, words precede numbers. Interpreting the spatial symbols, one may see the left representing the past, origins, the mother, regression, introversion. Borges does not indicate who wrote those words and numbers, but they must refer to his ancestors and his parents.

Are the Japanese doors related to María Kodama, in terms of love and care? They are sliding doors, they offer a way out, and they move; time, however, has elapsed, and now they are rusty. Aar and Zwingli are not, of course, the first and last words in a Spanish dictionary, except for Borges. Curiously, they define the time of his teenage years in Swizerland, where he attended secondary school, where he had friends that he always remembered and where he had his first sexual experience. Cryptically refering to this first experience in the story "The Other," he imagines a dialogue with the young Borges, who, refers to the shelves of his father's library and says, " 'hidden behind the other volumes, [there was] a book in paper covers about sexual customs in the Balkans. Nor have I forgotten one evening on a certain second floor of the Place Dubourg.' 'Dufour', corrected the other. 'Very well, Dufour. Is that enough now?' " Near the Place Bourg Du Four, in Paris, there were bordellos where, according to Rodríguez Monegal, Borges had his sexual initiation. [22]

Aar is a river in Switzerland and Zwingli is the Swiss religious reformer. Borges attended a conference on Calvin in Geneva. His dream says of Zwingli that he was very distant. Is Borges now very distant from adolescence, from engaging in reform, from rebelling from the Father-based religion in which he had been indoctrinated? Concerning the divine command and the divine prohibition, which was which? Adolescence precisely marks the time and space of greening in all activities of life: love, science, work, art, poetry. Adolescence is the period when the Ego identifies with idealized creative individuals and with teachers. Peter Blos points out that narcissistic and bisexual patterns are abandoned during adolescence, thus preparing the development and consolidation of heterosexual ones. [23] Artistic creativitythat may have been sketched during the period of latency and hesitatingly brought to the surface by puberty break out vigorously in adolescence. Baudelaire thought that adolescence is an important component of the genius of man. During adolescence, he said, objects leave their imprint on the tender and fragile spirit, colors are striking, and people speak a mysterious language.

"On another oversize blackboard the word 'Neverness' is written." This "strange word" is the only one which in the original is written in English, the language of Borges's early childhood. "Neverness" signifies what must not be possessed or passed beyond. It sounds like a command, a prophecy, a prohibition, a taboo. "The entire course of [his] life" is condensed in such boundaries, in such a threat. Borges never left the garden and the library: there is a streetcorner he avows not daring to cross. "Neverness" is the signifier, the navel of the dream. The prohibition in the Edinburgh dream reminds me of the generic prohibition in Kafka's *The Castle*. When K, pretending to be a subordinate, calls and asks: "When can my boss come to the castle?" the answer is "Never." He says, "All right," and hangs up.

"Neverness" evokes "Everness," the title of one of Borges's poems, where he writes:

> One thing does not exist: Oblivion.
> God saves the metal and he saves the dross.[24]

Is he the dross that could never satisfy the expectations of his forebears, those giants? He alludes to something beyond measure, and this suggests the figure of the Devil, who in legends tends to appear building gigantic walls and bridges. Dante describes Lucifer as a giant in *The Divine Comedy*. The Devil displaced the giants of ancient mythologies. He appears at night in the guise of a dead man.

> I am not the one who engenders you. The dead do.
> My father, his father, and his forbears... [25]

Such a sinister engendering by the dead appears in the nightmare, like a deep traumatic inscription. Was Borges ever like the boy he describes in "Dr. Brodie's Report"?:

> Every male born into the tribe is subjected to a painstaking examination; if he exhibits certain stigmata, the nature of which were not revealed to me, he is elevated to the rank of king of the Yahoos. So that the physical world may not lead him from the paths of wisdom, he is gelded on the

spot, his eyes are burned, and his hands and feet are amputated. Thereafter, he lives confined in a cavern called the Castle ('Qzr'), into which only the four witch doctors and the two slave women who attend him and anoint him with dung are permitted entrance. [26]

This is an incredible version of a sinister fate, and the nightmare speaks the same language. *Dreamed in Edinburgh* reminds me of the static paintings by Chirico–if these were done in black and white. They have no inhabitants, they are full of the shades of objects, things, numbers, ciphers, and words, like the hallucinating vision of a desert, a dusty warehouse, a barracks or a schoolhouse, all empty. The dream surprises and overwhelms the dreamer. It overwhelms the reader as well: what seems to be an intellectual adventure turns out to be a real nightmare.[27]

This dream sounds like a premonition of Borges's death in Geneva— in the land of the Aar and Zwingli. Borges avoided dying and being buried where his parents were. He went away, got married, then died. He called his friends to say good-bye; they all said he sounded very happy. His death in Europe, far from his native country, appears it would seem as a gesture of liberation, not tolerated by some. Argentinians felt wounded and abandoned. Critical opinions and judgments were expressed, and Borges was called ungrateful, a fraud and a coward. Should we see in this nightmare a veiled, resigned complaint about his destiny? "A destiny is no better than any other, but a man must obey the one he bears inside."[28]

Borges chose to die in Switzerland, his other fatherland, as he called it, of which he had dear memories. Perhaps he did not want his body to rest in the same land where his mother was awaiting him. (She said: "He was born in the same house I was born.") Two services were offered, an Anglican one (for his British grandmother) and a Catholic one (for his Spanish mother). Borges died on June the fourteenth; his father had died on the fourteenth day of February. A footnote in "The House of Asterion" reads: "The original says *fourteen*, but there is ample reason to infer that, as used by Asterion, this numeral stands for *infinite*."[29]

> Perhaps on the other side of death
> I will know whether I have been a word or somebody."[30]

José, the Dreamer

> Aiax: Ai, ai! Who would have thought
> my name and fortune
> Could square so well together!
> My name is Ajax:
> Agony is its meaning.[31]

For the publication of his *Obras completas* (*Complete Works*) in 1974, Borges toyed with what might become part of a biography after his death. He wrote, "We transcribe here an entry of the *Enciclopedia Sudamericana_* that will be published in Santiago de Chile in the year 2074: 'Borges, José Francisco Isidoro Luis: author and self-taught man born in 1899 in Buenos Aires, at the time the capital of Argentina...' "
Yet his name was Jorge. Why did he write "José"? His full name included his father's name, Jorge; his paternal grandfather's, Francisco; his maternal grandfather's, Isidoro, and Luis, the name of an uncle who was an Uruguayan doctor of jurisprudence and a diplomat. Borges wrote insightfully about names. In a brief essay with the title "*Historia de los ecos de un nombre* (History of the Echoes of a Name)," he refers to the answer that God gave Moses when asked whatwas his name, "I am who I am." Borges says, "Before examining these myterious words, we would do well to remember that in magic or primitive thought, names are not arbitrary symbols but a vital part of what they define. Moses, like the Egyptian sorcerers, would have asked God what his name was in order to hold power over him."[32]

One wonders why Jorge Luis Borges would no longer be Jorge after his death but would become José. Is he finally breaking the mirror, ceasing to be the Jorge who is infinitely reflected in Borges? Is he no longer the echo of those two other great Jorges, his father and grandfather? In an interview with Fernando Sorrentino, Borges said: "Jorge Luis Borges has a harsh sound; José Luis Borges is much smoother. Why repeat such an ugly sound as 'orge'? I don't think it is urgent to repeat "orge," no? I think in the long run I will be referred to in the history of literature as José Luis Borges."[33] The reasons Borges offers are rather naive, but this passage is typical of the verbal pranks he was fond of.

Indeed, names and jokes are not "arbitrary symbols but a vital part of what they define." I advance a few hypotheses on Borges and his names. His paternal grandmother, Fanny Haslam, repeated by heart to little

Georgie long verses from the Bible where the figure of Joseph must surely have occured. Joseph was the eagerly and long awaited firstborn son of Jacob and Rachel. The story goes that Jacob, encouraged by his mother and in complicity with her, deceitfully obtains the blessing from Isaac, who is nearing death. Thus he displaces Esau, the firstborn. Later, Jacob falls in love with his cousin Rachel, but her father demands that, as a condition of her hand, Jacob work for seven years, and when this period elapses, forces Jacob to marry Leah, his elder daughter. After another seven years, Rachel finally becomes Jacob's wife. For a long time she does not bear a child, but, finally, "God remembered Rachel, listened to her and opened her womb." Joseph was born, his father's favorite. Arrogant and vain, Joseph dreams that the sun, the moon and the stars bow down before him. For this reason, his half-brothers call him "the dreamer." Jealous and angered by his arrogance, they hate him and secretly contrive to sell him as a slave to Ishmaeli merchants who in turn offer him to Potiphar, a eunuch who was the captain of the guard for the Pharaoh. Once in Egypt, Joseph underwent harsh vicissitudes but, thanks to his cleverness and his daring, finally became the Pharaoh's minister.

This famous Biblical story has been for centuries a paradigm of the hero. Joseph interpreted for the Pharaoh the dreams that his own magicians were not able to decipher. Among these was the well-known dream about the seven fat cows that went up the river and were devoured by seven skinny cows, as well as the dream about the seven full ears of corn devoured by another seven small and sun-beaten ears. Freud found the character of Joseph intriguing and identified himself with him in some respects: "It will be noticed that the name Josef plays a great part in my dreams. My own ego finds it very easy to hide itself behind people of that name, since Joseph was the name of a man famous in the Bible as an interpreter of dreams."[34]

In the associations stimulated by one of his dreams, Freud evokes the image of a friend whom he names Joseph. This was the name of an uncle considered dishonest by the family on account of his business. Freud's recollections bring back to his consciousness an occasion when, as a young man, his indiscretion created hostility between two common friends. This aroused intense feelings of guilt, and he felt dishonest. Later, he collaborated with his friend Joseph in research done in Doctor Brüke's laboratory, and he concluded that there was fraternal jealousy between them with regard to their mentor. Finally, connected this rivalry to an earlier one he had had vis-à-vis his nephew John, who was only a year older and took the role of elder brother and was his close friend throughout their childhood. Actually, by reporting the faults he thought he had detected in them, the Biblical Joseph constantly caused ill-will between his brothers and his father. Freud referred to the story of Joseph several times. There is a curious reference to it in a letter written to Thomas Mann in november of 1936, concerning Mann's famous tetralogy[35]: Freud's remarks concerning Napoleon's family life are extremely interesting; he deals with the influence on Napoleon of his older sibling, Joseph, who was at once Napoleon's model and rival for the duration of their lives, and he considers whether this was a factor in Napoleon's later love for Josephine.

Armando Hinojosa emphasizes the negative aspects of the figure of Joseph who was, he says, clever and cunning but dependent. "He never was who he pretended to be."[36]

Borges said that a boxer once mistakenly called him "José," and so he thought that, having been renamed by a courageous fighter, that should be his true name. A typically Borgean train of thought, I would say. The Biblical Joseph was not lacking in courage. Perhaps for Borges the name "José" expresses various desires for identification with "Joseph the Dreamer" who declares what is hidden, as the Bible says, and who seems to be present in Borges's dreams and nightmares, both fictional and real. "Joseph and His Brothers" (as in Mann's title) would be represented by the fictional epilogue (or prologue?) to be published in 2074; when he mentions his sister, Borges adds "q.v." (*quod vide*, equivalent to English "See... ") taking it for granted that she also could be expected to have her own encyclopedia entry. "Joseph and the Pharaoh" leads us to an ambivalent position with regard to paternal authority and to a secret desire on Borges's part for omnipotence and domination. The deeper reason for his renaming himself as "José" may have to do with the neurosis of destiny, the iron destiny that imprisoned Borges. But destiny tricked him, because, by choosing to be José, he became once more his own self, Jorge Luis Borges.

Postcript
Two Versions of the Same Dream

After the first Spanish edition of this book was published, I found another dream by Borges, almost identical to the one I analyze in this chapter, with the title of "A Dream in Germany."[37] Having two versions of the same dream makes it even more intriguing, because it allows me to penetrate better the interplay of the unconscious and censorship. While "Dreamed in Edinburgh" was published in 1985, the version I present here appeared in 1984.

A Dream in Germany

> This morning I had a dream that left me overwhelmed. Later I started putting it in order. Your elders engender you. In a far frontier of deserts there are dusty classrooms, or maybe, dusty warehouses with parallel rows of blackboards whose length is measured by miles or by hundreds of miles. No one knows the exact number of warehouses, but there are certainly very many. In each one, there are nineteen rows of blackboards. Someone has loaded them with words and Arabic numerals, written with chalk. Each classroom has a metal Japanese sliding door. The metal is rusty. The writing begins on the left edge of the blackboard and starts with a word. Below, there is another, and they all follow the rigorous alphabetical order of encyclopedic dictionaries. The first word is, let us say, *Aachen*, the name of a city. The second, immediately below, is *Aar*, the river of Berne. In the third place is Aaron, of the Levitic tribe. Then come *abracadabra* and *Abraxas*. After each one of these words, there is set the precise number of times you will see, hear, remember or pronounce them in the course of your whole life. There is an indefinite cipher, yet surely not an infinite one, for the number of times you will utter, between cradle and grave, the names of Shakespeare or Kepler. On the last blackboard of a remote classroom is written the word *Zwitter*, which in German means hermaphrodite, and below is indicated the number of images of the city of Montevideo that has been set for you by destiny; you will exhaust that number, and you will continue living. You will exhaust the number of times set for you to sound off this or that hexameter, and you will continue living. You will exhaust the number of times given for your heart to beat, and then you will have died. When this happens, the letters and the numbers traced in chalk will not be immediately erased. (Every instant of your life, someone modifies or erases a cipher.) All this serves a purpose that we will never understand.

The reader will perceive similarities and differences between the two versions. The one just transcribed, which was the first, suggests to me the following reflections. The number of rows of blackboards is nineteen: see Chapter 6 for its occurrence in connection with Emma Zunz. Why does Borges omit it in the second version? And why are the blackboards "worn out" in the Germany dream? In a lecture he delivered on July 8th, 1985, with the title "My experience in Japan," Borges referred to his journey there with María Kodama. When asked what had most impressed him, he said, "Well, Nara impressed me more than anything else. We spent one night at a Japanese inn: sleeping on the floor, the sliding rusty doors... ." In the Edinburgh dream (the second version), Borges adds: "The entire building is circular and so huge that the circularity cannot be perceived from outside. It is seen as a straight line. The crammed blackboards are taller than a man and they reach up to the gypsum ceiling, whitish or gray." This passage confers fantastic, regressive and sinister resonances to the text. The crammed blackboards that reach up to the ceiling are like partitions designing a labyrinth from which it is very difficult to escape. This detail does not figure in the "Dream in Germany," where, however, similar fantasies are also present. In the Edinburgh dream, the curve and the straight line coincide: that happens as the circle becomes infinite. The fifteenth century philosopher, Nicholas of Cusa, who coined the expression *coincidentia oppositorum* (coincidence of opposites), thought the infinite is the divine place where the unity of opposites is achieved. The oxymoronic Borges dreamed of that infinity where the supreme truth resides, where all contradictions are resolved. Such a desire is revealed in "The Theologians," a story that ends as follows: "It is more correct to say that in Paradise, Aurelian learned that, for the unfathomable divinity, he and John of Pannonia (the orthodox believer and the heretic, the abhorrer and the abhorred, the accuser and the accused) formed one single person."[38]

Yet no sooner does this thought appear in the dream than contradiction occurs once more; there is the image of the gigantic blackboards that tabulate everything. In the first version, Borges wrote "parallel rows of blackboards." Parallels converge in the infinite. With this we come close to the ideas associated with the words *Abraxas* and *Zwitter*. They manifest the Borgean garden of forking paths that can only meet at an infinite point of convergence, or after death. There are words in the "Dream in Germany" that do not appear in the second version: *Aachen, Aaron, Abracadabra, Abraxas*. *Aachen* is a German city that was once the capital of the Germanic Roman Empire. It evokes times of coronations and glory, all in the past. *Aaron,* of the Levitic tribe, was Moses's elder brother. Borges may be betraying here his delight in sounds associated with Spanish *ver* (to see): *Le vi,* Berna, "*verás*" (you will see), Monte<u>video</u>. Another possible association is the inverted reading of Aaron, i.e. Norah (see the analysis of Emma Zunz, in Chapter 6).

Abracadabra was used in the Middle Ages as a magic utterance. Its origin is the Hebrew *abreq ad habrd*, which means "send your ray until death." In the Cabbalah it corresponded to an inverted triangle imagined to have healing properties for some diseases. *Abraxas* is a Gnostic symbolic word that expresses the course of the sun every day of the year. Borges mentions it in "*Una vindicación del falso Baquílides* (A Vindication of Basilides the False)": "The numeric cosmogony of the beginning has degenerated toward the end to numeric magic: 365 levels of heaven, at 7 powers per heaven, require the improbable retention of 2,555 oral amulets—a language that the years reduced to the precious name of the redeemer, which is Kaulakau, and to that of the immobile god, which is *Abraxas*."[39] Serge Hutin says in *Las sociedades secretas* (The Secret Societies) that the gems known by the name of *Abraxas* had a role in Gnostic initiation rites.[40] They had engraved schematic figures, allegorical animals such as the serpent or dragon that bites its own tale (ouroboros), the scarab, the solar disk, etc. Instead of Neverness (in the Edinburgh dream), we find in the "Dream in Germany" the word *Zwitter* with its meaning spelled out by Borges as hermaphrodite. The shy, proper Borges may have substituted Neverness in the second version of the dream. He referred to Neverness in an interview by a Japanese journalist, Mie Uchida, as follows:

> **UCHIDA**: Eternity meaning that everything happens simultaneously has much in common with Shintoist doctrine.
> **BORGES**: I agree. Do you know Bishop Wilkins? He was an English philosopher in the seventeenth century. He invented a very beautiful word. It is equivalent to "eternity," and its origin is not Latin. No one has used it again after Wilkins—"everness." Don't you think it is much better than "eternity," which has been overused and has lost its force. Everness and neverness. Don't you think these two words by themselves make a poem? "Neverness" is a terrible word. To love a woman and have it never realized... Wilkins invented that word, but later poets, out of fear, could not use it. After him, it does not appear in any book. I found it in a dictionary. I have looked it up in all the other dictionaries, including the big Oxford English Dictionary, and could not find it. Could there be any other expression so strong and so concise?[41]

On March 7th, 1980 the poet and playwright Shuji Terayama asked Borges,

> **TERIYAMA**: If all men were about to forget all words and could save only one, which word would you choose?
> **BORGES**: A word that Bishop Wilkins created in the seventeenth century, which no poet has had the courage to use, is a terrible word and replaces "eternity," that is to say, it constantly occurs. That word is "everness." It is not one word but two. The other word is even more terrible, it makes us shudder with terror: "neverness." I don't know how it could be translated into other languages. No one has used it. Those who followed Bishop Wilkins realized that this word canceled everything. I have gathered the courage to pronounce it, but it worries me to think what might happen."[42]

These remarks serve to confirm the interpretation I propose. It is surprising to find the word *Zwitter* (hermaphrodite), after words such as *Abraxas*. Significantly, Gnostic gems with this name carried the engraved image of the *ouroboros*, a serpent or dragon biting its own tail, one of the most ancient magic symbols. It appears in the eleventh century Codex Marcianus with the epigraph "The one, the whole." Jung comments: "He is the hermaphrodite that was in the beginning, that splits into the classical brother-sister duality and is reunited in the *coniunctio*, to appear once again at the end in the radiant form of the *lumen novum*, the stone. He is metallic yet liquid, matter yet spirit, cold yet fiery, poison and yet healing draught—a symbol uniting all opposites).[43]

Even as the *ouroboros*, endogamic marriage closes the circle upon itself, since its nature is hermaphrodite. An androgynous person is entranced by his own image. What seems bisexual is, in fact, unisexual, because the fantasy implied in naming both sexes only pursues the negation of the difference. It is a paradisiac vision originating in early infancy, when the child is fantasized as the mother's penis. Julia Kristeva says: "The androgynous makes a reality of what he imagines his mother to experience; androgyny, a realized fantasy, is the deviation that comes closest to psychosis."[44]

The androgynous is afraid of the words that differentiate, identify, sever. Neopythagoreans conceived divinity as hermaphrodite. In the Cabbalah, Adam Kadmon is the unity of being, a "Primordial Androgyne" consisting of Binah, female passive principle and Hokhmah, a male, active principle of wisdom.[45] In Greek mythology the androgynous

Hermaphroditus was born from the union of Hermes and Aphrodite. There is archaeological evidence of androgynous representations of divinities dating as far back as the seventh millenium B.C.E. Reflecting on the compulsion to repeat returning to a prior state, Freud refers in *Beyond the Pleasure Principle* to the theory that Plato puts in the mouth of Aristophanes in his dialogue, *The Banquet*. In the beginning, humans were androgynous, and every part of their bodies was double: they had four pairs of limbs, two faces, double genitals, etc. Then Zeus decided to divide them by severing them into halves. Ever since, each half yearns to be reunited to the other, the halves hold hands, they desire to be fused into one single being.[46]

Was Borges, the dreamer, traumatically fixated on this bridge? Was this the corner he could never cross but could sublimate and spiritually crystallize? The word *Zwitter* in the first version of the dream denotes the unity that is everything, and he substitutes in the second version Neverness, "that terrible word which [Wilkins realized] cancels everything." This dream speaks about the finite number of perceptions, emotions, thoughts, and human vicissitudes that we will exhaust before we die. So does "Circular Time," written by Borges in 1935.[47] Is destiny memory? "A Dream in Germany" seems to convey in its conclusion the hope that writing will not die with the writer, a hope never made explicit by Borges. When he concludes this dream saying, "all this serves a purpose that we will never understand," does he mean the irreparable fading of ciphers and of all-devouring time—the cruelty of old age?

Edgar Allan Poe may suggest a clue to the dream, as he places the words *Zwitter* and Neverness prominently in "The Purloined Letter." Is the obvious reality (which we fail to perceive) that the dreamer never had the courage to make love to a woman and as a consequence needed to find comfort in loneliness? In a poem quoted in Chapter 9, Borges says, "A woman's name has me in thrall. / A woman's being afflicts my whole body."[48]

Notes

1. Pedro Calderón de la Barca, *La vida es sueño* (*Life Is A Dream*), trans. Roy Campbell, in *Life Is A Dream, and Other Spanish Classics*) ed. Eric Bentley (New York: Theatre Book Publishers, 1959), 223.
2. Jorge Luis Borges, "The Keeper of the Books," *In Praise of Darkness* (A bilingual edition), trans. Norman Thomas di Giovanni (New York: Dutton, 1974), 73.
3. Borges, "Poem about Gifts," *Dreamtigers*, transl. Mildred Boyer and Harold Morland (New York: Dutton, 1964), 55.
4. Borges, *El libro de los sueños* (Buenos Aires: Torres Agüero, 1976).
5. He delivered this lecture, "The Nightmare," in June of 1977. The newspaper *Clarín* carried it the next day (16th June, 1977).
6. Borges, "The Zahir," *Labyrinths: Selected Stories and Other Writings*, trans. Donald A. Yates and James E. Irby (New York: New Directions Publishing, 1964), 164.
7. Borges, *Obras completas 1923-1972* (Buenos Aires: Emecé, 1974), 1022.
8. Sigmund Freud, *Beyond the Pleasure Principle*, SE 18: 20
9. Laplanche, J. and J.B. Pontalis, *Vocabulaire de la psychanalyse* (Paris: P.U.F., 1967).
10. J. E. Gedo Beyond, *Interpretation* (New York: International Universities Press, 1979).
11. C. Hollande et M. Soulé, *"Pour introduire un colloque sur la compulsion de répétition,"* *Revue Française de Psychanalyse* 3 (1970): 373-406.
12. Jones, Ernest, *On the Nightmare* (New York: Liveright 1951).
13. Ibid., 76.
14. Ibid., 85.
15. Cited by J. Delassus, *Les incubes et les succubes* (1987), 34.
16. Richard Burgin, *Conversations with Jorge Luis Borges* (New York, Chicago and San Francisco: Holt, Rinehart and Winston, 1968), 45.
17. Piera Aulagnier, *La violence de l'interprétation* (Paris: P.U.F., 1975), 85-86.
18. Borges, *El libro de los sueños*, 7.
19. María Esther Vázquez, *Borges, imágenes, memorias, diálogos* (Buenos Aires: Monte Avila, 1977).
20. Borges, *Los conjurados* (Buenos Aires: Alianza, 1985) 67.
21. The etymology of Teiresias (cf. the Greek verb *tereo*) points to one who watches, observes.
22. Emir Rodríguez Monegal, *"Una biografía literaria,"* *El Periodista,* 12-18 June 1987, 144, writes: "Borges confided to several friends that his Father once took him to one of those obliging Geneva girls whose clients tend to be foreigners, lonely men or eager youths. Georgie played his role so speedily that the intensity of the orgasm overwhelmed him. What the French call "little death" came for

him too close to real death. After that, Georgie was afraid of sexual intercourse. There is another facet to this incident, one that could have had more complicated consequences. Being initiated into sex by his father, Georgie must have assumed that the Geneva girl was giving him the same services; sharing the same woman with his Father was something that disturbed ingrained taboos."

23. Peter Blos, *On Adolescence: A Psychoanalytic Interpretation* (New York: Free Press of Glencoe: 1962).

24. Borges, *Selected Poems 1923-1967*, trans. Richard Wilbur, ed. Norman Thomas di Giovanni (New York: Delacorte/Seymour Lawrence, 1972), 187.

25. Borges, "*Al hijo*," "*El otro, el mismo*," *Obras Completas*, 948.

26. Borges, *Dr Brodie's Report*, 113-114.

27. Another passage of *Dr Brodie's Report* confirms what Jones points out as the incest fantasies underpinning nightmares: "In another Castle lives the queen, who is not permitted to see her king. During my sojourn, this lady was kind enough to receive me; she was smiling, young, and, insofar as her race allowed, graceful. Bracelets of metalwork and of ivory and necklaces of teeth adorned her nakedness. She inspected me, sniffed me, and, after touching me with a finger, ended by offering herself to me in the presence of all her retinue. My habit [my cloth] and my habits [my ethics], however, forbade me that honor, which commonly she grants only to the witch doctors and to the slave hunters, for the most part Muslims, whose caravans journey across the kingdom. Twice or thrice she sank a gold pin into my flesh; such prickings being tokens of royal favor, the number of Yahoos are more than a few who stick themselves with pins to encourage the belief that the queen herself pricked them." Ibid. ,114. [Slightly modified to preserve Borges's pun (habit/habits). Translator's note.]

28. Borges, "Biografía de Tadeo Isidoro Cruz," *Obras completas*, 561.

29. Borges, *Labyrinths*, 138.

30. Borges, "*Correr o ser*," "*La cifra*," *Obra poética*, (Buenos Aires: Emecé 1977), 604.

31. Sophocles, *Ajax*, trans. John Moore (Chicago: University of Chicago Press, 1957), 430-31.

32. Borges., "*Otras inquisiciones*", *Obras completas*, Buenos Aires: Emecé 1974), 750.

33. Sorrentino, Fernando, *Siete conversaciones con Borges* (Seven Conversations with Borges) (Buenos Aires: Pardo 1964), 13.

34. Freud, "Interpretation of Dreams," SE 4: 334; 5, 484.

35. Thomas Mann, *Joseph and His Brothers*, transl. of *Joseph und seine Brüder,* Vienna 1936 (New York: A.A.Knopf, 1948).

36. Hinojosa, Armando, "*Psicoanálisis de la historia de José*," *Revista de Psicoanálisis, Psiquiatría y Psicología* 3 (Mexico: Fondo de Cultura Económica 1966), 83.

37. Borges, *Obras completas*, 418.

38. Borges, *Labyrinths*, 126.

39. Borges, "A Vindication of Basilides the False," *Borges: A Reader*, ed. Emir Rodríguez Monegal and Alastair Reid (New York: Dutton, 1981), 26.
40. Serge Hutin, *Las sociedades secretas* (Buenos Aires: Eudeba Cuaderno 47, 1984), 19.
41. Guillermo Gasio (ed.), *Borges en Japón* (Buenos Aires: Eudeba 1988), 80
42. Ibid., 112.
43. Carl G. Jung, *Psychology and Alchemy* (New York: Princeton U. P., 1968), 293, 295.
44. Julia Kristeva, *Historias de amor* (Mexico: Siglo 21, 1987), 60.
45. Beatriz Borovich, *La cábala*, (Buenos Aires: Lumen, 1990), 52.
46. Freud, "Beyond the Pleasure Principle," SE 18: 57-58.
47. Borges, *"El tiempo circular," "Historia de la eternidad," Obras completas*, 393.
48. Borges, *"El amenazado* (The Threatened One)," *The Gold*, 22-23.

Chapter 11

Borges, Author of *Hamlet*: Pathology of the Ideal

> There is always a feeling of triumph when something in the Ego coincides with the Ego Ideal, and the sense of guilt (as well as the sense of inferiority) can also be understood an an expression of tension between the Ego and the Ego Ideal.
>
> Sigmund Freud[1]

Having analyzed in Chapter 2 particular aspects of enumerations, I begin here by citing once again Umberto Eco on the subject: "There is nothing more wonderful than enumerations, which are an admirable instrument for the most perfect hypotyposes."[2] In Borges's autobiographical poems and stories, one often finds enumerations.

> I cannot execute a new action,
> I weave, weave again the same fable.
> Repeat a repeated hendecasyllable,
> Say what others said to me,
> Feel the same things at the same
> Time of day or of abstract night.
> Every night the same nightmare,
> Every night the labyrinth's rigor.
> I am the fatigue of an immobile mirror
> Or dust in a museum.[2]

The question that constantly haunts Borges is: Who am I? His many answers are both similar and different. He says in "The Thing I am":

> I have forgotten my name. I am neither Borges
> (Borges died in La Verde, before the bullets)
> Nor Acevedo, dreaming up a battle,
> Nor my father, bent over a book,
> Nor Haslam deciphering the verses
> Of the Gospel far from Northumberland
> Nor Suárez of the spear-charge.
> I am just the shadow cast by
> Those intimate intrincate shades,
> I am their memory, yet I am the other.
> . . . .
> I am the one who knows he is nothing but an echo.[3]

In "Yesterday" we read:

> I am the false memory of an engraving
> In the room which my eyes
> Now dimmed saw clearly:
> The Horserider, Death, and the Devil.
> I am that other who looks to the desert.
> I am a mirror, an echo. The epitaph.[4]

The conclusion of "*El Hacedor* (The Maker)" is striking:

> Echoes, silt, sand, lichen, and dreams.
> Nothing am I but those images
> Shuffled by chance and named by tedium.
> With them, blind and broken as I am,
> I must forge the incorruptible verse
> And (it is my duty) save myself.[5]

These lines suggest to Willy Baranger[6] something like the "oceanic sentiment" that Freud, somewhat skeptically, mentions in a reply to Romain Rolland who related it to religious belief or belief in "eternity."[7] Such "oceanic sentiment" belongs to a very early stage of Ego development which is practically a pleasure Ego, and which will after its first frustrations project outwards whatever is menacing and painful. In the adult, the "oceanic sentiment" would aspire to reestablish an unrestricted narcissism. For Freud, this early infantile helplessness is at the source of religious attitudes, mystic states, and states of trance and ecstasy. Dealing with the "oceanic," we approach the problems of autism. When the individuation process proves to be difficult to effect, autistic cores tend to reestablish the union with the object, but only regressively. Describing infantile autism, Leo Kanner points out two pathognomic traits: extreme isolation and an obsessive insistence upon identity.[8]

Guy Rosolato states, elaborating on Freud's theories, "The pleasure proper to art is closely related to what Freud called the oceanic sentiment. It is related, also, to the mystic enterprise, its subjectivity and its ineffability."[9] As he creates fascinating dreams and hallucinations, Borges tries consciously and systematically to achieve the oceanic through his themes and chosen rhetorical forms (see Chapter 2).

The images in "The Maker" take us from the oceanic to the sinister: "*resaca, arena, liquen* (silt, sand, lichen)." They call up unfamiliar images of the unreal, the untouchable, the despicable. They give evidence not only of suffering but also of struggle, Borges's struggle to rescue himself, "though blind and broken," as a subject. In his "Poem about Gifts," Borges appears a king amid echoes and dreams, amid "resaca", silt on the shore, and "gelatinous and parasitical lichen," amid what merely reflects, what is dependent and despicable:

> An old Greek story tells how some king died
> Of hunger and thirst, though proffered spring waters and fruits.

Why such a derogatory self-image, such low self-esteem? Is this the expression of a self-deprecatory delirium, an illusion of melancholic insignificance? Is it the product of identification conflicts between the Ego and the Ideal?

Heritage and Destiny

Freud inquires into some of the vicissitudes of the structuring of an Ego in "Introduction to Narcissism": "If we look at the attitude of affectionate parents towards their children, we have to recognize that it is a revival and reproduction of their own narcissism, which they have long since abandoned."[10]

Jorge Francisco Isidoro Luis Borges was, from the moment he was born, linked to the gleaming necklace of names tying him to two genealogical trees. He was called Jorge for his father (and received the nickname Georgie to avoid confusion); Francisco, for his paternal grandfather, a colonel; Isidoro, for his maternal grandfather, a colonel, too; and Luis, for his paternal uncle, a doctor of jurisprudence.

> Beyond the name there lies what has no name;
> Today I have felt its shadow stir the aim
> Of this blue needle, light and keen, whose sweep
> . . . .
> Homes to the utmost of the sea its love,
> Suggestive of a watch in dreams, or of
> Some bird, perhaps, who shifts a bit in sleep.[11]

We understand Borges when he says that he is subjected to the discord of two lineages: he was linked to the Borgeses by intelligence, to the Acevedos by courage. "The father has transmited to the son his unfulfilled desire, and this desire, fascinating the son, led him to an existence also imaginary," says Didier Anzieu.[12] The narcissistic mirror identification of Georgie with Father Jorge is compounded by the painful heritage of their nearblindness. Yet the blindness was not the determining factor. Borges was the last descendant in a lineage where fathers bequeathed to their sons a script, a destiny.

María Esther Vázquez reports that Borges said: "When I was still only a boy I felt that my destiny was literary. My father had always longed to be a writer and he was a writer to a certain extent, and because he had wanted to be a writer, it was more or less assumed that I had to fulfill that destiny."[13]

Borges's history, it seems, starts from this pact with his father. "Borges must write for his father and with his name. Heritage and destiny involve a promise, or rather, a debt."[14] Borges is a man of paradoxes and moves amid the paradoxes of family myth, rooted, on the one hand, in the heraldic memory of conservative Argentine aristocracy, and, on the other, in world literature, especially the English. His two lineages used two languages, Spanish and English. Is it this doubly imagined existence in the form of a dream of the father and a dream of the mother, a dream of both paternal and maternal forebears, that one day disturbs him as an echo—as a plurality of echoes—and perhaps as "*resaca, arena, liquen, sueños* (silt, sand, lichen, dreams)"? He is the object of the desire of others, a subjected subject painfully chained to a destiny.

"Words, displaced and mutilated words, words of others, were the poor pittance left him by the hours and the centuries."[15]

An Echo of Other Echoes

In the prologue to "The Other, The Self," Borges wrote: "What is strange and what I cannot fully understand is that my second versions, like dimmed and involuntary echoes, are usually inferior to the first." [16] This is actually true for the dream of the tiger in *Dreamtigers* (see Chapter 1). He says that when childhood passed so did his fascination with tigers, yet they were still present in his dreams:

> At that submerged or chaotic level they keep prevailing. And so, as I sleep, some dream beguiles me, and suddenly I know I am dreaming. Then I think: This is a dream, a pure diversion of my will; and now that I have unlimited power, I am going to cause a tiger.
> Oh, incompetence! Never can my dreams engender the wild beast I long for. The tiger indeed appears, but stuffed or flimsy, or with impure variations of shape, or of an implausible size, or all too fleeting, or with a touch of the dog or the bird.[17]

Borges feels he is an echo. And everything that is his would seem to become in turn an echo, progressively deteriorating. An echo of echoes, his very memories and desires will fade away. "Resaca," mud that rivers deposit on the shore and sand, eroded rock that runs through the fingers. The deposit will form deserts, which are a symbolic destiny of the destruction of the body for the salvation of the soul. As lichen is a symbiotic union of algae and fungus, a parasitic dweller on walls and trees, slippery, fleeting—so are dreams. Could it be said more beautifully? In "The Circular Ruins" we read:

> Not to be a man, to be a projection of another man's dreams—what an incomparable humiliation, what madness! Any father is interested in the sons he has procreated (or permitted) out of the mere confusion of happiness; it was natural that the wizard should fear for the future of that son whom he had thought out entrail by entrail, feature by feature, in a thousand and one secret nights.[18]

"Yesterdays" also speaks of being and not being, being just "the servitude of two sunsets." Is this the source of his self-deprecation?

> I am and I am not my real stock.
> It is my father's voice I still hear.
> . . . .
> I am what philosophers have told me.

> Chance or destiny, those two names
> Of some secret we do not know.
> . . . .
> I am the hollow solitary dream
> Where I lose myself or try to,
> The servitude of two sunsets.
> . . . .
> I am nothing else but those images
> Sorted by chance and named by tedium.
> . . . .
> With them, though blind and broken,
> I am to work the incorruptible verse.
> And (it is my duty) save myself.[19]

Notwithstanding the disorientation of chance, notwithstanding his "not being," Borges expresses his determination to save himself. For Nietzsche an animal, a species, an individual that lose their instincts, and thus choose what is harmful to themselves are corrupted. Borges's incorruptible poem would be one not alienated from the life instincts. It would be a poem he could sense as his own, coming from him alone, not dictated by other voices, by the memory of other poets, by the desire of his parents. He adds "it is my duty" in parentheses, as if another part of himself were admonishing him. He is determined to save himself, always, and only, through his poetry.

Borges and Melanie Klein

For Didier Anzieu, Borges may be better understood from a Kleinian psychoanalytic approach. He states, "The genius of Borges allowed him to discover, at the same time as Melanie Klein and independently from her, similar ideas; to fashion a new form of literature which is both an imaginary realization and a symbolic representation of some of her findings."[20] I concur with Anzieu in that the Kleinian approach yields a better understanding of the profile of so-called schizoid personalities many of whose characteristics I find in Borges. As we know, the emotional life of these individuals is controlled by an intense fear of suffering narcissistic wounds. For this reason, they block their ability to love. Object relations are felt as imprisoning and stifling, because the object has been highly idealized. Actually, because of dissociating mechanisms, the internal world of a schizoid individual is filled with figures either extremely good or extremely bad. They exhibit an exaggerated persistence of the early oral situation, with long-term effects. Among these, I mention only the particularly incorporative relationship and the attitude where the fear of giving prevails so that self-exhibition replaces real giving.

These characteristics have special meaning for the states of plenitude and emptiness (Borges's "Everything and Nothing"). Giving becomes equivalent to draining oneself of worth and lessening one's self-esteem. "When they [schizoid personalities] give, they feel impoverished, because they do it at the expense of their internal world."[21] For instance, a schizoid woman giving birth does not experience the gaining of a child but rather the losing of a content, with the consequent feeling of emptiness. Something similar occurs to the artist who pretends to devalue his creation to mitigate the feeling of impoverishment. Falling in love is for a schizoid personality an experience of persecution, an assault on his or her identity, sometimes accompanied by the notion of being influenced and controlled by the significant other with whom the schizoid individual feels fused. Ideas and thoughts, overvalued and highly libidinized, are substitutes that compensate for emotional problems.

Borges's exceptional memory and erudition might be said to have ingested, devoured wisdom. Paradoxically, memory motivated in him the feeling of an empty Ego, and the image of himself as a plagiarist, as he once confessed, one who possesses only because he has deprived others. He felt himself an echo of other echoes, a memory of other memories, as if held in the possession of the memory of others. Feelings of futility, typical of schizoids, are apparent in Borges, as are their unconscious counterparts: fantasies of having been despoiled by the object who first penetrates the intimacy of the subject and then leaves, taking away all that is worthy.

In the story "Everything and Nothing,"[22] a character (who turns out to be Shakespeare) feels he is nobody, that he is *a dream dreamt by no one*. He is like a dream without desire. Hence his desperate search for an identity. After believing at first that all people were like him,"the astonishment of a friend to whom he had begun to speak of this emptiness showed him his error and made him feel always that an individual should not differ in outward appearance." What does it mean that an individual should not differ "from the species"?[23] Did this character feel that he was different, knowing that he must be like the others? This problem is inherent in man's eternal conflict between himself and the others, the struggle between his need for similarity and his desire for difference, or, as in this story, between the evidence that he is different and his desire to be similar. Such a conflict haunted Borges ever since he was a young boy.

> Once he thought that in books he would find a cure for his ill and thus he learned the small Latin and less Greek a contemporary would speak of; later he considered that what he sought might well be found in an elemental rite of humanity, and let himself be initiated by Anne Hathaway one long June afternoon.

Yet this experience neither soothed his pain nor gave an answer to his search. Then he decided to become an actor, someone

> ... who on a stage plays at being another before a gathering of people who play at taking him for that other person. His histrionic tasks brought him a singular satisfaction, perhaps the first he had ever known; but once the last verse had been acclaimed and the last dead man withdrawn from the stage, the hated flavor of unreality returned to him. He ceased to be Ferrex or Tamerlane[23] and became no one again. Thus hounded, he took to imagining other heroes and other tragic fables. And so, while his flesh fulfilled its destiny as flesh in the taverns and brothels of London, the soul that inhabited him was Caesar, who disregards the augur's admonition, and Juliet, who abhors the lark, and Macbeth, who converses on the plain with the witches who are also Fates.[25] No one has ever been so many men as this man, who like the Egyptian Proteus could exhaust all the guises of reality. At times he would leave a confession hidden away in some corner of his work, certain that it would not be deciphered; Richard affirms that in his person he plays the part of many and Iago claims with curious words 'I am not what I am.' The fundamental identity of existing, dreaming and acting inspired famous passages of his.

Here Borges seems to stand between warrior-like omnipotence, cruel and tyrannic, and impotence; between everything and nothing. "Shakespeare," finally in the presence of God, says: "I who have been so many men in vain want to be one and myself." God comforts him saying, "Neither am I anyone; I have dreamt the world as you dreamt your work, my Shakespeare, and among the forms in my dream are you, who like myself are many and no one."

It needs to be emphasized that Borges is contrasting "one" and "I," not "many" and "no one," nor "everything" and "nothing." Does being everything for his parents mean he is nothing for himself? Everything and nothing is equivalent to many and no one. Borges's need to be someone different is apparent, but, one wonders, different for whom? Considering this sad reality, does he find comfort in the thought that God is not himself either?

I have referred above to the poem with the paradoxical title "*El hacedor* (The Maker)"[26]

> I who have in vain been so many men
> Wish to be one and myself.[27]

Projective identification is a complex process in which the unconscious "if I were the other" becomes "I am the other." Borges-Shakespeare locates himself in the other and, for this reason, suffers pain and inclines to conflicts that create anxiety, guilt, fear, and difficult relationships with many people. Melanie Klein studied two literary works, *The Portrait of Dorian Gray* by Oscar Wilde, and Julien Green's *If I Were You*. She explains that the mechanisms involved in cleavage are produced by greed and envy.[28] Bion writes, "I expect to show also that the mechanism of cleavage is in place to control the patient's greed.... This mechanism is the result of a project that may be verbally expressed as the intention of being as many persons as possible in order to enter into as many places as possible and obtain as much as possible, for the longest possible duration—actually forever."[29]

I Offer Shakespeare's Memory for Sale

I find an illustration of greed, memory, and a tortured search for personal identity in a story that was also its author's nightmare, "Shakespeare's Memory."

> I still possess two memories, mine, which is personal, and the memory of that Shakespeare which I am. I should rather say that two memories possess me. In a certain zone they are fused. I do not know in which century I should place a certain woman's face. In the first state of the adventure I felt the bliss of being Shakespeare; in the last one, I feel oppression and terror. First the two memories were not confluent; as time elapsed, Shakespeare's great river threatened, nearly flooded, my modest body of water. I fearfully realized that I was forgetting my parents' language. Because personal identity is based upon memory, I feared for my sanity. My friends came to see me, and I was surprised when I saw that they sensed I was in hell. I ceased understanding the

everyday things around me. One morning I would get lost among great shapes of iron, metal, and crystal. It took me an instant (which may have seemed infinite) to going through the turnstiles in the Bremen station. As the years go by, every man is compelled to carry the growing burden of his memory. Two were weighing me down, sometimes blending my own memory and the memory of the other, which was incommunicable.

I have forgotten the date when I decided to liberate myself. Would you like to have Shakespeare's memory? I know that what I am offering you is burdensome. Paradoxically, I felt both the nostalgia of the book I should have written but was barred from writing and the fear that the host, the specter, would never leave me.

That method and other methods were useless. Everything led me to Shakespeare.30

"Shakespeare's memory" is a rich signifier for Borges: possessing Shakespeare's memory means being Shakespeare, and this is an oneiric desire that serves as basis for the story. This memory invades, floods, and confuses him, because it is connected with his yearning for a "heroic identification" which indeed floods his Ego. Edmundo Gómez Mango calls this process "literary melancholy." "Tradition, the classical authors—deceased—, books, become the Ideal of the Ego. In its presence, the writer's Ego fades away."31

Ideal Ego and Ego-Ideal

The ideal of narcissistic omnipotence, of being that *other* hero or famous writer, represents the Ideal Ego that Freud studies in his *Introduction to Narcissism*, where he says, "the subject's narcissism makes its appearance displaced onto this new Ideal Ego, who, like the infantile Ego, finds itself possessed of every perfection that is of value."32 Other authors have further developed Freud's, ideas proposing a conceptual differentiation between Ideal Ego and Ego-Ideal. Whereas for Nunberg the Ideal Ego is simply the union of Ego and Id, D. Lagache states that the Ideal Ego implies something else that is fundamental, a "primary identification with that other person invested with omnipotence, that is to say, the mother."33 Thus the Ideal Ego becomes the basis of what he describes as "heroic identification" with exceptional and prestigious characters.

This Ideal Ego of primary identification, invested with the idealized apparel of the mother, actually involves a lack. It characteristically includes strong dependence from the object, (which becomes indispensable) and operates using absolute categories such as being and not-being, presence and absence, everything and nothing, good and evil. There is also insufficient discrimination between being and having, self and non-self.

Borges has superbly expressed this lack of discrimination in "The Circular Ruins" and in "Tlön, Uqbar, Orbis Tertius," where we read in a footnote, "All men, in the climactic instant of coitus, are the same man. All men who repeat one line of Shakespeare are William Shakespeare."[34] The conclusion that follows is that if repeating is being, differences are erased and creative paternity is canceled. "Narcissism," says André Green, "sustains the illusion of an "An-Oedipus" (not an "Anti-Oedipus" but a "Non-Oedipus") because it knows only the "myself-self." Even as God, the "myself-self" feels self-engendered, asexual."[35]

Jacques Lacan makes this distinction between the Ideal Ego and the Ego-Ideal: "One is on the imaginary level and originates in the stage of the mirror; the other on the symbolic level, since the demands of the Ego-Ideal are located in the totality of the demands of the law."[36] That is to say, with the ability to symbolize, in the Oedipal situation, the Ego-Ideal apears. It serves as a model, a condition to which the human being must conform. Yet its validity will depend on whether the subject has progressed from a totalizing absolute discourse ("everything or nothing") to a discriminating language.

Freud considers Ego-Ideal and Superego still as synonyms in *Ego and Id*. Only in 1932, in *New Introductory Lectures on Psycho-Analysis* does he make a distinction between the two. The Superego involves three functions: "self-observation, moral conscience and the function of an ideal."[37] In other words, feelings of guilt relate to the Superego's moral conscience, but feelings of inferiority have to do with the Ego-Ideal.

Borges concludes a poem with the title "Matthew XXV: 30" as follows:

> In vain have oceans been squandered on you, in vain
> The sun, wonderfully seen through Whitman's eyes.
> You have used up the years and they have used up you,
> And still, and still, you have not written the poem.[38]

For "the poem" I understand the absolute, the unique, the unsurpassable poem. Matthew XXV: 30 reads: "And cast ye the unprofitable servant into outer darkness: there shall be weeping and gnashing of teeth." These three factors: Ideal Ego, Ego-Ideal, and

Superego, seem in Borges to have converged to impose upon him conditions that made libidinal satisfaction difficult and to cast a shadow on his self-esteem, burdening him with infinite guilt.

Self-Identity

As we know, self-identity ("*Selbstgefühl*") is augmented by new shoots of primary infantile narcissism, by every remainder of the primitive feeling of omnipotence corroborated by experience (namely, the Ego-Ideal), and by sexual gratification from the object of love. It follows that self-identity essentially depends upon narcissistic libido. Borges might have the highest self-image, if it related only to the intellect and to literary success. Yet this does not happen, because he has not written yet *the poem*.

Gabriela Massuh has studied "The Approach to al-Mu'tasim," "The Zahir," "The Aleph," "Undr," and other stories where the search for the word as an absolute, as the highest synthesis of perfection, reaches obssessive levels. The word is One and Everything, and it brings Borges, in his endeavor to verbalize the experience of divinity, close to the mystics. Are we in the presence of word as fetish? It is possible. The search for unity in the word leads him to an obssessive megalomania which I see as one of his defenses against anxieties of depression and fragmentation. He writes in "Undr":

> In the course of time I have been many men; it was a whirlwind, a long dream, but all the while the main thing was the Word. From time to time I disbelieved in it. I kept telling myself that to renounce the beautiful game of combining beautiful words was senseless, and that there was no reason to search for a single, and perhaps imaginary, word. Such reasoning was vain.[39]

In this quotation, the compulsion to repeat is apparent, ranging from the absolute to the demonic, even to the neurosis of destiny. In the prologue to the Spanish edition of "Dr. Brodie's Report" Borges writes, "A few plots have pestered me all along; I am definitely monotonous." "Beyond the pleasure principle," he returns in search of someone who will liberate him from an alienating desire. He is like Asterion in his labyrinth. The cleavage of the Ego retains an Ideal Ego fixed at the level of primary identification, and he is compelled to a painful repetition of a family myth from which he cannot free himself. Freud wrote, "The realization of impotence, of one's own inability to love, in consequence of mental or physical disorder, has an exceedingly lowering effect upon self regard."[40] Borges illustrates this statement by Freud in "The Sect of the Phoenix" where "the Secret" is sexual intercourse: "A kind of sacred horror prevents some faithful believers from performing this very simple rite; the others despise them, but they despise themselves even more."[41]

The greatest lack of Borges is the body and its shadow, which is love. Did the mother not know how, or was she unable to cathexize, eroticize, narcissize her body?[42] Is this the reason for the precocious emergence of disappointment and hatred?

Melancholy Depression

Since Freud wrote *Mourning and Melancholia*, much more has been written attempting to distinguish the two patterns. Both typically involve a deeply painful state of mind, a lack of interest in the outside world, the loss of the ability to love, and the inhibition of numerous functions.[43]

In Spanish, the word, "duelo" has two different connotations: "grief" and "duel." I have pointed to both connotations as positively and negatively revealed in the Borgean narrative. (See the chapter on "Borges, The Man at The Pink Streetcorner" and "The Unnamable.") Both may apply simultaneously to the ambiguous Spanish term, "duelo." There is in the normal process of grief—in addition to the pain suffered because of the loss of object and parts of the Ego—a "struggle" to disconnect oneself from persecutory aspects and assimilate the benevolent aspects of the lost object. Freud emphasized that whereas, in normal grief, loss is conscious and produces the feeling that the world has been left "impoverished, empty"; in melancholy the object lost seems to be an unconscious loss which is introjected into the Ego, leaving the Ego feeling impoverished and empty.

André Green states, "The narcissist character is more independent but more vulnerable. While the Ego is disappointed in front of the Ego-Ideal that becomes its object, the Ideal Ego loses its fragile equilibrium. Two outlets are available: depression, due to disappointment in front of the object ... or fragmentation."[44]

In melancholy depression, the presence of early narcissistic injuries becomes manifest and therefore an oral mechanism is revealed which, biting its own tail like the *ouroboros*, bespeaks the refraction of aggression onto the subject. In Borges, self-denigration results from narcissistic, melancholy subjection, and is expressed in a typically schizoid code. Borges does not openly complain about or blame his parents. He regrets not having satisfied them in their idealized desires. and so he writes the eloquent sonnet entitled "Remorse."

> I have committed the worst sin
> A man may commit: I have not been happy.
> Let glaciers of oblivion mercilessly
> Drag me away in destruction.
> I have betrayed them. I have not been happy.
> My parents brought me into this world
> For life's play, full of risk and beauty..
> For earth, water, air, fire. Their young aim
> Was not fulfilled. My mind stubbornly
> Stuck to the symmetrical
> Enterprises of art, weaving nothing into nothing.
> They gave me courage, and I was not bold.
> The shadow does not leave me, the shadow
> Of having always been unhappy, always at my side.[45]

Franz Kafka, another tortured soul with his own labyrinths, writes:

> I am my parents' offspring, I am bound to them and to my brothers by our bloodline... deep down I respect them more than I think I do. Some times I also pursue them with hatred... And if my father, on the one hand, and my mother on the other, have also destroyed (almost inevitably) my will, then I also want them to deserve what they have done. They have cheated me, and yet I cannot rebel, without losing my mind, against the law of nature; thence more hatred, and only hatred...[46]

How close is this passionate reproach from Borges's distressed regret? Are these two ways of expressing the same sentiment?

Notes

1. Sigmund Freud, "Group Psychology and the Analysis of the Ego," SE 21: 131.
2. Umberto Eco, *The Name of the Rose* (*Il nome della rosa*), trans. William Weaver (New York: Harcourt Brace Jovanovich, 1983).
3. Borges, "Ecclesiastes 1.9," "La Cifra," *Obra poética* (Buenos Aires: Emecé, 1981), 569.
4. Borges, "The Thing I am," "*Historia de la noche*," ibid., 543. Several poems on these themes have English titles in the original.
5. Borges, "Yesterdays," "*La Cifra*," ibid., 585.
6. Willy Baranger in a personal communication to the author.
7. Freud, "Civilization and Its Discontents," SE 21: 64-65.
8. Leo Kanner, *Psiquiatría infantil* (Buenos Aires: Paidós, 1966), 533.
9. Guy Rosolato, "*Présente mystique,*" Nouvelle Revue de Psychanalyse 22 (Paris: Gallimard 1980): 22. Published in Spanish as "*Presentación de la mística*," *Revista de Psicoanálisis* 40 (1983): 945-1002.
10. Freud, "On Narcissism: An Introduction" SE 14: 90-91.
11. Borges, "Compass," *Selected Poems 1923-1967*, ed. Norman Thomas di Giovanni, transl. Richard Wilbur (New York: Delacorte/Seymour Lawrence, 1972), 97.
12. Didier Anzieu., "*Le corps et le code dans les contes de J.L. Borges,*" *Nouvelle Revue de Psychanalyse* 3 (1971): 192.
13. María Esther Vázquez, *Borges, imágenes, memorias, diálogos* (Buenos Aires: Monte Ávila, 1977).
14. Ricardo Piglia, *Ideología y ficción en Borges*, Colección Capítulo (Buenos Aires: Centro Editor de América Latina, 1981).
15. Borges, "The Immortal", transl. J. E. Irby, *Labyrinths: Selected Stories and Other Writings*, trans. Donald A. Yates and James E. Irby (New York: New Directions Publishing, 1964), 118.
16. Borges, *Obras completas*, 857.
17. Borges, "Dreamtigers," *Dreamtigers*, 24.
18. Borges, "The Circular Ruins," *Ficciones*, ed. Anthony Kerrigan (New York: Grove Press,1962), 62.
19. Borges, "Yesterdays," "La cifra," *Obra poética*, 587.
20. Anzieu, "*Le corps et le code,*" 203.
21. Wilfred R. Fairbairn, *Estudio psicoanalítico de la personalidad* (Buenos Aires: Hormé, 1962), 26.
22. This is the original English title of this piece by Borges. The citations that follow are from: Borges, "Everything and Nothing," transl. J. E. Irby, *Labyrinths*, 248-49. An earlier collaborative paper by the author on this story was read at the XIIIth Latin American Psychoanalytic Congress, Rio de Janeiro, 1980: Woscoboinik-Kancyper, "*Aproximación psicoanalítica a la obra de Borges.*"

23. For Otto Rank (*Don Juan et le double,* Paris: Payot, 1973) the double indicates "the eternal conflict of man with himself and with the others, the struggle between his need for resemblance and his desire of difference. On account of this conflict Borges toys with the creation of a spiritual double that will ensure the perpetuation of the self, since mortality implies the cancellation of the physical double. One of the numerous and diverse interpretations of the myth of Narcissus is that of Enrique Pichon-Rivière, who believes that the image of the "double" represents the mother who conceived her son, Narcissus, in the water of a stream. The double metamorphosis of Echo and Narcissus would in turn be the expression of guilty feelings and incest's punishment. Cited by David Liberman, "*Autismo transferencial,*" *Revista de Psicoanálisis* 15, 4 (1958).

24. Tamerlane was a ruler of the Tartars who in the fourteenth century subdued Persia and India and challenged the Turks and the Egyptians. In his 1972 poem, "Tamerlan," *El oro de los tigres* (*Gold of The Tigers*), *Obras completas,* 1083-84, Borges addresses an imaginary Tamerlane who "had read, at the end of the nineteenth century, Marlowe and historical treatises."

25. Does Borges think that brothels are the places where "the destiny of the body" is accomplished?

26. Borges, "*El Hacedor,* (The Maker)."

27. A Presocratic philosopher, Parmenides, considered "the One" or primordial unity" as a property of everything that is, of the universe as a whole. The Parmenidean doctrine of Truth is based upon his concept of the One. What is cannot be multiple because the One is opposite to the Multiple, which is the realm of illusion. The One is pure identity, pure simplicity, and pure uniformity. For Plato what matters is "not that a being be a being but that it be One;
signifies the union of human nature with the Divine Verb.

While some see the One as meaning "everything and nothing," others dispute that statement because speaking of the One as this or that entails a metaphor. Speculations on the One are based upon a concept of unity either as identity or as harmony. For Hegel the One is fundamental, since it is the point of convergence and conciliation of the opposites.

28. Melanie Klein, "*Sobre la identificación* (On Identification)", *Nuevas Direcciones en Psicoanálisis* (Buenos Aires: Hormé, 1964).

29. Wilfred Bion, "*Le langage et le schizophrène,*" *Psychanalyse et Langage* (Paris: Dunod, 1977), 199.

30. Borges awoke from a dream saying, "I Offer Shakespeare's Memory for Sale." Cited from Antonio Carrizo, *Borges el memorioso* (*Borges The Memorious*) (Buenos Aires: Tierra Firme, 1982*).*

31. Edmundo Gómez Mango, "*Borges et la mélancolie littéraire,*" *Nouvelle Revue de Psychoanalyse* 32 (1985), 155.

32. Freud, "On Narcissism," SE 14: 94.

33. D. Lagache, *La psychanalyse et la structure de la personnalité* (Paris: P.U.F., 1958).

34. Borges, "Tlön, Uqbar, Orbis Tertius," trans. Alastair Reed, *Ficciones*, 27.
35. André Green, "*L'angoisse et le narcissisme*," *Revue Française de Psychanalyse* 43 (1979): 83.
36. Jacques Lacan, *Le séminaire. Livre I. Les écrits techniques de Freud* (Paris: Éd. du Seuil, 975), 154.
37. Freud, *New Introductory Lectures on Psycho-Analysis*, SE 22
38. Borges, *Selected Poems*, transl. Alistair Reid, 93.
39. Borges, "Undr," *The Book of Sand*, trans. Norman Thomas di Giovanni an ox, but one ox." (New York: Delacorte/Seymour Lawrence, 1972), 81
40. Freud, "On Narcissism: An Introduction," SE 14: 98.
41. Borges, Jorge Luis, "The Sect of the Phoenix," *Ficciones*, 165.
42. Piera Aulagnier said in a lecture delivered at the Asociación Psicoanalítica Argentina (Buenos Aires, 2 April 1983): "The relationship of the subject with his body is the matrix that leads him to confront reality."
43. Freud, "Mourning and Melancholia," SE 14: 237-258.
44. André Green, "*L'angoisse*," 56-57.
45. Borges, "Remorse," in "*La moneda de hierro* (The Iron Coin), *Obra Poética* (Buenos Aires: Emecé 1987), 486.
46. Franz Kafka, "Journal," *Complete Works* (1973) vol. 1:1125-1127.

Chapter 12

Circular Time: Another Borgean Tautology

The notion of cyclic time is closely related to the space of narcissistic circularity in *"El tiempo circular,"* where Borges says, "... in the world of Heraclitus, which is engendered by fire and which the fire devours cyclically..."[1] Thus Borges expresses his preoccupation with the notion of a time that both generates and devours. In the same essay, he writes, quotation Ten years later, however, in *"Nueva refutación del tiempo* (A New Refutation of Time)" he avows that "In the course of a life dedicated to letters and (at times) to metaphysical perplexity, I have glimpsed or foreseen a refutation of time, in which I myself do not believe, but which regularly visits me at night and in the weary twilight with the illusory force of an axiom." [2] Here is a game of negations played by a hermit in silent isolation.

The representation of time, supported in the beginning of life by the biological cycle of corporal needs, satisfied by the mother, is gradually acquired in the course of the child's psychological development. Time follows along in the shaping of a vital space and so it is marked, lost, and recovered in the critical junctures of presence-absence of the first, indispensable object. It is precisely in those moments of absence that hallucinatory gratifications are increased, that what is forever present, immobile, "immortal," is manifested in a negation of time. The vicissitudes of the growing process and especially the relationships with the father gradually shape a resolution of the mirror situation and make feasible waiting, delaying, and trusting.

The child enters into chronological time as he accepts the double Oedipal taboo. In an adequate process of maturation, the past, present, and future of time become meaningful to the degree that differences are recognized, that frustration and grief are elaborated to deal with all that has been lost because it was not achieved or because it is not such as the One, or the Ideal, desired. Finally, an acceptance of the irreversible course of time occurs. Time is at the core of the riddle of the Sphinx that Oedipus could decipher. The answer to the riddle was "man," yet man set in time.

Borges, seeking shelter in the cleavage of circular time, writes:

> Let us consider a life in whose course there is an abundance of repetitions: mine, for example. I never pass in front of the Recoleta[3] without remembering that my father, my grandparents and great-grandparents are buried there, just as I shall be one day; then I remember that I have remembered the same thing an untold number of times already; I cannot walk through the suburbs in the solitude of the night without thinking that the night pleases us because it suppresses idle details, just as our memory does; I cannot lament the loss of a love or a friendship without meditating that one loses only what one really never had; every time I cross one of the street corners of the southern part of the city, I think of you, Helen; every time the wind brings me the smell of eucalyptus, I think of Adrogué in my childhood; every time I remember the ninety-first fragment of Heracitus "You shall not go down twice to the same river," I admire its dialectical dexterity, because the ease with which we accept the first meaning ("The river is different") clandestinely imposes upon us the second ("I am different") and grants us the illusion of having invented it; every time I hear a Germanophile vituperate the Yiddish language, I reflect that Yiddish is, after all, a German dialect, scarcely colored by the language of the Holy Spirit. These tautologies (and others I leave in silence) make up my entire life."[4]

It is an intimate confession. What one has really had is never lost: it remains in the eternity of memory. What one repeats again and again, without remembering, is what one has not had, or has had imperfectly, with trauma or unhappiness. Freud's title "Remembering, Repeating and Working Through" (SE 12:147) is well known. In the context I have been describing, we should rephrase it as "remembering and repeating without oblivion and without the grief of working through." Redirecting the process in this manner helps to stop time, deny losses, and avoid the anxiety and pain of frustrations, the successive time of growth and change.

Societal development in its early stages requires the shaping of tradition. Reiteration establishes, consolidates, and signifies its institutions. In cult the dead become ancestors; each ritual sacrifice mimics and restates the original mythic sacrifice. If the recurrence inherent in tradition becomes stereotyped and rigid, progress is impaired. When archetypes prevail and paradigmatic gestures impede renewal, the future is seen as an extension of the past. The myth of eternal return, studied among others by Mircéa Eliade, projects this pattern onto a cosmic background. It represents the cancellation of time. [5]

Borges expresses that notion in "*La noche cíclica* (The Cyclical Night)":

> They knew it, the fervent pupils of Pythagoras:
> That stars and men revolve in a cycle.
> . . . .
> In my blood: Laprida, Cabrera, Soler, Suárez...
> Names in which secret bugle calls are sounding,
> Invoking republics, cavalry, and mornings,
> Joyful victories, men dying in action.
> . . . .
> It returns, the hollow dark of Anaxagoras;
> In my human flesh, eternity keeps recurring
> And the memory, or plan, of an endless poem beginning:
> "They knew it, the fervent pupils of Pythagoras: [6]

Time, Destiny, Identity

By citing Marcus Aurelius's well-known statement (*Reflections*, 14), Borges intends to extoll the present: "No one loses the past or the future, for no one can take from him what he does not possess... Even though the years of your life were three thousand or thrice three thousand, remember that no one loses any life but the one he has now, nor does he live any other but the one he loses." [7] Borges omits consideration of the moral conveyed by this message and, focusing on the generalizing value of the statement (i.e., "no one"), draws the conclusion that "all human experiences are somehow analogous." Recognizing that this may appear as an impoverishing thought, he resorts to Schopenhauer's eternal essence: "... this lion is the same he was a thousand years ago. I have always been myself; that is to say, all who said "I" during that time, were no other but I."

Yet Borges's pendular thinking goes back and forth between statement and denial, interweaving time and destiny, memory and oblivion, being and not being. Even though in "The Doctrine of the Cycles" he rejects ironically the theory of eternal return, upon which Nietzche, he says, "who wanted to be Walt Whitman... confers the atrocious lucidity of an insomniac," later he applied the idea of eternal return as often as he refuted it. [8] It helped him to shun (at least temporarily) "the intolerable presence of the successive," as he says in the prologue to "History of Eternity." [9] Borges crafted in "The Aleph" a splendid instrument for just this purpose, condensing the universe into a single point. In "The Secret Miracle," a minute may last a year, allowing Hkadik to finish his writing before being executed.

Vincent Moon (In "The Shape of the Sword") says, "those nine days in my memory form one single day." In the story "*El fin* (The End)" the seven years elapsing between the musical dialogue and the duel at knife-point are for the character Martín Fierro seven days. In literary creation, just as in dreams, the impossible becomes possible. Well-known examples are drama within drama (Hamlet the spectator of *Hamlet*), or the reshaping of classical tragic characters in a new plot.

> Is not one single repeated term sufficient to break down and confuse the series of time? Do not the fervent readers who surrender themselves to Shakespeare become, literally, Shakespeare? [10]

Like his character Tsui-Pen, Borges, the maker, believed in an infinite series of times like divergent and convergent parallel mirrors. [11] Yet when he manages to wake up from his stubborn nightmares, he says:

> And yet, and yet[12].... Denying temporal succession, denying the self, denying the astronomical universe, are apparent desperations and secret consolations. Our destiny ... is not frightful by being unreal; it is frightful because it is irreversible and iron-clad.

And then, as if "the other Borges" were speaking, he adds,

Time is the substance I am made of. Time is a river which sweeps me along, but I am the river; it is a tiger which destroys me, but I am the tiger; it is a fire which consumes me, but I am the fire.

Finally, he finds himself: "The world, unfortunately, is real; I, unfortunately, am Borges." [13]

Notes

1. Jorge Luis Borges, "*El tiempo circular*," "*Historia de la eternidad*," *Obras completas* (Buenos Aires: Emecé, 1974), 394.
2. Borges, "A New Refutation of Time," *Labyrinths: Selected Stories and Other Writings*, trans. Donald A. Yates and James E. Irby (New York: New Directions Publishing, 1964), 218.
3. A national cemetery in Buenos Aires, with tombs of prominent historical figures and funeral vaults belonging to a limited number of traditional families. [Translator's note.]
4. Borges, "A New Refutation," 223-24.
5. Eliade, Mircéa, *The Myth of the Eternal Return*, trans. Willard R. Trask (Princeton: Princeton University Press, 1965).
6. Jorge Luis Borges, "Cyclical Night," trans. Alastair Reid, *Selected Poems 1923-1967*, ed. Norman Thomas di Giovanni (New York: Delacorte/Seymour Lawrence, 1972), 80-81.
7. Borges, "*El tiempo circular*," *Obras completas*.
8. Borges, "The Doctrine of Cycles," *Borges: A Reader*, ed. by Emir Rodríguez Monegal and Alastair Reid (New York: Dutton, 1981), 69.
9. Borges, *Obras completas* (Buenos Aires: Emecé, 1974), 351.
10. Borges, "A New Refutation of Time," *Labyrinths*, 224
11. Borges, "The Garden of Forking Paths," *Ficciones*, trans. Anthony Kerrigan (New York: Grove Press, 1962), 89-101.
12. These words are in English in the original. [Translator's note.]
13. Borges, "A New Refutation of Time," *Labyrinths*, 233-234.